After Queer Theory

After Queer Theory

The Limits of Sexual Politics

James Penney

www.plutobooks.com

First published 2014 by Pluto Press
345 Archway Road, London N6 5AA

www.plutobooks.com

Distributed in the United States of America exclusively by
Palgrave Macmillan, a division of St. Martin's Press LLC,
175 Fifth Avenue, New York, NY 10010

British Library Cataloguing in Publication Data
A catalogue record for this book is available from the British Library

ISBN   978 0 7453 3379 3   Hardback
ISBN   978 0 7453 3378 6   Paperback
ISBN   978 1 8496 4985 8   PDF eBook
ISBN   978 1 8496 4987 2   Kindle eBook
ISBN   978 1 8496 4986 5   EPUB eBook

Library of Congress Cataloging in Publication Data applied for

This book is printed on paper suitable for recycling and made from fully managed
and sustained forest sources. Logging, pulping and manufacturing processes are
expected to conform to the environmental standards of the country of origin.

10   9   8   7   6   5   4   3   2   1

Typeset from disk by Stanford DTP Services, Northampton, England
Simultaneously printed digitally by CPI Antony Rowe, Chippenham, UK and
Edwards Bros in the United States of America

Contents

Acknowledgments

I wish to thank the Social Sciences and Humanities Research Council of Canada, whose Standard Research Grant assisted in the completion of this project.

Some of the chapters in this book were previously published in shorter versions. I thank the following for permission to incorporate them here: The Johns Hopkins University Press, for Chapter 2, which appeared as '(Queer) Theory and the Universal Alternative', *diacritics* 32.2 (Summer 2002): 1–18; Taylor & Francis, for Chapter 4, which appeared as 'The Schizoanalytic Protest: *Homosexual Desire* Revisited', *Angelaki: Journal of the Theoretical Humanities* 9.1 (April 2004): 67–83; Joan Copjec, for Chapter 5, which appeared as 'The Sameness of Sexual Difference and the Difference of Same-Sex Desire', *Umbra: A Journal of the Unconscious* (2002).

Introduction
After Queer Theory – Manifesto and Consequences

Setting the Scene

This book makes the scandalous claim that queer discourse has run its course, its project made obsolete by the full elaboration of its own logic. Far from signalling the demise of anti-homophobic criticism, however, the end of queer offers an occasion to rethink the relation between sexuality and politics. Via a critical return to Marxism and psychoanalysis (Freud and Lacan), I argue that the way to implant sexuality in the field of political antagonism is paradoxically to abandon the exhausted project of sexuality's politicisation.

There are two principal premises from which I develop each chapter's discussion. First: queer theory was set in motion by transformative developments in Anglo-American sexuality theory in the early 1990s, inspired by decidedly post-Marxist currents in what is generally known as poststructuralism. Derived from these currents, the hegemonic assumptions of queer theory have proven to be irreconcilable with the premises of a generically emancipatory politics. Second: queer's demise presents a strategic opportunity to reconceive how we think about sexuality and politics. Indeed, a quite paradoxical truth is exposed. The sexual politics of both feminism and queer theory generally insist that sex is inherently political. I argue instead that the reverse contention – that politics is inherently sexual – inserts sexuality immanently within the field of political antagonism. By *sexualising the political*, it becomes possible to wrest sexuality discourse from its various minoritarianisms,

1

opening it up to a genuinely universal emancipatory struggle beyond the reach of capitalism's complicity with the continuing proliferation and deconstruction of sexual and gender identities. My alternative thesis further exposes the underwhelming political implications of sexuality, as queer theory has generally understood this term – that is, as a discourse in the vague sense of the social constructionists and the more carefully articulated sense of Michel Foucault's poststructuralist historicisation.

Some context: on the left today, one hears from time to time that the gay and lesbian movements of the 1960s and 1970s featured a broader political horizon, linked to their organic relation to feminism and the New Left, than the more lifestyle-oriented, theoreticist and narrowly defined interests of the more recent queer agendas. There were remnants of authentic socialist praxis among members of the first post-Stonewall generation, and it's still possible to find work by writers who remain faithful to varying degrees to this seminal moment.[1] Even in the best-case scenarios, by contrast, poststructuralist queers tend merely to add 'class' to the end of their long list of preferred categories of social difference to which they lend their reformist attention.

But there is a second reality, much more paradoxical, which has been left largely unobserved to this day. Whereas previously politicised gay and lesbian communities, founded on generally unproblematised ideas of (minority) sexual identity, saw inherent links between their own ambitions and those of other oppressed constituencies (in particular straight women and people of colour), more recent queer writers and activists, asserting identity's inherently normative and exclusionary workings, have been comparatively self-concerned, reluctant to forge alliances with groups that don't define themselves in sexual terms. This has remained the case despite the often universalising reach of their claims (i.e. everyone is actually or potentially queer). To be sure, queer theory has been more interested in complex theoretical articulations and transgressing presumptive identity categories, than in thinking through its relation to the historical social movements that made queer possible in the first instance.

Counterintuitively, the subversion of sexual identity has turned the sexually marginal inward. With few exceptions, the queer contingent has been less willing than its predecessors to articulate its concerns to those of other groups, particularly geopolitically distant ones whose marginality takes a more conventionally material, that is to say socioeconomic, form. As a theoretical discourse, the queer project has primarily addressed itself to an Anglo-American academic readership. More specifically, particularly during its early history, it has been situated in elite centres of academic capital in the United States. For these reasons, it should hardly come as a surprise that queer discourse in general reflects the interests and investments of this group of privileged academics and students in the global North.

The advent of queer saw a project coupling minority sexual identity with a wide-reaching emancipatory political agenda, cede ground to an approach that wed sexual identity's immanent subversion and a vision of the universal implications of queerness with an issue- and lifestyle-oriented micro-level politics, alarmingly distanced from the critique of capitalism or any programme for thoroughgoing social change. Far from forging broad political alliances, the project of identity's subversion has had the unanticipated effect of strengthening the boundaries that separate a given identity, however problematised or deconstructed, from the wider social field. Meanwhile, in the world of academic publishing, queer studies and queer theory are intellectually dead discourses. Excluding for the time being its elite theoretical vanguard, recent queer textual production can be divided into two moribund categories: introductions and textbooks that repeat old mantras from the 1990s, and a range of largely untheorised studies of cultural phenomena featuring non-normative sexual content, otherwise fully conventional in scope and aim.[2]

For its part, the vanguard of queer theory has most recently turned its attention to what we might loosely call the negative. Shame, impersonality, the antisocial and 'the end of sex' are the new fashionable themes.[3] But these emergent tropes are still marked by the discourse's inherent contradiction. This contradiction can be traced all the way back to queer's dawning moment, when Eve Kosofsky Sedgwick asked if homosexuality is of universal or particular concern. In light of queer's subsequent history, we can ask: is sexuality inherently, universally, queer? Or should it rather name a distinguished minority, an elite experimental constituency pushing the boundaries of community, social life, politics and subjectivity?[4]

This book suggests that these questions are no longer productive because they assume a false dilemma. If the former is the case, then we lack a rationale for queer's existence as a special field of inquiry and, in any event, we already know all about it from Freud's strong theses about a constitutive bisexuality in the subject, and the drive's resistance to reproductive normalisation.[5] Even more importantly, on the level of theoretical practice, the premise of queer universality – the idea that sexuality is inherently queer – demonstrates against its own intentions how sexuality is an inauspicious starting point for a project invested in genuine social change, one which addresses itself to a humanity generically conceived. This is so because the universality premise implicitly desexualises expressions of political interest that don't make explicit reference to sex. In other words, sexual politics is viewed as a subspecies of a generic politics, which implies unhelpfully that there's a politics that has nothing to do with the libido. For their part, artists and critics who opt for the alternative minoritising option have produced texts that are not without interest. Because they adopt a mode of aesthetic and experiential analysis limited to merely sexual or erotic utopian horizons, however, work in this mode fails to qualify as political in any genuine, that is to say socialist, sense of the term.

After Queer Theory foregrounds the strong, if not absolute, determination of sexual identities by economically structured social relations. Sexual identities, however deconstructed or problematised, are always in a significant sense responses to developments in the relations of capital. This is to say that the discourses of sexuality and sexual identity are necessarily ideological. As Bolshevik feminist Alexandra Kollontai argued with respect to women, *class antagonism has always-already divided the 'queer community' from itself.* Or, perhaps more accurately, the identification of class antagonism places the queer on the side of what we used to call the bourgeoisie. Class is a diagonal difference that cuts through all the other differences – with the exception of sexual difference – that queer theory and poststructuralism have alternatively valorised.

Each of the chapters that follows this introduction seizes upon a significant aspect of the queer argument, exposing its inconsistencies and problematic political assumptions. Each then begins to propose challenging alternatives inspired by a critical return to the psychoanalytic and Marxist traditions. Although the elaboration of these alternatives has barely begun, *After Queer Theory* aims to clear the terrain for a fresh start. It looks forward to the day when the concern for sexuality in cultural and political studies is wedded to a genuinely emancipatory and transformative vision of anti and post-capitalist social change.

Six Points

The argument this book develops can be summarised in the form of six main theses. Each is outlined below, followed by a condensed exposition. I revisit each argument in more detailed and complex ways throughout the rest of the book. Everything relates back in one way or another to these key points. Some readers may wish to return periodically to this section as they work their way through.

1. *All the valuable points queer theory has made about human sexuality were previously made by Freud and developed in (aspects of) the psychoanalytic tradition.* For instance, the foundational claim that queer theory 'politicizes sex, gender and sexuality in a way that severs the notion of identity from any stable reference points'[6] fails to add substantial insight to the argument of *Three Essays on the Theory of Sexuality*. In fact, Freud's theory is more radical than at least this particular queer iteration. Rather than assume that sexual identities slide promiscuously and unpredictably from one 'reference point' to another, psychoanalysis posits instead that sex is coterminous with the immanent subversion of each and every such point. Sex is the obscene shadow of every social identity; it presents the constant threat of collapse into nonsense, non-meaning.

2. *The promise of queer universalism – that everyone is (potentially) queer – is compromised by both an identitarian gesture of self-privileging and a reference, tending towards paranoia, to the quasi-omnipotence of heterosexism or 'heteronormativity'.* To rationalise its distinct existence, queer generically references a style or aesthetic, a (non)identity, a set of affects or feelings, a politics, or a mode of sociality or relation, which it then routinely differentiates from an idealised and hostile adversary, the social and psychical purchase of which is unhelpfully exaggerated. To be clear, I don't wish to minimise the sometimes lethal effects of homophobia. The point is rather that the premise of

a heteronormativity embedded in the very fabric of culture, society, 'power', or subject production is both incorrect and self-defeating.

Here again, psychoanalysis is more instructive. It first takes the homosexual current of the libido *as such* as a foundational and universal fact of psychic life, and then sets out to analyse its manifold vicissitudes. There is no non-libidinal, non-sexual obstacle to homosexuality. The corollary of this is that any such obstacle is already homosexual. Further, the psychoanalytic claim that sexuality is neither primarily reproductive nor naturally heterosexual is generic in nature. There's no such thing as reproductive or fully heterosexual – 'normal' – sex. In this precise sense, *sex as such is queer* and, despite the protestations and asceticisms of various moralistic would-be legislators, there's no actually existing normality against which it might be contrasted. Sex is always-already transgression of the norm. This also implies that there's no such thing as (a particular) 'transgressive sexuality'. As a result, the injunction to (be) queer tends to have perversely normalising effects. This is the case, for example, with the various queer vangardisms that wish to normalise promiscuity, inveigh against same-sex marriage, or impose regimes of aesthetically-conceived forms of alternative social being.

3. *No positive social or political claim can be made in the name of queer when queer is defined, as above, as the generic real of sex.* Further, there is nothing in this claim that in any way hinders the war against homophobia, which should and will continue. The proper way to pursue the intersection of sex and politics is to inquire after the libidinal logic, the unconscious fantasies, that buttress particular political judgments and desires.

Speculatively, the imperative is to theorise and instantiate new forms of liberatory sublimation. As Alain Badiou has forcefully argued, the truths from which can be deduced the project of human emancipation from oppression and inequality are generic, universal in their address.[7] Generic humanity is sexed (*sexué*, as the French say), and *in this precise sense only*, queer. The corollary of this is that political programmes that fail to acknowledge human sexuality in this way (for example, programmes that normalise heterosexuality and legislate against 'deviations') are fundamentally illegitimate, and can be shown to be illegitimate without arduous effort.

4. *There can be no meaningful, specifically sexual, utopianism from an authentic psychoanalytic perspective.* This doesn't imply that properly political utopias of all kinds are inherently and always undesirable. Although his misinformed polemic against psychoanalysis continues to have disastrous effects on the study of sexuality, Foucault was well placed historically to draw the lesson of the various ill-fated 1960s and 1970s lifestyle vanguardisms. Utopianisms centred on erotic subjectivity remain without exception tied to liberal or libertarian individualisms, which can only detract from a meaningfully political horizon of social transformation.

5. *Properly formulated, the psychoanalytic idea of sexual difference is neither heterosexist nor anti-feminist.* The various anti-oedipal and gender theory arguments animate a wish-fulfilment fantasy of infinite sexual and gender possibilities, which solves only a false problem. For psychoanalysis, there are only two possibilities for sexuation, for *failing* to achieve a sexual identity. That these possibilities are masculine and feminine in no way establishes a sexual relation, nor does it impose a putative 'compulsory heterosexuality'. There is no necessary connection between either biological and psychical sex, or psychical sex – masculine or feminine – and the biological sex of one's partner(s).

Usually taken to mean that men and women are neither sexually complementary nor naturally inclined to one another, Lacan's dictum 'there is no sexual relation' must inevitably relate to same-sex partners also. Same-sex partners are neither more nor less naturally suited to one another than their heterosexual counterparts. Freud was right to insist that there are fundamental psychical differences between the sexes, and in this precise sense only they're unequal. This inequality, however, carries no *necessary* political or social consequences. Nor is it even necessarily hostile to programmes based on the feminist principle of 'equality between the sexes', which usually acknowledge anyway that sexual equality is contingent on the recognition of particular differences between the sexes, however these are conceived.

6. *The recent queer interests in affect and the negative are politically inadequate.* The affective turn is apolitical and narcissistic because it ignores the psychoanalytic insight that affect – with the exception of anxiety – is always connected to an unconscious object that has been

disguised or distorted in order to break the barrier of repression. Unanalysed, affect is fundamentally a mechanism of defence. For its part, the so-called antisocial thesis in queer theory is desirable to the extent that it lays bare the connection between, on the one hand, the drive's involuted, nonsocial, incommunicable qualities and, on the other, the constitutive antagonism of the social, that is the inability of the social world to organise itself into a consistent, unbroken whole.

The antisocial current has also provided a refreshing alternative to the bourgeois and assimilationist trajectory of the (post) gay movements, at least to the extent that we discount the bourgeois, primarily American, academic milieu to which its purchase has largely been limited. Politically, however, both tendencies leave much to be desired. The cult of the death drive offers only a decadent nihilism, which casts any and all references to futurity as abstractly reactionary.[8]

Alternatively, when antisocial queer theory acknowledges the need for a dialectical counterpart to the negative, it produces only elitist programmes for vanguard social life or alternative aesthetic programmes with political implications that are ambiguous at best. Any politically significant discourse on social negativity must acknowledge its relation not only to psychical antagonism, but also to the antagonisms of capitalism, both internal and external. The internal antagonisms pertain to how capitalism's conflict with itself creates a dependency on crisis, imperialism and war; the external to how capitalism necessarily produces a class conflict, on which it must expend tremendous resources in order to disguise its workings from the oppressed.

The following five chapters offer detailed examinations of specific sites of discourse that raise central questions concerning the relation of queer discourse to the Marxist and psychoanalytic traditions. Each chapter makes suggestions about how the anti-homophobic project can integrate itself with a new political discourse that extends beyond the limits of the queer problematic. The concluding chapter resumes where the first chapter leaves off: it examines one final thematic in contemporary queer discourse – so-called antisocial queer theory – and elaborates on the parameters of a new way of thinking about the place of sexuality in transformative political thought.

1

Currents of Queer

This first chapter consists of four sections, each of which takes on a key emergent tendency in the most recent queer-theoretical work. In each discussion, I try to articulate the argument and its significance, offer criticisms from both psychoanalytic and Marxist perspectives, and then suggest alternative avenues of interrogation, which go beyond the limits of queer discourse as I see it.

The main trends I consider are the resurgence of phenomenology, the inquiry into affect or emotion, and finally the discourse of 'homonationalism'. A further emergent trend of today, the so-called antisocial turn, is taken on and contextualised in the concluding chapter. By necessity not without an arbitrary quality, the selection of texts aims to be representative rather than exhaustive, both with respect to each considered author's body of work and the queer theory field in general. Throughout, I attempt to relate the author's most foundational assumptions to particular illuminating details of their discussion as a means of clarifying the concrete political implications of general theoretical ideas. In the first section, I consider a recent example of the queer discourse on identity and community, perhaps its most consistent and dominant thematic. The example gains in significance in light of its concern for the British, rather than the hegemonic American, political context.

Community and the Subversion of Identity

Arguably, the most paradigmatic gesture of queer theory since its inception has been to insist that gender and/or sexuality subvert claims to identity. Pre-queer activists and critics tended to assume that an idea of gay or lesbian identity was required in order to resist the pathologisation of non-normative sexualities, make claims for civil rights, and gain legal protection from discrimination. With the deconstructionist and Foucaultian turns of queer theory, however, the emphasis shifted to considerations of how all social identities, even minority ones, are unstable social constructions and/or productions of power, viewed as 'discourse'. In Foucault's later work, power carries a disciplinary function, and in this precise sense is always normative. In the shadow of latently homicidal state policies developed in the early days of the HIV/AIDS crisis, queer theory began to consider all invocations of gay and lesbian identity and citizenship as more or less inherently oppressive. This tendency developed in conjunction with a poststructuralist feminist theory that similarly began to consider all invocations of 'woman' as essentially exclusive of 'other' women, in particular lesbians and women of colour. Many queer authors justifiably enlisted psychoanalysis to support the claim that sexual identities and orientations are never stable because they are subordinated, as Freud consistently claimed, to a primary psychical bisexuality.

Taken to its logical conclusion, the thesis that sexuality is antithetical to identity makes it impossible to ground a restricted notion of community on sex. In other words, it's impossible to ground a notion of community on queer, if queer is what stops you from identifying any quality its members might share. If everyone is potentially queer, then there are no definite exclusions by means of which that community might be defined against society, or the people, at large. And yet, it's impossible to deny that wide swathes of queer theory manage to do just that, even when it explicitly endorses the position that sex subverts any and all identity claims.

At the root of queer-theoretical production lies an unrecognised contradiction. Queer insists that the gay and lesbian identities of previous generations functioned in an unacknowledged normative way, implicitly excluding men and women of colour, transsexuals, transvestites, femme lesbians, butch fags, the poor and any other identifiable marginalised group or subgroup. On its more theoretical register, however, queer claims that sex disturbs attempts made by language, discourse, the ego or power to fix identity to stable terms of reference. But even the most sophisticated queer theorists rely on an implicit distinction between what is queer and what is normative, the latter often rendered as 'compulsory heterosexuality' or 'the heterosexual matrix', for instance.[1] Even the distinction queer tries to make between itself and its more fixed generational predecessors requires the most fundamental gesture of identity construction, namely differentiation from an 'other'. After all, it's much easier to define yourself by specifying what you aren't than by identifying essential qualities that don't depend on a contrast with something else. In short, queer wants to subvert identity and have it too. It qualifies queer as groundless as a means of compensating for prior political blind spots, while at the same time positing a queer ground defined against a 'normativity', the status of which is never clearly defined.

Now, the introduction to a relatively recent UK-published queer theory reader can serve as an example of this persistence of identity and community in queer work. Authored by Iain Morland and Annabelle Willox, the essay also emblematises the kind of false politicisation of sexuality that I set out to challenge in this book. I should signal here that I chose this particular text because it concisely expresses the difficulties that underlie the logic of queer discourse's approach to the identity and community issue. The essay also gains in importance to the considerable extent that the political moves its argument makes are generally characteristic of dominant queer discourse as a whole.

Morland and Willox's discussion pivots around former UK Prime Minister Tony Blair's response to a spate of nasty homophobic hate crimes, which took place in London in April 1999. The central event was a bomb attack at the Admiral Duncan pub, an establishment in Old Compton Road, historic centre of gay life in west-central London's Soho district. The perpetrator of a whole series of attacks designed to stir up homophobic and ethnic resentments, known neo-Nazi David Copeland detonated a nail bomb in the pub, killing three people and wounding about 70 others. In conjunction with the Prince of Wales's visit to the attack's survivors, Blair made a public statement condemning the anti-gay violence that plagued Britain that spring. 'When the gay community is attacked and innocent people are murdered', Blair proclaimed, 'all the good people of Britain, whatever their race, their lifestyle, their class unite in revulsion and determination to bring the evil people to justice'.[2]

To all appearances, the Blair statement was designed to teach a version of the lesson of universalism that queer theory itself, at least in certain of its iterations, wants to teach: homosexuality, as well as the prejudice against it, should be of concern to everyone, not just the 'community' to which Blair's words also allude. The prime ministerial proclamation rests on the assumption that even though homophobic violence is targeted against a particular group of people, the implications of this violence, and therefore the ethical duty to speak out against it, pertain to everyone equally. Further, this remains the case in spite of the various differences, including those of sexuality (the 'lifestyles' cited by Blair), that distinguish us from one another.

Without question, Tony Blair has been among the most cynical and hypocritical world leaders of recent memory, guilty in particular of deliberately misleading the British public in order speciously to justify a nasty and racist neo-imperialist war. But this aspect of Blair's politics is not what's of interest here. Rather, I wish to examine details of the critical view of Blair's statement expressed by Morland and Willox. They begin by granting the argument that the statement 'would seem to mark the success of queer activism' because it gives voice to 'the official view that the gay community [is] a respectable minority' (3), albeit one, I've already noted, whose victimisation should be of concern to all. In light of the anti-identitarian claims of queer theory, one might reasonably assume that the editors' difficulty with Blair's statement would lie in what might be construed as a simplistic or essentialist reference to a 'gay community'. Indeed, many queer theorists might justifiably want to argue that the seemingly innocuous phrase marginalises lesbians and/or women, not to mention all the other varieties of sexual nonconformity on which the queer movement has striven to shed light.

Curiously, however, the authors' criticism raises instead questions of invisibility and sexual erasure. On the one hand, Morland and Willox argue that Blair's reference to a gay community subsumes the apparently unpalatable realities of gay sexual life under a putatively less offensive reference to 'lifestyles'. In other words, the phrase 'gay community' works to dissimulate from a potentially hostile public what gays actually do with one another in bed. On the other hand, however, Morland and Willox use the problematic term themselves when they affirm in the next paragraph that 'in an important sense queer politics is about shared lifestyles'. They even go as far as to attribute ambivalence to Blair's statement concerning whether or not 'the killing of homosexuals should incite revulsion' (3), basing this judgment on what is very likely a misreading of what he said. Without providing contextual evidence to support their interpretation, the editors make the rather paranoid assumption that Blair's reference to 'innocent victims' is meant to include only the heterosexual dead.

In any case, the fact that Blair's statement in the editors' view is 'couched in terms of *everything but* sexuality' poses unanswered, and perhaps unanswerable, political questions about 'a diversity of identities' and 'a cultural diversity that surpasses the notion of identity'. They conclude their discussion with a question: 'Is queer still queer, and is it important for "queerness" to refer always to the same communities, acts, and beliefs?' (3). These last formulations confusedly convey the full extent of queer theory's underlying ambivalence towards the idea of community. Arguably, 'gay community' or 'queer community' may indeed attenuate the potentially corrosive force of sexuality on specifically heterosexist interests, the former perhaps more than the latter. Further, such constructs provide tangible targets in the social world for homophobic violence which, as the London attacks demonstrate, routinely hit even persons who don't identify as homosexual or queer. All the same, queer discourse clings anxiously, if ironically, to the idea of an 'us', apparently unable to let go of the notion despite the lack of convincing political or theoretical arguments in its favour.

This curious ambivalence becomes even more pronounced as Morland and Willox's own analysis of the bombing shows that the target of homophobic violence isn't really even a community in the sense in which they use the term. The authors' laudable insistence on foregrounding the unsettling social impact of the very notion of queer sex suggests that anti-gay violence results from a fantasy of an 'other' jouissance, which both fascinates and repels. From the psychoanalytic perspective, the gay pub, or even the 'gay community', is a material or social stand-in for a properly psychical object – that is to say, the traumatic object of enjoyment that the ego attempts to jettison from consciousness with the associated forces of repression and idealisation. It doesn't require an investment in psychoanalysis to think that by detonating the bomb, the perpetrator seeks unknowingly to cleanse himself of his own unconscious 'queer' sexual fantasies. Indeed, queer universalism can be put in this instance to a different use, more subversive than its mobilisation in queer theory itself. Queer inheres most essentially in the subject who seeks to destroy it, through acts of homophobic violence or pseudo-therapeutic processes of hetero-sexualisation, for instance. Queer becomes truly universal precisely at the moment when it's targeted for elimination as a perverse, impure, community-destroying anomaly. Paradoxically, the universal reach of queer is only underscored by its motivation of the very 'acting out' that seeks to eradicate it.

In this light, it's hardly coincidental that the homophobic bomber was also a neo-Nazi racist. Racism, too, targets an object that can't be equated with persons or communities. Rather, racism is set in motion by fantasy perceptions of ethnicised and racialised enjoyments; constructions of 'other' satisfactions associated with incomprehensible languages, spiced or differently spiced foods, traditional collective customs and rituals, and the like. Or, more precisely put, such fantasies are projections onto the Other of the subject's own disavowed enjoyments, which can be conveniently rejected by the ego as foreign and obscene. Marxism surely adds to this line of analysis the insight that such fantasy perceptions are often directed across the traumatic psychosocial dividing line of class.

The general theoretical point to be made in this context for anti-homophobic work is that a notion of a gay community, or even of the queer person, isn't required to denounce, as of course one must, symptomatic acts of homophobic violence. Indeed, the fact that a bomb going off in a queer establishment will almost always impact heterosexual persons as well betrays the disjunction between the true cause or object of homophobic violence – a psychical object of fantasy – and the actual, 'real-life' persons whom it affects. The anti-identitarian logic of queer theory, the logic it so routinely fails to follow to its proper conclusion, should ultimately imply that the queer person, with his or her distinguishing marks of lesbian, gay or transsexual jouissance, exists only in the homophobe's head. Never, however, does queer theory entertain the corollary that both the idea of a 'gay/queer community', and the 'compulsory heterosexuality' that forms its negative ground, might in fact exacerbate, rather than attenuate, homophobic passion.

In the final analysis, however, the most basic and egregious problem with the Morland and Willox essay lies in its misidentification of the political. As for much of queer theory, politics for these authors signifies only the ambivalent struggle with notions of community and identity, as well as the proclamation of their immanent, but nonetheless provisional, subversion. As we've considered, the authors reproach Blair's speech for whitewashing the obscene realities of gay sex with politically correct talk of a multiplicity of lifestyles. At the next moment, however, they're embracing an idea of politics *as* lifestyle, and then inventing a provisional notion of community to give it form. Like so much of queer theory, their discourse never extends beyond the innocuous horizon of lifestyle politics, with its implicit or unconscious call to the Other for recognition, for sanction, for integration with dominant social norms. This call persists beneath what appears, and is consciously intended, as its opposite. After all, it's not at all clear why it would be so important for queer politics that Tony Blair openly disclose what lesbians, for example, do in bed, either on the occasion of the commemoration of an act of homophobic violence or, for that matter, at any other time.

Psychoanalytically, this brand of queer pseudo-politics can be linked to an anxiety arising out of the impossibility of *speaking* sexual experience, of transcribing the real of sex into the order of the signifier. For Lacan, sex signals the disjunction between jouissance – that is, the ecstatic experience of the body – and what can be articulated logically in language, in speech, and therefore consciously known. That this disjunction is indifferent to what is understood as sexual orientation – although not to sexual difference, but that's another story[3] – is but a further indication that sexual identity can't form the basis for political subjectivation, that is for a truth procedure in Alain Badiou's sense of the phrase. Because both queers and non-queers alike experience it 'in the defiles of the signifier',[4] as Lacan put it, sexuality can't be directly politicised. But this statement isn't tantamount to claiming that sex is entirely severed from politics. Rather, sex is what haunts the expression of all political judgment. It's the excess that estranges political articulation from itself; the surplus showing that political judgments always contain latent sexual significance.

And from the perspective of Marxism, queer politics fails because the difference upon which it rests (queer vs 'heteronormative') carries no necessary relation to class antagonism, to the mode of production in its determination of the relations of capital. Non-heterosexuals are widely distributed across the range of material privilege. In fact, what's so politically disconcerting about queer is the largely academic and upper-middle-class origin of so much of the discourse, not to mention its serious lack of geopolitical mobility and awareness. To be sure, there is no doubt that in the liberal and 'post-oedipal' global North, there are concrete material advantages to be gained from engaging in the queer lifestyle of which Morland and Willox speak. The queer is not only unburdened by conventional family obligations or the monogamous relationship. Also, the lifestyle values he or she embraces are inherently synchronous with the flexibility, mobility and precariousness on which contemporary capitalism so exploitatively thrives.

Phenomenally Queer

One of the better-known queer theory figures based in the UK, Sara Ahmed has made a substantive contribution to one of the discourse's newer and alternative currents. Ahmed draws from the phenomenological tradition in philosophy, more specifically from three of its usual suspects: Husserl, Heidegger and Merleau-Ponty. Although Elizabeth Grosz's writing can be credited for initially charting this direction,[5] I've chosen to focus instead on a selection from Ahmed's work for three, somewhat arbitrary, reasons: its contemporaneousness, its emergence from outside the American academic context, and the clarity with which it brings forward numerous problems in contemporary queer theory as I see it.

Ahmed is interested in what phenomenology might have to say about the idea of orientation. She premises her elaborations on an understanding of space which, viewed from the psychoanalytic perspective, fails to take account of the effects of the unconscious. But the difficulty with Ahmed's work isn't merely theoretical in nature. Indeed, the phenomenological assumptions that ground her argument are characteristic of much hegemonic queer theory, the political implications of which I find deeply problematic. Counterintuitive though it may sound, queer phenomenology effects a desexualisation of cultural analysis, which has the strange consequence of rendering banal both the term 'queer' and politics as such. In line with mainstream opinion, Ahmed's view of queer politics remains, like Morland and Willox's, entirely within the horizon of lifestyle choices. For this reason, her discourse presents no significant threat to the status quo, including in particular the forces of heterosexism that her own analysis sets out to attack.

Ahmed inquires after the implications of the phenomenological current for today's discourse of sexual orientation, taking into consideration that this latter term carries a quite particular meaning in the philosophical tradition. In very general terms, phenomenology sets out to offer an alternative to the Platonic and Cartesian traditions in philosophy which, notoriously for some, privilege the abstract realm of the idea above the data of sensation and perception. Ahmed seeks to appropriate for the study of queer bodies and sexualities ideas from phenomenology concerning how human perception relates to its objects through the intentionality of consciousness – the orientation of consciousness, that is to say, in space and time. Potentially, at least, the queer subject for Ahmed has the capacity to orient him or herself within these mediums in counterhegemonic or non-normative ways. Further, this alternative orientation – *dis*orientation, actually – carries, for her, a significance she describes as political. 'If orientation is a matter of how we reside in space', she writes, 'then sexual orientation might also be a matter of residence, of how we inhabit spaces, and who or what we inhabit spaces with'.[6] One of the tasks a critical reader must therefore set himself is to question how Ahmed makes the link between the philosophical understanding of spatial relations and the terrain of political conflict.

Ahmed wants to 'queer' phenomenology. This means that she intends to read the discourse against the grain, discovering moments of confusion, for example, in what it says about orientation. To this end, Ahmed develops a novel reading of a passage from Husserl, which describes the philosopher sitting at his desk, philosophising about his consciousness of the objects around him as he writes. Husserl's discussion appeals to Ahmed because it shows how 'consciousness is always directed toward objects and hence is always worldly, situated, and embodied' (544). For instance, Husserl describes how, ensconced in his study, he can allow his attention to wander from the page to the window, taking into view his grandchildren at play in the garden. The example is meant to show how perceptual consciousness is always spatially directed, and focusing on, *intending*, particular objects. For Husserl, however, the intentionality of the mind's attention is also mobile; it changes shape in accordance with shifts between objects, just as these objects themselves change in consciousness. Ahmed 'queers' this element of Husserl's discussion by underlining how certain marginalised or forgotten objects will be sidelined or remain unperceived. In other words, it's not only a question for Ahmed of the unfixed plasticity of consciousness; that consciousness will bear different qualities in accordance with its grasp of different objects. More importantly, other objects 'are relegated to the background', she writes; 'they are only ever co-perceived'. Ahmed wants to extend the phenomenological analysis so that it stops looking only forward through the philosopher's study. Instead, she wants it to turn around so that, as she puts it, it 'faces the back' (546).

I have two main objections to the phenomenological tendency in queer theory as Ahmed formulates it. The first is philosophical or ontological in nature; it has to do with how psychoanalysis questions the most basic assumptions of phenomenology concerning the subject's relation to space and time. I've developed a version of this argument elsewhere in the form of a critique of the resurgence of phenomenology in film theory,[7] so a brief overview will suffice here. In short, phenomenology inadequately problematises the subject's relationship to space, and Ahmed's presentation of the tradition only exacerbates this inadequacy. Lacan argues that phenomenology misconceives space as empirical and geometrical.[8] As her discussion makes clear, Ahmed imagines a subject for whom appearances can be taken for granted, a subject whose mastery of space is limited only by the objects that remain unseen at any given time. If only this subject could see in every direction at once, space would unfurl in a way fully given to intentional consciousness.

For Lacan, in contrast, the subject's grasp of the world is always mediated and limited by language, an elemental fact of human existence the impact of which phenomenology consistently underestimates. Because of language, according to Lacan, objects appear suspicious, ungrounded to the subject, as if they conceal something more desirable or satisfying behind them. Freud's work on voyeurism and exhibitionism influenced Lacan to emphasise our uncomfortable unconscious awareness of our unmasterable visibility in the world, as well as the neurotic resistance we put up against this irreducible condition of our existence.

Even eminent phenomenologist Maurice Merleau-Ponty, whom Ahmed cites in her discussion, stresses how the subject is fundamentally given-to-be-seen. For Merleau-Ponty as well as for Lacan, this condition of general visibility is logically prior to our comparatively vulnerable faculty of sight. Further, no psychoanalytic critique of phenomenology would be complete without mention of the fact that language's mediation of the world causes objects to appear to the subject in a way that's shaped and distorted by their signifier, and even more importantly with this signifier's associations with other signifiers in the unconscious. With its focus on the relation of consciousness to the outside world, phenomenology for psychoanalysis forgets about what Freud called internal stimulation, that is to say the perceptions, linked in a complicated way to both memory and fantasy, that manage to break out of the unconscious mind in censored form. Husserl's relation to his table, for example, can be overdetermined by its signifier's relation to other signifiers in his unconscious in a way that bears no direct relation to either experience, perception, or even 'meaning' as it is conventionally understood.

More germane to the immediate concerns of queer theory, however, is the curious fact that Ahmed's own orientation towards the term 'orientation' effectively desexualises it. I've already shown how Ahmed wants to claim queer as a kind of disruptive or against-the-grain practice of reading – one that seeks to destabilise any semblance of order that a text, on this view, might be construed to set up. Ahmed advances that what's queer in phenomenology is its attempt to think through what she calls an 'intellectual experience of disorder' (544). This is arguably the main anti-Platonic objective of the phenomeno-logical tradition writ large: to allow the object to skew the alignment of perception in such a way that the sense data this object sends off to consciousness begin to overwhelm the object's properly ideational or intellectual determinations. In Lacanian vocabulary, phenomenology wants to prioritise sense data over the signifier. But what exactly is to be gained by 'queering' phenomenology – that is, by referring more or less uncritically to an intact aspect of an existing canonical philosophical tradition with a new word, one which it has never used itself? In this precise sense, Ahmed's reading of phenomenology is thoroughly conservative. Indeed, a cynic might conclude that the whole exercise amounts to a word game enlisted for a marketing strategy:

to sell more books, 'queer' can sex up a philosophical tradition that makes for remarkably dry reading. Misleadingly, however, 'queer' in this instance has nothing whatsoever to do with sex.

This criticism notwithstanding, it would be disingenuous to leave the reader with the impression that Ahmed fails even to detect heterosexism in the texts of phenomenology. To be sure, the identification of straight bias in the texts of culture is one of the hallmarks of queer discourse, particularly in its less theoreticised, and more pragmatic, cultural studies mode. But there's a problem here as well. Not only does the queer tradition overestimate the general political importance of such acts of unmasking explicit or implicit heterosexism. Additionally, more often that not the force of this heterosexism – that is, its powers of determination over the argument's conceptualisation and development – is counterstrategically exaggerated.

To shed light on this politically problematic exaggeration in her work, I propose to examine a personal anecdote Ahmed offers in her text as a counter-example to the Husserl-in-his-study scenario I referred to earlier. What importance does Ahmed's drawing out of Husserl's heterosexual investments bear for either his general contribution to phenomenology, or the struggle against homophobia? Does Husserl's writing impose or reflect what Ahmed and other queer theorists have termed, after Adrienne Rich, compulsory heterosexuality?

Here is the alternative philosophical scene related in the text. Ahmed is seated with her parents and siblings around a family dinner table in her parents' garden. Like the table, and the food and drink resting upon it, any given world of things comes along with scripts and rituals, Ahmed argues. The objects of the world prescriptively direct the attention of those who come into perceptual contact with them. Pointing to two of Ahmed's nephews seated next to the table on the grass, one of her sisters exclaims, 'Look, there's a little John and a little Mark', remarking on the boys' physical resemblance to their respective fathers, the author's brothers-in-law.

Echoing Judith Butler's development of the role played by 'citationality'[9] in the perpetuation of gender norms, Ahmed goes on to argue that her sister's utterance is an example of the kind of direction or orientation of consciousness which, consolidated through repetition, reinforces the power of heterosexual relations. Indeed, the verbal acknowledgment of paternity implicitly forges a path leading first to the boys' own eventual fatherhood, and then to a forever expanding family tree. 'We can think of such an utterance as performing the work of alignment', Ahmed suggests. 'The utterance positions the child and the not-yet-adult by aligning sex (the male body) and gender (the masculine character) with sexual orientation (the heterosexual future)' (557). In short, for Ahmed the world of objects in the family abode normatively directs the subjects who inhabit it towards a straight and reproductive future.

There should be little question that the situation Ahmed describes can put tremendous pressure on those who suffer from the burden of heterosexual convention. As we've seen, the family home for Ahmed is a space populated by objects that have the power to set thoughts and actions moving in particular directions. In order to describe this space as normatively (or even compulsorily) heterosexual, however, Ahmed has to extract her own being from it, in effect describing it from the outside as if she were an invisible, disembodied and mute presence at the al fresco supper party. As an intellectual woman, established professor, and 'out' (public) lesbian, Ahmed is unusually privileged and insightful about her situation as a queer woman in (what I presume to be) a traditional family. But, even if we were to replace Ahmed with a younger, closeted, vulnerable young woman or girl, her presence would still have an impact, phenomenologically speaking, on the way the other family members perceive the objects in the room, including my hypothetical alternative Ahmed herself.

Quite clearly, her presence might also help to shape the way these objects 'orient' the other family members in Ahmed's sense of the term. When the sister points at the boys and makes her comment, for instance, my alternative closeted Ahmed might spontaneously react by looking away too soon and perhaps refilling her drink. Her actions and expression might betray discomfort or unease with the familiar patriarchal scene, and the mother, for example, noticing that discomfort, might now be forced to re-evaluate her initial perception of her other daughter's remarks. Ahmed's phenomenological analysis of the family celebration remains unpersuasive to the extent that she fails to take her own presence at the table into account.

Readers familiar with Ahmed's work might object at this point that my criticism misses the nuance of her evocative analysis. For example, it could be pointed out that Ahmed is always careful to remark that, despite their considerable power, non-alignment with the heterosexual orientations she depicts will often occur; as she puts it, such non-alignments can have a 'queer effect' (557). But Ahmed also writes that '[straight] tendencies enable action, in the sense that they allow the straight body, and the heterosexual couple, to extend into space'. By contrast, 'the queer body does not extend into such space' (559). With these remarks in mind, Ahmed's reader is left trying to make sense of an autobiographical description of a publicly known lesbian academic participating in a family gathering at which her body strangely fails to extend into space. Elsewhere in her essay, Ahmed refers to Merleau-Ponty's idea that consciousness is shaped by the body's 'task and situation' (561), what the philosopher calls the virtual body. If only she had applied this notion to her own embodied presence at the dinner table, and thought through the transformations brought to her own consciousness as it engages with the objects on the table, Ahmed might have produced a subtler, more dialectical account of what, from the psychoanalytic point of view, is always a necessary antagonism between sexual desire and social convention.

Focusing in such detail on this aspect of Ahmed's discussion would hardly be worthwhile in this context if it didn't hold a paradigmatic importance for hegemonic queer theory writ large. The ritual reference to compulsory heterosexuality, here extrapolated by Ahmed into a general phenomenological law of spatial extension (i.e. only heterosexual objects are allowed extension through space), enables the deployment of an at once self-aggrandising and self-victimising discourse of injury and transgression. Conveniently sidestepping the logical problem of the production of the queer subject, however injured, by a matrix qualified as exclusively heterosexual, queer discourse is able to denounce a heterosexist world from which it excludes itself, all the while claiming subversive political significance for a privileged and exceptional queer existence left largely unexplored and unexplained. Indeed, the empty political claim enabled by queer's exaggeration of heterosexuality's power of discursive production and spatial extension leaves the status and purchase of this power entirely unquestioned. Too often, the logic of queer theory departs from the unpromising and unnecessary premise of a compulsory heterosexuality, the existence of which is belied by the very existence of the queer subjects whose experience it apparently sets out to theorise.

Ahmed herself treads onto this terrain when she comments critically on conservative literary critic Bruce Bawer's suspicions about the minoritarian and anti-normative thrust of queer theory. In his own presentation of the issue at hand, Bawer compares the social marginality of the anti-assimilationist homosexual to the placement of the kids at the children's table at the extended family gathering. Bawer argues that if homophobic prejudice is the force that banishes the queer subject from the adults' table in the first place, then only this same prejudice can account for the desire to stay on the sidelines with the children. The tendency towards self-marginalisation among members of the queer community, in this view, is the result of something like a disavowed internalised homophobia. Citing the supreme poststructuralist value of difference, Ahmed disagrees. For her, Bawer's strategy implies 'becoming part of the family and becoming like the family, which is itself predicated on likeness (being with as being like)' (568).[10] In other words, there is no possibility for Ahmed of simultaneously occupying the adults' table and resisting the heterosexist norms according to which it functions.

Left unexplored in Ahmed's rejoinder is the invigorating and authentically subversive possibility that when the queer subject insists on sitting at the big family table, the nature of the table itself, the logic by which it operates, changes. The at-the-table queer forces the others to re-examine their understanding of the family. Even more importantly, queer self-inclusion exposes the family's own difference from itself – that is, the ways in which its members have already transgressed the patriarchal rules according to which the family is officially supposed to function. Rather than risk such confrontation, however, Ahmed's queer phenomenologists are happy to remain at their own small table in the shadows, talking politely and inconsequentially among themselves. Even more problematically, Bawer's gay conservative contingent is left to dominate discussion as they are left unchallenged as the token gays at the grown-ups' table.[11]

Finally, an even more unfortunate element of Ahmed's phenomenology is its endorsement of a limited and familiar lifestyle politics not unlike the politics of the Morland and Willox piece considered earlier. Indeed, Ahmed's work evacuates from the understanding of politics any meaning that the Marxist tradition would be capable of recognising. The best way to develop this last criticism of

Ahmed's work is to focus on another of her illuminating examples. This one speciously puts the Marxian vocabulary to decidedly un- or post-Marxist use. Ahmed draws on Adrienne Rich's work to develop what she calls a 'political economy of attention' (547). Incorporated into Ahmed's discussion as a counterweight to Husserl's philosophically canonical account, the Rich passage in its original context makes a strong feminist point about the difficulty mothers of young children can face when they sit down to write. In Ahmed's discussion, however, Rich's valuable insight is 'phenomenologised', as it were. That is, Ahmed uses Rich's discussion not to decry the numerous obstacles that have confronted women writers historically, but rather to convey an abstract theoretical point about how there can be, as she puts it, 'an uneven distribution of attention time among those who arrive at the writing table' (547).

Although Ahmed's discussion is clearly not without relevance, its placement under the heading of a political economy of attention not only dulls the edge of Rich's original materialist, and more significantly political, feminist argument. Additionally, this placement brings to the fore the failure of Ahmed's discussion properly to contextualise itself with respect to both history and economic relations. Ahmed construes labour in phenomenological terms as a quantity of abstract perceptual attention which can be directed in a variety of different directions. By sharp contrast, Marxism's more political understanding ties labour to the human energy expended in the production process, and quantified by capitalism in a way that materially disadvantages the worker. Here a properly Marxist feminism – not to mention Virginia Woolf's, from the heights of its bourgeois Bloomsbury privilege – delivers more valuable insights. The alternative Marxist perspective has the advantage of adding to both Rich's original account and Ahmed's appropriation of it much-needed analysis of the material reasons why women writers have faced more distractions, have been so much less voluminously published, than their male counterparts.[12] Marxism's account of the sexual division of labour remains unhindered by the philosophical abstraction of Ahmed's account. Even more importantly, it wonders about the specific social conditions that would have left Rich no alternative but to try desperately to write while having to mind her child.

In short, Ahmed's discussion of queer disorientation proceeds as if the critique of ideology had never taken place. Instead of asking why the queer subject experiences what she experiences in the way she does, Ahmed rather takes this experience at face value, assuming in the process that politics amounts to a set of lifestyle choices. Disorientation, Ahmed writes, is 'an effect of how we do politics, which in turn is shaped by a prior matter – how we live' (569). Quoting Judith Halberstam, Ahmed defines queer politics as 'the potentiality of not following certain conventional scripts of family, inheritance, and child rearing' (569).[13] At the root of such formulations is a naïve voluntarism that Marxism and psychoanalysis both reject. These alternative discourses instead choose a more complex and dialectical way of thinking about the relation of consciousness to the real in its interrelated psychical and socioeconomic aspects. In the final analysis, it's not at all clear that the decision merely not to follow certain conventional lifestyle paths amounts to a politics that will in any way threaten the social and economic status quo.

However we decide to think about what some will insist on calling 'queer experience', this experience remains both historical and overdetermined by the unconscious. Not only is the cultural significance of homosexual desire packaged and presented to the subject in particular ways at particular times, but this packaging is part and parcel of an ideological apparatus that works to dissimulate how the mode of production, including our libidinal complicity in its workings, functions in the interests of some, against those of many.

Ahmed sums up her doctrine of queer disorientation by invoking the 'desire lines' of which some landscape architects speak. These are the paths through a landscape design that direct our attention and our experience of it, sending us first in one direction and then in another. Ahmed's project aims to trace new, uncharted lines, rather like the lines of flight of which Gilles Deleuze and Félix Guattari memorably write.[14] The problem, however, is that the space itself stays the same; the logic according to which all possible paths can be charted is left unaddressed, unquestioned. Instead, the queer landscape needs to be razed. Only in this way will paths inconceivable in the old landscape make themselves available to thought.

Queer Affect's Effects

The affective turn in queer theory shares a number of traits with its phenomenological kissing cousin. Significantly, these include a feeling of fatigue with respect to the emphasis in previous-generation queer theory on language and discourse. This emphasis was heavily influenced by the work of Derrida and Foucault as well as, to a lesser extent, by psychoanalysis. The turn to affect can be traced to a desire for immediacy; for a way to talk about the experience of our engagement with the world. Tired of having to work with heady abstractions like 'the signifier' or even Foucault's elusive notion of power, I want the chance to talk about myself, about my innermost feelings and intimate experience.

From the perspectives of psychoanalysis and Marxism, this is bourgeois psychology by another name. Set free from the need to abstract from experience and emotion in order to gain knowledge of their unconscious and material determinants, I can engage in a practice that feels more authentic, more reflective of my life's particular concerns. The main problem of this approach is that it takes phenomenal experience, including the seductive but misleading realm of feeling, at face value. It fails in this way to heed the elementary lesson of a disappearing generation's ideology critique: I experience the world in the way capital and my ego investments want me to experience it. To the extent that I remain at the affective level, I miss the opportunity not only to discover how my personal reality functions to dissimulate my unconscious libidinal investment in an unjust status quo, but also how the world as it appears compensates for violent antagonisms and conflicts of interest, which it seeks at all costs to obfuscate and repress.

The later work of the late Eve Sedgwick gains particular interest in this light not only because it presents an unusually intelligent iteration of the affective turn, but also because it returns to psychoanalysis – a discourse more or less summarily rejected in 1990's seminal *Epistemology of the Closet* – to question the assumptions of the tradition that her earlier work so influentially inspired. Before her untimely death, Sedgwick evidently had grown tired of queer theory, and she offers a critique of it which, surprisingly, shares some of the views I've put forward myself.[15] Despite the undeniable salience of her diagnosis of queer theory via Melanie Klein, Sedgwick's affective discourse exhibits the same inward and in many ways quintessentially American political naiveté that has characterised her work from the beginning. In the end, Sedgwick's politics unfortunately retains a properly narcissistic resistance to the power of the universal, precisely the sort of pseudo-politics, typical of queer discourse, that this book sets out to leave behind once and for all.

We can begin by considering the details of Sedgwick's psychoanalytically informed critique of earlier queer theory, including her own. As mentioned, Sedgwick draws inspiration from noted Austrian-born British analyst Melanie Klein (1882–1960), whose work, despite enjoying a resurgence in the past decade or so, hasn't had an especially significant impact on theoretical discourses in the humanities. Describing a world of fantasmatic objects – objects internal to the psyche – and the usually violent relationships the subject entertains with them, Kleinian discourse has much to say about the dynamics of intellectual work. Provocatively, Sedgwick speculates that this facet of Kleinian analysis in fact explains critical theorists' reluctance to take it up: it hits too close to home. At any rate, the aim of Sedgwick's engagement with Klein is not only to uncover how earlier queer theory went wrong, but also to speculate about how its project might be renewed. And for Sedgwick, there's a Kleinian concept available to accomplish each of these tasks: the paranoid/schizoid position for the first, and the depressive position for the second.

A central concept of Kleinian psychoanalysis, the paranoid/schizoid position describes the original predicament of the subject. Klein's development of the concept borrows significantly from Freud's idea of the oral stage, and the closest analogue in the Lacanian tradition is no doubt his concept of the imaginary. The paranoid/schizoid position is characterised by the subject's insistence on dividing up the world into two by establishing a firm boundary between what is inherently beneficial and what is clearly dangerous. This is the principle that supports Klein's discussion of her well-known notions of 'good' and 'bad' objects. These two types of object are linked to two opposite but complementary compulsions: good objects must be devoured and incorporated into the ego; bad objects must be kept at bay at all costs. While the subject must incorporate the good objects into itself, the bad objects threaten to incorporate the subject, thereby presenting the terrifying prospect of its being's very obliteration. The logic at work echoes the binary of activity and passivity that Freud attributes to his drives. Similarly, Klein stresses that both the incorporative passion to devour and the traumatic prospect of being devoured are vicissitudes of the same fundamental fear. This is ultimately the subject's fear of its own powers of destruction and dominion, powers it wants ambivalently to embrace and disavow.

Even readers unfamiliar with this facet of her work may not be surprised to learn that Sedgwick goes on to reproach previous queer theory for getting psychically stuck, as it were, in this paranoid/schizoid position. Famously, Foucault in *The History of Sexuality*'s introductory volume debunked what he calls the repressive hypothesis: the classical idea, many will recall, that sex and power work at cross-purposes; that power functions to repress sexuality.[16]

In her last writing, Sedgwick comes to acknowledge the limitations of Foucault's massively influential displacement of the understanding of power from a force that limits and constrains to one that enables and produces. Foucault appears 'to be far more persuasive in analyzing this massive intellectual blockage [set up by the repressive hypothesis]', she writes, 'than in finding ways to obviate it'.[17] In consequence, queer theory became mired in 'those circular Foucaultian energies' (294). In Sedgwick's view, these energies can do no more than insist, however correctly, that any attempt to break through the apparently limiting force power exercises on sexuality winds up reinforcing the strength of the repression that the attempt initially set out to overcome.

It's then up to Sedgwick to link this impotent logic to the mechanism of projective identification, which Klein finds to be inherent in the paranoid/schizoid position. The schizoid subject shows 'a terrible alertness to the dangers posed by the hateful and envious part-objects that one defensively projects into the world around one' (295), Sedgwick writes. The provocative implication is that Foucault and his legions of queer followers fall into this trap. Their projective identification causes them to misperceive the internal objects of their own psychic life as external and nefarious productions of power, which seek oppressively to normalise heterosexual relations.

It's to her tremendous credit that Sedgwick stresses the significance of the American political context to queer theory's earliest days. As members of the first generations afflicted with the HIV crisis, many early queer theorists, Sedgwick included, participated in activist groups, which found themselves up against a virulently phobic political environment characterised, as she memorably puts it, by 'prurient schemes for testing, classifying, rounding up, tattooing, quarantining, and otherwise demeaning and killing men and women with AIDS'

(297). Still, it's impossible to consider Sedgwick's rationale for queer paranoia in isolation from the affect-based psychoanalytic theory upon which she bases her argument. It may be necessary to clarify at this juncture that neither I nor Sedgwick (as I read her) is claiming that the hostile political situation bravely stared down by first-generation AIDS activists and queer theorists was merely conjured up, in whole or in part, in their heads.

In retrospect, however, it's become clear that the Foucault-heavy theoretical lens through which the HIV crisis was initially critically analysed, particularly within groups such as ACT UP familiar with then-emergent queer academic discourse, wasn't especially conducive to the creative imagination of strategies for countering the effects of the deathly state-sanctioned public indifference to the crisis. As Sedgwick insightfully argues, this apparatus tended to produce a paranoid and abstract vision of power, which actually worked against the development of productive strategies of resistance. By emphasising the determinative impact of power over the creation of positive alternatives, the Foucaultian framework created conditions that worked against the negotiation of relations and alliances. These alliances might have called into question the entire Orwellian complex through which health care provision is distributed, highly differentially of course, in the American national context.

The application of Klein's paranoid/schizoid idea to queer theory evidently yields remarkable critical insights. Sedgwick's appraisal of the significance of the alternative depressive position, by contrast, betrays the same resistance to politics that we've seen in the other queer authors considered thus far. Unlike the paranoid/schizoid position, the depressive position, Sedgwick writes, 'is conceived as virtually intersubjective, profoundly ambivalent, and a locus of anybody's special inventiveness' (287). It therefore carries positive implications for theoretical work as Sedgwick construes it.

Unfortunately, however, when it comes to outlining these implications, Sedgwick can offer only vague allusions to the overcoming of depressive affects through 'intellectual creativity', 'challenges to a normalizing universality', and 'pedagogy' (295, 299). At this stage in her discussion, Sedgwick misses a golden opportunity to link the affective vicissitudes of subjectivity to a more social and political understanding of intellectual work and the teaching vocation. This is what's wrong with Sedgwick's analysis: the passionate attachment to her own archive of feeling tethers her argument to the focal points of her limited political knowledge and experience. It seems logical to conclude that such passionate investment in one's own affective history discourages interest in locales, times and experiences other than one's own.

In fact, Sedgwick says as much herself. To introduce her interest in the Kleinian understanding of affect, she relates a memory from her early childhood. A consideration of Sedgwick's evocation and analysis of this memory will allow for the development of my contention about the link between affective self-concern and the elision of politics proper in queer theory discourse. Told by her parents that she must accept her elder sister's doll instead of the new, larger one she prefers, the young Sedgwick sinks 'into the awful whirlpool of tantrum mode' (284), convinced that the old doll is much too small for a girl of her age. For Sedgwick, the recollection's significance lies in the evidence it provides for what she dramatically calls 'the almost grotesquely unintelligent design' (285) of the human mind, a design well placed to remind us of the fundamental psychoanalytic insight that infantile wishes, unanalysed, continue to have their impact on the psyche far into adulthood. Sedgwick's trip down the dark lane of memory leads her to quote American author and naturalist Henry David Thoreau's famous surmise that the majority of human lives are led in quiet desperation. She proceeds to ask herself 'whether or not [hers] is part of that majority' (285), going so far as to insinuate this question into the heart of her investigation of Klein's work.

Sedgwick tells us that she likes to read Klein because 'she is one of the people who most upsets' her, and Klein does this by reminding her of Thoreau's troubling question. There then follows a line that's truly remarkable in its monumental political obliviousness. Klein unsettles Sedgwick's emotional equilibrium 'vastly more than Freud or Lacan does', she writes, 'and even more than the Marxist or anticolonial perspectives from which [her] preoccupations are so effectively made to feel marginal, even to [her]' (285). Unfortunately, Sedgwick's professed inability to imagine how her intellectual concerns might relate to class struggle and colonial history tells us all we need to know about her deepest political convictions. In particular, her inability to see any relation between her own involvement in the HIV/AIDS crisis in the United States and the obscene devastation inflicted by that same crisis, especially in sub-Saharan Africa, is deeply objectionable to say the least.

In fact, one begins to wonder if Klein's writing proves so seductive for Sedgwick not because it allows her to work through or overcome the infantile affects that haunt her, but rather because it provides a sort of intellectual alibi for wallowing in them, sheltered from any reminder that they might in part be determined by forces outside the boundaries of her own limited and very bourgeois construction of her intellectual identity. In short, Klein allows Sedgwick to take the sense data of her feelings at face value, reneging on the political and analytic responsibility to question the ideological parameters that set the terms of her experience of them.

Why exactly does 'girl Sedgwick' want a doll, anyway? What do the qualities of the doll (about which we learn nothing) tell us about the young Sedgwick's position in the social hierarchies and relations of power of the day? How does the doll work as a symptom in her psychical economy – function, that is to say, as a dissimulated expression of the enjoyment about which she would prefer not to know? An interrogation of affect isn't necessarily ancillary to the answering of these questions. But they'll remain unanswered for as long as we fail to move beyond the personal realm of affect, psychologically conceived, and into more materialist and authentically analytic forms of inquiry.

The Homonationalist Critique

The recent appearance of Jasbir Puar's work on the queer theory scene was a significant event in the discourse's history because it introduced geopolitical concerns, in particular the question of the racialisation and sexualisation of the 'terrorist', which, with precious few exceptions, have previously been left unaddressed. Indeed, queer work continues overwhelmingly to be confined to an ideological landscape dominated by a Euro-American history of anti-homophobic activism, a Judeo-Christian genealogy of attitudes towards homosexuality, and a liberal political framework of civil rights and state recognition. By contrast, *Terrorist Assemblages* brings to the fore how globalisation has effectively spread anti-homophobic critique and paradigms for activism to world diasporas shaped by religious and cultural traditions that have been all but invisible throughout the short history of queer discourse.

Further, Puar's book was among the first to acknowledge, however critically, the significance of the historically unprecedented reality of legitimated queer subjects: men and women fully, although also very selectively, recognised by a small number of the most socially liberal state regimes. In the past few decades, these men and women have been endowed with the legal right to marry or to participate in a civil partnership, thereby gaining access to rights of citizenship – spousal benefits and tax exemptions, for instance – which were previously unavailable to same-sex couples. Deploying a sophisticated, but also jargon-heavy and irritatingly opaque, theoretical artillery derived from a familiar and trendy mix of Foucault, Derrida and the Italian philosopher Giorgio Agamben, this new paradigm in queer theory – more worldly; more attuned to differences of race and nation; clearly impacted by post-9/11 modulations of Western orientalisms and Islamophobia – seemed poised to enable the illumination of queer's scandalous geopolitical blind spots. Here, finally, was a book that could talk back to Sedgwick's spectacularly self-concerned bewilderment at how anticolonial theory and the critique of capitalism could possibly relate to her own queer-theoretical thoughts.

Unfortunately, however, despite the undeniable importance of its contribution, Puar's work is too bogged down by the confused obscurity of its poststructuralist biopolitical apparatus, and too marked by the overwhelmingly inward gaze of its own American academic context, to rescue the queer project from its increasingly apparent Eurocentric and bourgeois limitations.

Apart from the significant problem of its complicity with queer theory's inherent reluctance to look beyond America's borders, my main criticism of Puar's project will be that its adoption of a Foucault-derived conception of biopower conditions two main weaknesses. First, the relentless emphasis on power's production of both normalised ('homonational') and queer ('terrorist') subjectivities is badly positioned creatively to imagine the new forms of political organisation that contemporary socialism so desperately needs at the present moment.

Second, these same biopolitical premises obscure the valuable psychoanalytic insight about the properly *symptomal*[18] relation between, on the one hand, the patriotic – and even sometimes 'gay-positive' – construction of the good American citizen and, on the other, the 'queer' racialising terrorist fantasies on which the image of the patriot secretly depends. By positing the latter as the *truth* of the former, psychoanalysis uncovers the disavowed enjoyments that support the racist and homophobic fantasies buttressing the US imperial agenda Puar so rightly wants to decry.

A more detailed run-down of Puar's main argument will prove helpful, however, before I proceed to support the criticisms I've just enumerated. As is widely acknowledged, the biopolitical turn in the work of the later Foucault, and further developed by Agamben, reconceives the relation between power and subjectivity as productive rather than repressive.[19] A complex amalgam of state and non-state discourses create, and at the same time discipline, possibilities for subjectivity not by setting limits, passing laws and constraining freedoms, but rather by promulgating notions about optimising the possibilities for life through the tethering of the human desire for enrichment and improvement to abstractly conceived regimes of surveillance and normalisation.

In short, biopolitical power exercises its force not by limiting or threatening life, but rather by creating and then colonising the desire to live it to the fullest. On the level of its content, Puar's project intervenes in a variety of US-based 'multicultural' or diasporic sites, from the complicity of a growing and normalised conservative gay/queer constituency in both the US and Europe with the racialising and Muslim-bating discourse of counterterrorism, to the 2003 *Lawrence and Garner vs Texas* ruling, which decriminalised sodomy between consenting adults, only to reinforce norms of citizenship premised on the ownership of property and the cultivation of bourgeois, psychological ideals of relationship intimacy.

Tying Puar's project together is an abiding concern for the way in which discourse, in its productive management of the very possibilities for life, produces hierarchies of normality for subjectivity. These hierarchies separate good citizens from bad by promulgating ideals of exceptional citizenship to which we are enjoined to adhere. In the process, such hierarchies draw lines even between members of the variously conceived non-heterosexual constituencies. An example indicative of the general approach is Puar's analysis of how the efforts of

US-based Sikh organisations to defend the image of the turban-wearing man against associations with fundamentalist terrorism draw on what she calls 'heteronormative victimology narratives'.[20] These are the very same constructions that queer and feminist diasporic groups and critics routinely condemn as patriarchal and heterosexist.

Puar's central notion of 'homonationalism' develops out of a quotation from the work of Amy Kaplan, in which the American studies scholar justifiably attacks the conservative appropriation of the thematic of 'coming out' from modern lesbian and gay politics.[21] The target is a column by journalist Charles Krauthammer. In this column, Krauthammer claims that the taboo discouraging explicit celebration of the American empire has diminished or disappeared during the past decade, as a result of changes in the geopolitical situation connected to the events of 9/11. Kaplan incisively remarks on the political irony of Krauthammer's imperialist coming out party against the backdrop of the notorious Clinton-era 'don't ask, don't tell' policy for the US military.

Although she endorses Kaplan's criticism of Krauthammer's hawkish militarism, Puar nevertheless reproaches her colleague in a familiarly politically correct way for harbouring an implicit racialising assumption. Although she offers no evidence to suggest that Kaplan set herself the task of addressing the problem of race in the military, Puar chastises her for failing to make explicit that 'the least welcome entrants into this national revelation of pride [will] be queer people of colour'. Adding a climactic poststructuralist flourish, Puar avers that both Krauthammer and Kaplan 'execute a troubling affirmation of the teleological investments in 'closeting' and 'coming out' narratives that have long been critiqued for the privileged (white) gay, lesbian and queer liberal subjects they inscribe and validate' (2). In short, not only does the 'out' American imperialist inappropriately borrow the language of gay pride. According to Puar, he additionally draws on a discourse of homosexual affirmation, which implicitly reinforces white racial privilege.

I bring out these details of Puar's analysis because they set the stage for her definition of the homonational with respect to 'three imbricated manifestations – sexual exceptionalism, queer as regulatory, and the ascendancy of whiteness' (2). Although the discussion lacks clarity, sexual exceptionalism appears to refer to what Puar considers an implicit legitimation of homosexuality in Krauthammer's appropriation of the coming out narrative for the millennial celebration of American hegemony. That right-wing defences of American economic and military imperialism routinely issue from sources with overwhelmingly socially conservative views doesn't seem to be taken into account. At any rate, this is the project Puar's theoretical machinery sets out to realise, one she shares with a panoply of similarly pedigreed poststructuralist queer work: to uncover the implicit forces of exclusion and marginalisation that accompany the various historically unprecedented cultural and legal accommodations of homosexual and post-homosexual identities in the liberal Western countries. For Puar, even queer discourse effects such acts of exclusion. More dramatically, she adds that hegemonic anti-homophobic programmes carry an unacknowledged and neo-fascist genocidal fantasy of racial purification.

Now, the classical Marxist response to Puar's nonetheless admirable insistence on reading race into the queer problematic would no doubt be to reproach it for being too abstract. More precisely, Puar's approach to race, typical of critical race discourse in the US, errs where it abstracts racialisation from concrete forms of socioeconomic marginalisation – including in particular the histories of colonialism, imperialism and slavery – with which race is always intricately 'imbricated', to use Puar's own term.

For Marxism, structural inequalities directly linked to the history of the mode of production are then 'racialised' at a second moment of determination. British racism during the Raj, for instance, can't be considered outside the history of imperialism and colonialism in India. The competing view holds instead that an abstract racism is primary, and this racism then somehow causes racialised economic stratification more or less on its own. In sum, Puar's vague evocation of a discursive force of racialisation does little to improve our understanding of how intertwined material and psychodynamic causes contribute to the dismaying intractability of racialised hierarchies of economic privilege, which are scattered so widely, even universally, across the globe.

Further, surely it's unhelpful to link the anti-homophobic project as such to what Puar insists on calling, against all available demographic data, the 'globally dominant ascendancy of whiteness' (2). It's imperative that we create a discursive space on the left where it's possible to decry the bourgeois fetishisation of whiteness in so many non-white social contexts, and at the same critically read hyperbolic and counterstrategically abstract charges of racism such as the one Puar confusedly articulates.

But the more fundamental theoretical point to make here is that Puar's fashionable set of biopolitical assumptions can only produce further identifications of what she calls 'normative gayness, queerness, or homosexuality' (2). From the psychoanalytic perspective, such critical identifications, however valuable and to the point, remain stuck in the position of the hysteric, who passionately and unceasingly denounces the Other's imperfections in a way that only exacerbates her continued dependence on its sanction. The repressed underside of the poststructuralist discourse on heteronormativity and homona-tionalism is an unrecognised wish to be acknowledged as normal. The unconscious desire of this discourse is the creation of a worthy Other who will finally be able to recognise all subjects, no matter how obscenely 'queer', as legitimate.

Rather than simply join in on Puar's denunciations of a discourse which, on her view, can produce only 'liberal' queer subjects with questionable investments in whiteness, we must look instead at forms of oppositional political subjectivity that have already made themselves manifest – from Occupy and the Arab Spring, to the widespread popular resistance to the German-led programme of economic austerity in the Eurozone. The urgent imperative is to create new ways of transforming such subjective emergences into lasting forms of political organisation. I've already signalled how Badiou has tirelessly argued that the new political subjectivity must be universal in its address; must speak to the people in a way that communicates *in*difference to their 'small' differences from one another, in particular differences relating to sexuality. We can describe this form of universality queer – why not? – but only on the condition that it doesn't rest on a facile and pseudo-political gesture of differentiation with respect to a presumed instance, embedded in the very fabric of discourse and power, of heteronorma-tivity or homonationalism.

My alternatively universalising form of political subjectivation has the added benefit of specifying the logic of the relation, in Puar's argument, between the call to idealised patriotic citizenship and the tendency sexually to pathologise the (unpatriotic) terrorist. To clarify,

Puar's idea of homonationalism argues for a relation of complicity between what she calls the exception and the exceptional. The ensuing discussion reveals that Puar's appropriation of the exception theme in contemporary theory draws from two different sources. The first source is the long-standing tradition in American foreign policy of attributing, however implicitly, exceptional status to the American nation: as Americans, leaders of the free world, we have an inherent right to set the terms of international law, and it's the duty of all the other nations to obey it. This ethos of exceptionalism penetrates to the very core of the ideology of individualism: the realisation of the American dream requires heroic discipline and self-reliance; the ideal model of US citizenship is premised on a gesture of distinction vis-à-vis the unmotivated, state-dependent masses. The second source is the work of Agamben, who formulated the influential notion of the 'state of exception' to signify the naturalisation of technically illegal state measures in times of perceived crisis.[22] As one might imagine, the standard examples are the 'detention centres' of the US naval base at Guantanamo, Cuba, and the notorious Abu Ghraib prison complex in Baghdad, Iraq.

Puar rightly argues that the two forms of exceptionalism are intimately interrelated. As she writes, they work 'to turn the negative valence of torture' witnessed at Abu Ghraib, for example, 'into the positive register of the valorization of (American) life' (3). Although the logic of the connection is never clearly spelled out, Puar ties the attenuation of heteronormativity in the US – she seems to have in mind the abolition of sodomy laws and the legalisation of same-sex marriage or civil partnership in a select few states of the Union – to the thematic of exceptional citizenship. Somehow, it would appear, this uncharacteristic manifestation of homophilic generosity is part and parcel of a more general programme put in place by the US and its allies to enlist support for the occupation of Iraq and the associated global 'war on terror'.

But psychoanalysis makes the same point in a more forceful, clearer, convincing and politically salient way. For her part, Puar tries to spell out the logic of the relation between the exception and the exceptional with a vague reference to Derrida's idea of 'hauntology, in which the ghosts, the absent presences', she writes, 'infuse ontology with a difference' (4). While this reference to deconstruction offers only a philosophically sophomoric tie-in to the problem of being, psychoanalysis, through its concept of the symptom, precisely defines the contours of the relation between the two phenomena with which Puar is concerned. More specifically, psychoanalysis tells us *why* the fantasy construction of the ideal, counter-terrorist, patriotic and respectably homosexual citizen requires as its unacknowledged condition the obscene, sadomasochistic jouissance of Guantanamo and Abu Ghraib – that is, the flagrant violations of international law that have incensed so many around the world. Psychoanalysis teaches the invaluable lesson that the construction of the ego ideal – the symbolic point from which we can gratifyingly contemplate ourselves – goes hand in hand with the repression of a fantasy, which delivers the libidinal satisfaction such contemplation can only fail to acknowledge. Indeed, it's precisely this enjoyment, kept safely beneath the threshold of our awareness, that fuels our attachment to the ideals of US-style militaristic and Islamophobic patriotism.

We can relate this same logic to Puar's concern with how the fantasy-image of the terrorist is homosexualised. The psychical condition of possibility of the virile heterosexual patriotic male is the repression of a libidinal investment in his uncanny obverse, the subversive queer terrorist. The psychoanalytic wager is that the disclosure of this investment has the effect of dismantling the structure of the ego ideal. Confronted with knowledge of what actually took place at Abu Ghraib and Guantanamo, the patriotic subject has two options: either reinforce the power of repression, which aggravates his complicity with the intrinsic violence of the state of exception, or else allow the patriotic identification to come crumbling down, making possible very different acts of unpatriotic and properly political citizenship.

In Puar's argument, the relation between the exceptional and the exception remains unthought, couched in the vague terms of an apolitical philosophical ontology. Thankfully, psychoanalysis presents a coherent theory that not only outlines how the prestige of our highest ideals is maintained by a covert investment in their basest libidinal correspondents. Even more importantly, it instructs us that the disclosure of this repressed libido can liberate us from the tyranny – often of an inherently political kind – that binds us to their considerable and backhanded ideological force.

2

The Universal
Alternative

Gay Politics in America

Allow me to indulge in a brief personal anecdote to set the stage for this chapter. Over a decade ago now, in October 2000, just a few weeks before the US presidential election that would inaugurate the second Bush era, a young, fashionable, handsome man handed me a political leaflet as I crossed Christopher Street in Greenwich Village, New York City. I failed to give it much thought at the time: I was in transit to the subway and the Port Authority to catch a bus back to Ithaca, where I was working as a postdoctoral fellow at Cornell University. Weeks later, I had the idea to write the first of what would become numerous essays on the (largely missed) encounter between Marxism and queer theory. I wanted to make use of the pamphlet as an example, but I couldn't find it. My quite hostile original reaction to its content – irritatingly politically correct, exasperatingly conservative – had led, unconsciously it seemed, to its mysterious disappearance.

I found the leaflet later, in the chaos of my move away from Ithaca to another privileged but terminal postdoctoral position. It occurred to me then that my reaction to its reappearance had a hysterical quality: I was reluctant to address its traumatic content, unable to move beyond my frustration with the inanity of mainstream queer politics in America. Writing the original version of this essay, I took refuge in my status as a Canadian in the United States, albeit one who, leaving upstate New York, had barely even been across the border. At the time, I acknowledged, but also finally dismissed, 'the condescension of my fellow Canadian lefties towards the primitive, superficial, liberal (in the worst psychologistic sense), irremediably ideological and thoroughly depressing state of American political discourse'.[1]

Having come to the end of a six-year period as a foreign graduate student in the US, I had become deeply disillusioned with the dominant poststructuralist queer theory of the 1990s. That discourse had exposed me to the narrow political horizons of many of its most recognised practitioners. It had also highlighted the stark differences between the trajectories of the elite-educated Americans with whom I associated the queer academic project, and my own academic socialisation in a sprawling and comparatively underfunded public university in Canada, where there are still no private institutions of higher learning with any general credibility, and where the neo-Christian right-wing lobby has had a currently creeping, but comparatively insignificant, influence on social policy.

The general interest of this sort of autobiographical commentary is probably limited, so let's move on. What were the contents of the upsetting leaflet? What exactly was my problem with it? Published by a coalition of queer voters in New York called the Empire State Pride Agenda, its pages presented selective profiles of the main candidates, both Democrat and Republican, running for the offices of President, Senator, State Senator, and Member of the State Assembly. Each profile summarised the history of the aspirant's policy positions on issues of concern to gay, lesbian, bisexual and transgendered persons. No concerted effort was made to document the candidates' perspectives on any other issue: gun control, education, the death penalty, taxation, foreign policy or health care (generally speaking, that is beyond the specific concerns related to HIV/AIDS and reproductive rights). Only policies obviously related to civil rights for non-heterosexual citizens were meaningfully broached.

This briefest of summaries makes the leaflet's general strategy quite patent. But the devil, as they say, is in the detail. The Agenda's members made their endorsements on the basis of results from a questionnaire circulated to New York state queers. Questions covered 'the following topics: comprehensive civil rights protections; protecting students from anti-gay harassment in schools; funding for our health and human service needs; anti-discrimination protections in the issuing of insurance policies; funeral and bereavement leave for same-sex partners; opposition to the state anti-gay marriage bill;

support of multicultural curriculum in our schools; age-appropriate sex education; HIV transmission prevention and counselling for the seropositive; and recognition of our relationships through domestic partnership, civil union, and/or same-sex marriage legislation'. Bear in mind for the upcoming discussion that several topics on this list express interests that extend beyond the queer community strictly speaking, however one may wish to define it, to include the citizenry or people in general: health care, women's reproductive rights, multicultural and sex education, in particular.

On the level of its address, however, the pamphlet presupposed a specific, clearly delimited community subtracted from the whole. The members of this community expressed the interests of an explicit 'we'. The issues of health care and health insurance, for instance, were approached not as concerns that raise the general question of each and every citizen's access to the benefits they provide, but rather as a question of 'our' specific needs and right to protection from discrimination.

The exclusivity of the address works well in the instance of sex education: we can be confident that in our efforts to have educators broach strategies for safer same-sex relations, they won't forget to talk about contraceptive methods. (Note that my 'our' is different from the Agenda's in that it's more than likely that many straight people as well will undertake the efforts I refer to).

The case of health care is probably the one that most clearly brings out the strategy's most troubling political consequences. In the absence of any reference to the broad politics of health care as such, we're led to assume that all will be fine as long as we queers are protected from the phobic discrimination of private insurance providers and the ominously named American health management organisations (HMOs). To be perfectly explicit, the health care system's status quo is left entirely unquestioned; the frame is limited to the ambition of preventing discrimination against queers in the system as it currently stands. Also worthy of note is the tokenistic gesture towards multicul-turalism, made in acknowledgment of the fact that some of us are of colour. Parenthetically, this gives rise to a curious logical difficulty for non-queer non-whites, who belong to 'us' on the level of their racial difference, but are at the same time excluded for being straight.

The interest of the pamphlet lies in the sort of political subject it presupposes. Scandalised, I realised that it enjoined me implicitly to vote for the fiscally conservative homosexual or queer-friendly Republican (rare, but not non-existent) in favour of capital punishment and low corporate taxes, instead of the Democrat pushing for a patients' bill of rights and the regulation of the pharmaceutical industry, but who may have spoken out against gay marriage.

To be blunt, not having the right to vote in the election wasn't the saddest prospect. Yet, it also struck me that on the most fundamental level there was something even more disturbing about the picture the leaflet painted: its survey of gay-rights issues was utterly devoid of any critical or alternative horizon. It simply rehearsed the already existing binary of Democrat or Republican options, leaving without comment the massively circumscribed field of choices on offer. The pamphlet failed to offer any authentic *political* choice, betraying in the process an exasperating blindness. To limit sexual politics to the narrow horizon of American liberal democracy is to betray important elements of the tradition of sexual activism and critique to which its agenda, apparently unknowingly, was indebted. In other words, the Agenda's programme remained totally oblivious to the inspiration earlier generations of gay activists drew in both theory and practice from the socialist political tradition.

Let's imagine for a second an intrepid queer archivist of the current moment. Wanting to get to the source of what I'm going on about, he or she digs up the pamphlet, now already more than a decade old. Given the state of contemporary queer politics, I can almost hear this researcher raising their voice, objecting to my argument as outlined thus far. Does my reading not implicitly attribute a prescriptive dimension to a publication deliberately addressed to a specific audience united by a single set of concerns? I might also be reproached for a naïvety, for a lack of appreciation for certain American political realities. 'He's clearly unaware of the full diversity of forms of politicisation in the historical gay and lesbian movements', some might interject. There are, after all, lesbian Republicans, and an inclusive Pride Agenda should set itself the task of providing them as well with the information they need to exercise their constitutionally enshrined democratic rights.

Further, sceptics might reason that the leaflet makes no assumptions at all about its readers' other, non-gay-related, political convictions:

it simply presents itself as a resource to a constituency united by its concern for a particular experience of discrimination or marginalisation linked to homosexual desire. The difference of the group of individuals concerned, they might add, is different in an important way from that of other historically oppressed groups: women, Asian Americans or illegal immigrants, for example. The difference at issue is tied to the notion that those whom it marks experience desire in a way generally deemed inappropriate, and who have, since at least the moment of the famed Stonewall riots in New York City, emerged into political visibility in unprecedented fashion only during our relatively recent and unusually privileged millennial historical moment.

Post-Marxism and Homosexuality

It could indeed be claimed that queer people make up the most radically new of the new social movements of which Ernesto Laclau, Chantal Mouffe and innumerable others before and since have spoken since at least the early 1970s.[2] The historical novelty of a group of citizens who predicate their politicisation on a notion of sexuality could be submitted as evidence. As has been well documented, these newly audible political voices have justified, since the dawn of the New Left, the reorientation of Marxist and post-Marxist political discourses away from what had been, historically, their central concerns: a view of social antagonism and cultural production as determined predominantly by the economy; a critique of 'democracy' under the conditions of liberalism as democracy for the bourgeoisie, and in that sense disguised tyranny; and a utopian impulse positing a reconciliation of class antagonism under a revolutionary and non- or post-capitalist mode of production. 'What is now in crisis', Laclau and Mouffe wrote in 1985,

is a whole conception of socialism which rests upon the ontological centrality of the working class, upon the role of Revolution with a capital 'r', as the founding moment in the transition from one type of society to another, and upon the illusory prospect of a perfectly unitary and homogeneous collective that will render pointless the moment of politics. (2)

Replacing these allegedly metaphysical fantasies was an appreciation for the new proliferation of different identities. The concrete political demands coming from these new identities, it was suggested, were couched in a new set of assumptions. These assumptions moved beyond the conceptual reach of a Marxist tradition now exposed as insufficiently cognisant of cultural and sexual differences.

While there have been instances of the subversive eruption of feminine and minority voices claiming rights in the name of a variously configured difference throughout the modern era, including within Marxism itself, it's only since the invention of sexuality as a field of scientific inquiry in the nineteenth century that subjects have presented their interests in the public sphere as different, not on account of any objectively identifiable trait such as race or sex, but rather on account of their desire. Since then, this non-heterosexual desire has gone on to produce more and more numerous subdifferentiations. It's been in reference to this new sexual paradigm of difference that the numerous gay and lesbian movements of the past four decades have put themselves[3] forward as deserving gestures of cultural recognition and legal accommodation. These gestures have aimed to account for the particularity of their ways of being, and offer protection from social discrimination.

No doubt it's uncontroversial – banal, even – to claim today that the emergence into full visibility of self-identified sexual minorities coincides, in general historical terms, with the collapse of the Eastern bloc, the broad discrediting of Marxian political ideology, and the ensuing intellectual hegemony of a (neo)liberalism distinguished by how it links up in an essential way the purge-crazy totalitarianism of Stalinism to the very kernel, libidinal or conceptual, of the socialist utopian impulse. Already in the early 1970s, Gilles Deleuze and Félix Guattari had explicitly linked the 'deterritorialising' expansion of capital with a post-oedipal destructuring of not only the structures of kinship, but also the set of categories that serve to classify sex and sexuality.[4]

Further, the relative commercial success in the US of a film like *Before Night Falls* (2000), the Julian Schnabel-directed biopic about Reinaldo Arenas – an openly gay Cuban literary figure whom the Castro regime 'imprisoned' in 1973 – highlighted the increasing awareness in Western capitalist consciousness of the hostility orthodox

Marxist humanism had often shown to homosexual desire and the persons who experience it.[5] To take this evidence at face value is to conclude that you can't have an official Marxism and actually existing homosexuals in the same place at the same time. Further, if capitalism, as so much evidence does indeed show, has functioned historically to erode the bourgeois-patriarchal family structures that fuel the fires of homophobia, then it seems logical to conclude that the best anti-homophobic strategy is indeed a libidinally exuberant queer embrace of unlimited capitalist expansion.

These are perhaps only the most obvious reasons why one has been hard put, since the dawn of queer theory, to find an authentically radical socialist voice – one that goes so far as to seek after the material and historical conditions of possibility of the homosexual political movements. While they underscored what we might call the socially progressive power of capitalism with respect to conventional family forms and gender codes, Deleuze and Guattari influentially abandoned the properly Marxist project of capitalism's critique in favour of a celebration of capitalism's full anarchic potential.

It's been an equally challenging task over the past three decades to find texts that pose the touchy problem of the dependence of these movements on an implicit and largely unconscious acceptance of the bourgeois (liberal-democratic) political framework, beyond which it has proven so difficult to see. Moreover, those anti-liberal tendencies in queer theory that do exist tend towards a knee-jerk anti-statism, which implicitly confines their political reach to an ill-defined non-communitarian community or subculture.

In sum, since the dawn of queer theory, non-libertarian and non- or post-liberal – not to mention explicitly Marxist – approaches to homosexuality have been extremely rare.[6] Certainly, classical Marxism itself hasn't helped matters. With the exception of a smattering of quite banal, decidedly unscientific, homophobic comments in their correspondence, Marx and Engels themselves were significantly unconcerned with homosexuality. The historical record shows that this oversight has since led many major Marxist strategists and theorists to the silly conclusion that homosexuality as such is objectively reactionary or bourgeois.

Now, the work of Judith Butler immediately comes to mind when it comes to the productive encounter that has taken place between the concerns of the radical democratic left and the interests of the historically unprecedented sexual minority communities. For this reason, anyone who broaches the question of queer theory's problematic relation to Marxism has an obligation to take her work into account. Two of her texts from the millennium's turn – one questioning the implications for sexuality and kinship of the structuralist matrix of poststructuralist theory; the other presenting scrappy theoretical exchanges with two influential left-identified interlocutors – acquired tremendous significance by virtue of their effort to hook queer theory up with the major currents of progressive political theory at the end of the twentieth century.

It's become clear in retrospect that Butler's engagement with the category of the universal went a considerable way towards resuscitating it from its premature cardiac arrest at the close of a postmodern age, guilty of making a fetish of difference. Despite the massive impact of Foucault's reformulation of power on Butler's work in gender and sexuality theory, this turn towards the universal, quite surprising from this perspective, helped counteract the troubling inwardness that has significantly separated the imagination of queer theory's political future from the crucial debates around the ideas of democracy and communism, as well as the forms of national and supranational – state and non-state – power to which these categories are tethered. In short, the recuperation of the idea of the universal made it possible once again to connect the exercise of power to more concrete agencies – not the least of which being capitalism – than it was possible to do under the paradigm, massively influential for radical queer theory, of that omniscient but empty, subjective but non-intentional, discourse-power tandem that was Foucault's final and transformative theoretical contribution.

The publication during the same millennial year of Judith Butler's Wellek lectures on Antigone, and the 'dialogues on the left' between Butler, Ernesto Laclau and Slavoj Žižek, was important not only because it forced the 'issue' of homosexuality onto the broader terrain of contemporary political theory. Additionally, it presented, however potentially, an exciting opportunity to rescue queer theory from its increasing political irrelevance by coaxing it, kicking and screaming as it were, beyond the limits of the differentialist horizon within which, almost without exception, it had been confined.

Moreover, the dominant poststructuralist strand of queer theory set itself the goal of tracing the construction of the difference of non-heterosexual subjects within the existing discursive order without questioning this order's dependence on its socioeconomic base, however this dependence might be conceived. By contrast, the reactivation of the universal cleared a space for queer theory to ally itself with more politically challenging currents of thought. The question I wish to pose in this context is whether or not the neo-universalism set forth in *Contingency, Hegemony, Universality* might help set the conditions for a more thoroughgoing vision of general social emancipation which, ultimately, would be of benefit to everyone without exception – queer and unqueer alike.

Before considering how it might contribute to such a political reawakening, however, more details about the parameters of this redeployment of the universal will be required. More precisely, it will prove instructive to contextualise the nature and consequences of the theoretical conflicts that animate the debate, not only between the co-authors of *Contingency, Hegemony, Universality*, but also between the radical democratic discourse – in dialogue with both Marxism and psychoanalysis – and the dominant assumptions of queer theory, as they have influentially taken form over the last quarter century in Butler's work.

As I work my way through a selection of issues broached in *Contingency, Hegemony, Universality*, and further developed in Butler's *Antigone's Claim*, I'll aim to develop two main points. First, the battle between Butler and Žižek concerning the political stakes of the category of the real in Lacanian psychoanalysis, originally pitched two decades ago,[7] has to my mind been decisively 'won' by Žižek. By this I mean quite simply that the element of queer theory that has seen in the real a nefarious naturalisation of heterosexuality has based itself on an unpersuasive reading of Lacan. (There is indeed a low-grade heterosexism in the early Lacan, but it disappears in the later teaching, and is flatly contradicted in the major work on sexuation in the 1970s.) Indeed, it should now generally be acknowledged that Butler is a weak reader of Lacan. Further, the inability of Butler's argument to appreciate the agency of the real in sexual difference is closely related to her discourse's unwillingness to proceed to an examination of the consequences of the identification of capital or the market as a kind of real, against which the more challengingly welcome anti-liberal aspect of her discourse continually runs up. That is, an analogy can be drawn between how the real becomes a normative instance for sexuality in Butler, and how capital takes form as a horizon beyond which her thought chooses not to explore.

Second, queer theory discourse is so entrenched in the presuppositions of poststructuralism that it should simply be abandoned – left to those content with accommodating the demands of non-heterosexual constituencies within the general framework of the 'third way' liberal democracy originally promulgated in the Anglo-American world by Bill Clinton and Tony Blair. The poststructuralist notions that must be left behind include its latently identitarian anti-identitarianism (paradigmatically, identity is 'subverted' only to be brought in through the back door as contingent, strategic, multiform, incomplete, partial); its minoritarian and absolutist anti-statism (the state by definition seeks nefariously to normalise sexuality); and its lack of an anti-capitalist critical horizon. The current state of rights-based queer political activism, including that aspect of it that acknowledges the limitations of the liberalist rights framework, is so deeply mired in the exploitative logic of capital that the optimal radical strategy is actually to declare the whole category of sexual orientation irremediably bourgeois. This gesture of negation opens up a space for the creation of a different form of political thought in which sexuality plays a new, more politically consequential, form.

Already, I hear indignant protestations. 'Go back to your Reinaldo Arenas example', some might insist. Does his case not show how a 'totalitarian' regime that rejects rights-based discourse as bourgeois inherently tends towards the criminalisation of minority sexualities? Let's assume for the moment that there was indeed systemic discrimination against homosexuals in the early Castro era in Cuba. Is it not also possible to say that the logic that supports this oppression – not uncharacteristic, to be sure, of 'actually existing' socialist social policy throughout the twentieth century – is symptomatic of the Castro regime's failure to dismiss sexuality as a reliably descriptive political, or even sociological, category? In other words, surely it makes more sense to claim that the Cuban communists' error lay in their inability to accept a simple fact: if homosexuality is indeed a bourgeois phenomenon, then surely heterosexuality must be as well.

The objectively reactionary concept is therefore neither homosexuality nor heterosexuality, but rather the very idea of sexual orientation itself. More precisely, the authentic socialist insight is precisely the illegitimacy of *the move from an idea of sexual identity or behaviour to a determinate political judgment.* More strongly, as psychoanalysis would concur, the very premise that sexuality lends itself to identity categories and their deconstruction is what is most essentially bourgeois about the discourse of sexual orientation.

Post-Post-Marxism and Sexuality

We can now turn to the texts themselves. The three terms of the *Dialogues'* title – contingency, hegemony and universality – encapsulate what's at stake in negotiations of left or progressive political theory at a moment, marked still by the clash between orthodox Marxist historicist teleology (capitalism leads inexorably to its revolutionary overthrow) and the newer postmodern politics predicated on identity claims and their interrogation or subversion. We should also note the significance today of the postcolonial context and the question of the recognition of cultural and ethnic identities associated with the discourse of multi-culturalism – a half-century old story in the North American context, but still topical and controversial in Europe. A closer examination of the terrain occupied by our key titular terms is therefore in order.

First, *contingency*: for Laclau, Antonio Gramsci's significance for Marxist theory lies in his suggestion that a political subject, individual or collective, will bear no perfectly predictable relation to the material situation that surrounds it. Thus, 'there is no necessity whose consciousness exhausts our subjectivity – political or otherwise',[8] nor is it possible accurately to identify particular agents who would harbour special revolutionary investments in consequence of a putatively objective structural position in the mode of production. Laclau's Gramsci precociously deconstructs orthodox Marxism's idealisation of the proletariat as history's predestined collective actor. Given the failure of both second world Soviet-style economies and third world developing ones to delink successfully from the logic of global capital and the influence of neoliberal trade law, does it still make sense to uphold capitalism as a socioeconomic reality that can be transcended, overcome? Further, in light of the poststructuralist commonplace that identity claims are historically contingent, structurally incomplete or necessarily failed, is the traditional Marxist category of 'class' to be relegated to the same suspect status as the other, latterly more fashionable, iterations of difference, including in particular the category of sexuality from which queer theory has ambivalently sought an escape?

Next, *hegemony*: classical Marxism argued for the determination of superstructural social elements (state, civil society, public sphere, culture, etc.) by a base of factors constituting a society's means of production of the necessities (including, in late or advanced capitalism, the less necessary ones) of life. Laclau and Mouffe's work strove to cloud the transparency of this relation, uncovering the significance of what they considered the self-conscious, actively willed instances of political organisation that occur at least in part independently of structural determination. In consequence, these new political forms are able to convey, in their view, an extremely broad spectrum of public and private interests. Further, Laclau and Mouffe claimed to find a space of indeterminacy or impossibility in the social field characterised by an immanent and insurmountable antagonism, calling 'hegemony' the temporary and contingent filling in of this space by a particular set of political interests.

It's startling to think that a full quarter century has passed since Laclau and Mouffe put forth the view that the hegemony concept acts as a kind of vanishing mediator between orthodox Marxist class 'essentialism' and the world of free-floating post-industrial identities and competing ideologies which, so they claimed, replaced it. Their version of hegemony appealed to social constituencies inclined to think that the privileging of class struggle as the prime mover of history performs a kind of violence which targets the proliferation of differences. These differences should therefore absorb class to create a level playing field among the competing signifiers of social identity.[9]

Since this view's popular apogee in the 1990s, however, numerous critics, including myself, have concluded that this articulation of the hegemony concept was itself a product of the ideologies of liberal democracy and multinational capital. We began to wonder if the knee-jerk association of the revolutionary or anti-capitalist 'grand narrative', with the inevitability of crimes against difference, was simply one of the forms of liberal blackmail that police the boundaries of political thought. This association effectively forces us to abandon ambitious agendas for social change as the price paid for the defence of hard-fought victories on the terrain of race, gender and sexuality.

Finally, *universality*: in the last few decades, cultural critics on the left have increasingly argued that the postmodern emphasis on difference, specificity and particularity makes us lose sight of: (a) the socioeconomic realm, by turning a blind eye to the production of difference by a capitalist totality or world system; or (b) the sociopolitical realm, by misrecognising the fact that by virtue of the lack of closure of the general social field (the barred Other for Lacanians, the structural necessity of suture or articulation for the radical democrats) any expression of a particular political interest always manifests either an implicit call to the universal, or else a formally necessary gesture of universalisation.

But how exactly is this reference to the universal to be understood? Is the dimension of the universal akin to a neutral a priori structural gap or emptiness, as Laclau argues, whose position is then filled in by a hegemonic political formation? Or is it rather, as Žižek suggests, and as Butler seems to concur, the result of a primal or original gesture of violent exclusion? In the latter scenario, the very field of political hegemony depends on such a moment of exclusion, and features in consequence an irreducible dimension of historicity. In short, is the terrain of the universal a neutral but punctured Habermasian public sphere equally accessible to all? Or is it rather a pre-constituted field or logic, which decides in advance what is and what is not a legitimate candidate for universalisation?

There are some especially telling threads in *Contingency, Hegemony, Universality*, which link up not only with the concept of the universal, but also with the politics of kinship of concern to Butler in *Antigone's Claim*, and in queer theory more generally. Indeed, one of the motivations behind Butler's examination of the critical reception of the Sophocles tragedy is to develop how Antigone's defiance suggests a radical critique of kinship, one that denounces all efforts on the part of the state to normalise family structures through a process of selective legitimisation. The examples in question are the still-topical controversy in Western public opinion at the turn of the millennium concerning the desirability of the legalisation of gay marriage, and the more US-specific debate about the rights of homosexuals to join the military and be open about their sexualities (the notorious 'don't ask, don't tell' policy introduced under the Clinton administration). Although the gay marriage issue (along with its kissing cousin the civil union) has arisen in numerous jurisdictions outside the US, the timbre of Butler's discussion as well as the military element lend it a distinctively American feel. Still, the significance of these examples extends beyond America's borders by virtue of the fact that they feature (nationally) universal social 'forms' (again: marriage and military service, or at least the eligibility for it), which are essential to most modern liberal conceptions of citizenship. These conceptions are designed to dissimulate disavowed exclusions of particular constituencies (here: homosexuals).

The question arises as to whether or not the inclusion of the excluded particular within the realm of the universal has an inherent political effect. There then arises an even more crucial question concerning whether or not the very goal of inclusion sidesteps a more foundational issue regarding the constitution of the field of universality in the first instance. We can take the example of marriage as a means of working through these questions. The anti-homophobic critic who sets out to answer the first question will inquire after the effects of the extension of marriage rights to couples previously deemed ineligible. By contrast, the one who addresses the second will instead interrogate the ways in which the legal form of marriage, regardless of its particular content, discriminates – with respect to taxation and state or corporate social benefits, for example – against subjects who by choice or circumstance don't find their lives linked in such a special way to a single person.

Further, this latter line of inquiry has the benefit of emphasising that the discourse about 'gays in the military' glosses over the question of why they would want to be there in the first place, given in particular the long-standing hypocrisy of US foreign policy, the role of the US military in shady neo-imperial and terrorist activity around the world, and the long-standing and extraordinarily effective taboo against the politicisation of the defence budget in American public discourse. Butler is justifiably concerned about all of these issues when she underscores how the conceptual horizon of inclusion takes for granted – leaves unquestioned – the normative framework to which one, as an excluded subject, seeks access:

One might say that the advances that are sought by mainstream liberal activists (inclusion in the military and in marriage) are an extension of democracy and a hegemonic advance to the extent that lesbian and gay people are making the claim to be treated as equal to other citizens with respect to these obligations and entitlements, and that the prospect of their inclusion in these institutions is a sign that they are at present carrying the universalizing promise of hegemony itself. But this would not be a salutary conclusion, for the instatement of these questionable rights and obligations for some lesbians and gays establishes norms of legitimation that work to remarginalize others and foreclose possibilities for sexual freedom which have also been long-standing goals of the movement. The naturalization of the military-marriage goal for gay politics also marginalizes those for whom one or the other of these institutions is anathema, if not inimical. (160)

Before considering this argument in detail, I wish to signal one underlying problem I'll have occasion to develop at a later point. Butler's programme to dissect the machinations of power in the normative constitution of the universal has recourse to an ideal of sexual freedom as an ultimate good, which by default remains outside the realm of politicisation. This feature not only indicates how her framework never completely steps outside the liberal ideology she attacks, but also bespeaks a fundamental and quite dangerous misunderstanding of the failures of safer-sex education in the gay community, as well as the history of HIV transmission between men. It's also clear, however, that Butler's point carries a basic and irrefutable significance. To the considerable extent that mainstream gay and lesbian politics never stretches beyond the horizon of inclusion, visibility and equality, the more crucial question of the ideological context in which these ideas are posited is left entirely unexamined.

Take the example of early twenty-first-century US network television. Despite the clamorous protestations of right-wing evangelical and family-values groups, one can represent gays and lesbians – in fact, if one doesn't one can be subjected to effective consumer boycotts by groups such as the very Hollywood GLAAD (formerly the Gay & Lesbian Alliance Against Defamation)– as long as they're young, attractive, well-paid professionals living in impossible apartments; as long as their lives proceed without friction against the dominant corporatist and consumerist ethic; as long as their problems stay well within the limits of the familiar comedic-melodramatic, properly psychological, terrain of relationships and affairs of the heart, intriguing though these can surely be. In short, the legitimate concern here is for all those queer subjects who will never see themselves on TV.

Admirably, Butler's argument underscores how official forms of social legitimisation conferred by regimes of state and corporate power create a shadowy parallel universe of invisible and voiceless subjects, who are concretely oppressed by such instances of normative control. Also, and more radically, these subjects remain socially and culturally unintelligible; underneath the threshold of representability – that which conditions all recognisable forms of viable life.

In his final contribution to the *Dialogues*, Žižek latches on to Butler's provocative examples, and makes a subtle but powerful point upon which I'd like to elaborate. This point pertains not to the violent primal exclusions that a field of universal intelligibility effects as it takes form, but rather to the logic of the *relation* between these exclusions, as Butler defines them, and her views – communitarian, anti-statist, in short ambiguous – about concrete political agency in an era of increasingly unrestrained transnational capitalist expansion. Žižek reproaches Butler for harbouring a view of state power excessively indebted to late-period Foucault, whose argument (I suggested earlier) tends towards a paranoid construction of its unlimited productivity. Butler's construal of power's operation fails to apprehend how 'state power is split from within and relies on its own obscene spectral underside' (313), as Žižek characteristically puts it. What power thinks it's doing and what power actually does, in other words, are two very different things.

To some, this point might seem like an abstruse theoreticist quibble. Does it really make any difference to our understanding of politics whether state power is an unambivalent expression of the law's normative reach, or rather a force which is, you could say, structurally hypocritical – which depends upon, and works in tandem with, its own violation? The best example here is the Catholic church's institutional power. While it tells you how it fosters the spiritual growth of today's youth, and positions itself as a moral authority on the topic of child rearing, it has engaged in an alarmingly systematic practice involving the sexual abuse of children. I go along with Žižek when he protests that Butler's qualification of the relation between the normative instance of state power ('the law', in this context) and its register of abject exclusions as one of antagonism rather than *disavowed complementarity*, leads the American critic to underestimate the importance of addressing the normative instance itself. That is, very often the politically effective move involves acknowledging with psychoanalysis that transgression is already (unconsciously) taken account of by, and is therefore dependent on, the law. In consequence, the tactic of praising transgression – of positing a 'subversive' effect for the law's violation – can have the unexpected consequence of confirming the law's effective authority.

Wedded to Subversion

The example of gay marriage illustrates this last point in a particularly illuminating way. Marriage conventionally – heterosexually – conceived is almost universally viewed in both social and religious discourses to be the linchpin of the social bond; the unique relation that stands for the cohesion of the total set of relations making up the social as a whole. In universalist liberal rights discourse, the right to marry is often listed alongside the basic rights to life and liberty. The vocabulary of kinship cross-culturally is incomprehensible in the absence of the idea of marriage in its stunningly varied forms, including those it took in matriarchal societies. This was taken for granted even in earliest Marxism, most notably by Frederick Engels in his landmark text *The Origin of the Family, Private Property and the State* (1884). Few would disagree that marriage has functioned historically, and to a large extent even today continues to function even in the most liberal cultures and state regimes, as a precondition of political and cultural legitimacy, indeed of full citizenship as such.

Yet, if we suppose that marriage, considered as a form of state or civil discipline, produces as its social effect a set of abject or delegitimated subjects who carry subversive potentialities by virtue of their mere existence outside the norm, then we simply fail to appreciate the significance of how the marriage institution concretely enables its own adulterous transgressions. By this I mean not only that marriage in its modern bourgeois form has always worked at least in part in synchrony with the various forms of unfaithful enjoyment it enables. (How many such marriages have functioned, for example, as preconditions for a spouse's, usually of course the man's, heterosexual or homosexual dalliances.) Also, just as significantly, contemporary bourgeois marriage lays the groundwork for the establishment of an idle and dreamy vicariousness through which a spouse disguises his or her illicit fantasies about a single friend's sex life under condescending assurances that this same friend will soon find a splendid partner.

It's in this sense that marriage in its status as a legal contract assumes the function Žižek designates with a term from Hegelian logic: concrete universality. Marriage presents itself as a sort of allegory of the social bond. Yet, in the vast majority of jurisdictions, it's concretely available only to heterosexual subjects of acceptable amounts of generally acknowledged attractiveness, a minimal level of material comfort or social prestige, and an apparent conventionality of lifestyle. In light of this reality, we would be gravely mistaken to underestimate the political power that can be exercised when a covertly excluded party invades the terrain of universality.

Given in particular the conservative and deeply patriarchal mobilisation of the marriage institution in the US, it isn't difficult to envisage how the inclusion of same-sex couples within the set of marriageable partners can potentially discredit marriage in its very concept. Indeed, the notion that the legalisation of gay marriage will effectively ruin the institution, that it has the power to subvert marriage's very meaning for everyone, is a constant refrain of the widely broadcast family-values ditty. Cultural commentators of the moral majority persuasion have repeatedly pronounced that when same-sex partners are allowed to marry, 'marriage won't be marriage anymore'. The fact that gay marriage has now existed for several years in a number of nation-states, including Canada, without in any way destroying the institution, has made only negligible impact on the persistence of the dynamic I've just described.

The logic isn't difficult to appreciate. Social conservatives explicitly admit to the not-so-hidden truth of marriage when they recognise that the concept depends on what we could call its decreasingly dissimulated heterosexual essentialism. Despite the widespread acceptance of homosexuality in many parts of Europe and North

America, the fact that only a handful of nations have legalised equal marriage (as opposed to civil union) lends support to this last claim. Illogically, conservative pundits often proceed as if one can oppose gay marriage and remain immune to charges of homophobia and discrimination. Further, queer radicals often insist that arguments in favour of gay marriage voiced by homosexuals betray the dreaded 'internalised homophobia'.

In light of these realities, it's hardly counterintuitive to imagine that the apparently banal and conformist image of the suburban upper-middle-class homosexual couple with one point three children and two SUVs has the effect of radically calling into question the terms of the social bond as such. I would go so far as to argue that the hirsute leather-bound BDSM muscle daddy, or the pierced and tattooed biker dyke (also known to be leather-clad), is much less threatening to conventional morality than the couple who, despite their shared biological sex, look and behave 'exactly like us'.

Of course, it would make no sense at all to offer up this troublingly normal suburban pair as an ideal of progressive or revolutionary political praxis. Still, the paradoxical logic inherent in gay marriage's surprisingly subversive consequences no doubt accounts for the comparatively wider acceptance of domestic partnership and civil union across the liberal and secular West. The French even invented a new form of legal union – the PACS – to keep marriage safe from the homosexuals.[10] Widespread opposition to same-sex adoption, even in jurisdictions where gay marriage has been legalised, further underscores the powerful oppositional effects of a culturally normative homosexuality. Families headed by same-sex parents, in other words, expose the stubborn intractability of the modern family's heterosexual essentialism. Tellingly, in many jurisdictions, the figure of a committed homosexual couple raising a child together seems to be more threatening than that of a gay single parent.

These admittedly selective observations make it tempting to conclude that the more gay cultures are mainstreamed – not in the sense of the emergence of gay 'markets' in global capitalism (the 'pink pound' in the UK for instance) or of the representation of upper-middle-class homosexual characters on network television, but rather with respect to the increasing resemblance of many gay couples and families to their heterosexual counterparts across the socioeconomic strata – the more the most foundational assumptions about the cultural intelligibility of sexual identities are called into question.

Contrary to what Butler argues, and counterintuitive though it may seem, the best way to attack the marriage form as such may very well be through an act of straightforward (no pun intended) conformity or imitation. The result of the full integration of homosexual couples within the universal set of privileges accruing from the institution of marriage might give rise to the dissolution of this very field of universality – indeed, to the elimination of the bourgeois family unit as the linchpin of mainstream liberal politics. Potentially, the definition of marriage could expand beyond the same-sex couple in such a way that the institution's meaning becomes a question merely of legal rights and responsibilities between individuals, devoid of any normative content whatsoever concerning who these individuals must be.

Vicissitudes of Antigone

The political terrain of family and kinship is more broadly explored in *Antigone's Claim*, where Butler endeavours to trace contemporary attitudes on these topics through structuralism and German idealism, all the way back to the foundations of Western culture in Greek antiquity. Butler's reading of Antigone re-examines the concept of kinship in contemporary theory, its place in culture and civil society, and its relation to the forms of state power. Butler views Antigone's defiant action – recall that she contravenes king Creon's edict by burying her brother Polynices, an enemy of the polis – as an ultimately doomed effort to 'defy the state through a powerful set of physical and linguistic acts'.[11] These acts, for Butler, suggest a new kind of feminism, which she hopes will take on the power of the state to set the conditions not simply for legitimate kinship relations, but more fundamentally for basic political, social and cultural intelligibility. Butler sums up her view of the significance of Antigone's act when she identifies the two questions Sophocles' original play poses to the contemporary reader: 'whether there can be kinship without the support and mediation of the state, and whether there can be the state without the family as its support and mediation' (5).

As many have done before her, Butler finds in Antigone's defiance a protest against a certain authoritarian and patriarchal form of power. This power delineates a notion of the universal collective good and, through this delineation, sets up conditions of intelligibility for the expression of legitimate political interests. Antigone doesn't merely violate Creon's edict, in other words. More consequentially, she calls into question the entire ideological frame through which this edict can be read as an exemplar of that collective good. Butler reviews how references to Antigone's challenge are scattered widely across the texts that form the Western tradition of ethics (Hegel, Hölderlin, Lacan, among others). She traces Antigone's impact to the way her act of defiance exposes the parameters by means of which collective social norms are instituted and contested.

According to Hegel's famous interpretation of the tragedy in *The Phenomenology of Spirit* (1807), Antigone acts in accordance with an ethical law connected to both the feminine realm of the household gods of the family, and the unknowable dimension of death, the meaning of which exceeds the public arena of political citizenship and commercial exchange. The ethical law enters into conflict with the masculine and political law of Creon, ruler of Thebes, whose legislative edicts are designed to ensure the smooth functioning of the polis, as well as the limitation of individual freedom in the name of the collectivity's general well-being. A dialectical tension animates the relation between the two opposing laws. For Hegel, this tension occasions the destruction of the ancient ethical world in which everyone accepted their given place in society. This destruction engenders a new set of laws and customs with which subjects can no longer spontaneously identify. As a result, these laws and customs are newly experienced as constraints imposed by an alien authority. Coming into being here is the 'modern' conflict between individual desire and social law.

In Butler's view, the Hegelian reading brings into relief the ethical implications of the antagonism between the cultural forms of kinship and the regimes of legality enunciated in the state's name. In his seminar on psychoanalytic ethics, Lacan presents a trenchant critique of the Hegelian reading.[12] Butler takes this opportunity to link, in a first move, Antigone's heroic act to the emergence of the structuralist idea of kinship in Lévi-Straussian anthropology (and its enlistment as the taboo-as-threshold-of-culture paradigm in Freudian psychoanalysis), and to characterise, in a second gesture, the whole apparatus of Lacanian theory as an elaboration of ahistorical premises featuring putatively immutable sociosymbolic structures. 'Lacanians tend to sever the symbolic account of kinship from the social', Butler sums up, 'thus freezing the social arrangements of kinship as something intact and intractable' (14).

The problem here lies in Butler's assumption that the unnamed Lacanians to whom she refers are competent readers of Lacan. Butler misconstrues Lacan's concept of the real as banishing particular non-hegemonic forms of human life to a domain outside the field of culture, and therefore beyond the reach of social change. Further, she misunderstands Lacan's idea of the symbolic order as proceeding from the premise of an a priori cultural taboo against both homosexuality and the free expression of feminine desire. No wonder, then, that only an explicitly patriarchal and heterosexist social economy can emerge from Butler's distorted Lacanian assumptions. Both the symbolic and the real are normative in Butler's Lacan in a rigidly determinative sense.

In actuality, however, Lacan associated the real with the subversion of normativity as such. And as far as the symbolic order is concerned, its normative power is limited to the castrating function of the notorious father's name. Belying feminist protestations, this name ultimately refers only to the signifier that indexes to the subject, regardless of its biological sex, its own unconscious knowledge that it has been ousted from its privileged position as object of the mother's desire.

Butler's iteration of Lacanian concepts is based on a misapprehension of the relation between the symbolic and the real. Indeed, this 'relation' is finally not a relation at all, since Lacan consistently chose to evoke the real not as a confirmation of symbolic law, but rather as the law's undoing. The real, for Lacan, manifests the symbolic law's own externality to itself, its self-difference. The real imposes as the symbolic order's destiny the ceaseless repetition of its failure to totalise itself in such a way that it might impose a normative matrix for both sexual identity and kinship relations.

Viewed in this light, Butler's argument against Lacan rests on the false premise that an internally limited sociosymbolic structure – a structure that isn't constrained from the outside by power, but rather one that effectively subverts itself *from within* – will dissimulate the naturalisation of a normative power regime which transcends history and representation. This premise distorts Butler's view of what Lacan says about Antigone's defiance of the edict against her brother's burial. On one level, Butler's error lies in her assumption that the concept of the Lacanian symbolic is identical to a 'structuralist', putatively Lévi-Straussian, framework in which every possible sociosymbolic system imposes specific conditions of cultural intelligibility overseen by the prohibition of incest, the exchange of women between kinship groups, and the psychosocial repression of homosexuality. According to Butler, Lacanian theorists, despite their protestations to the contrary, readily slip from speaking of the normative agency's properly symbolic forms (i.e. the link between the 'name of the father' and any actual father is contingent) to statements that enforce concretely heterosexist social imperatives. 'The distinction between symbolic and social law', she concludes, 'cannot finally hold' (19).

Although Butler is certainly right to cast a suspicious glance at the sometimes quite ridiculous social prognostications of some psychoanalysts, Lacanian and otherwise, it's unclear where Butler finds the distinction she names, since Lacan himself never introduced such a concept as a properly social law in this sense. Lacan formulated the symbolic law's strange failure to legislate effectively not with reference to particular social conventions (which everyone knows are historically contingent), but rather vis-à-vis an agency both unchanging and resistant to articulation – the real. Indeed, one of the fundamental focus-points of Lacan's mid to later teaching is an elaboration of the consequences of the disarticulation of the symbolic from the real. This means that all possible sociosymbolic systems necessarily fail to conceal the traumatic eruption of the real, a central negativity which not only ensures the law's impotence to legislate against its own violation, but which creates *complicity* between the law's effective power and a supportive realm of obscene, socially disavowed transgression.

This logic of inherent transgression, which Žižek, for one, has vividly evoked in his work, must force queer theory to re-examine how its argument presupposes an extraordinarily determinative 'heteronormativity' against which its programmes of subversion acquire their intuitive appeal. To reiterate, a sociosymbolic system is limited not by an externally imposed regime of power, but rather by an internal impossibility, which splits power's expression from the field of its effects. It's precisely the 'space' of this impossibility, this region beyond or underneath the law, which Lacan wants to claim in his ethics seminar for Antigone's act. Rather than merely transgress the law, Antigone's act exposes, *signifies*, the disavowed dependence of the political good on often brutal programmes of exclusion, which selectively and violently delegitimise specific non-hegemonic forms of living being.

When he calls Antigone the guardian of her brother's being, Lacan assumes that this dimension of being is what every sociosymbolic system lacks. Recall that Lacan defines the subject with reference to an essential *manque-à-être*, or lack of/in being. Crucially, however, by insisting that Antigone, through her act, occupies this impossible place or limit, Lacan insists not only that the suspension or cancellation of any sociosymbolic order is concretely possible and even necessary, but also that every social system will in a sense objectively put forth how this suspension might be effected. It does this through the way it implicitly qualifies as criminal, impossible, or unintelligible particular avenues of thought and action. According to Butler, however, when Lacan claims that Antigone affirms in defiance of Creon's edict the properly transcendental value of her brother's being, 'he forgets that Antigone is also committing a crime' (53).

Yet, Lacan makes clear that this link between being's affirmation and the dimension of criminality is precisely his point. 'The fruit of the incestuous union [between Oedipus and Jocasta]', he says, 'has split into two brothers [Creon and Polynices], one of whom represents power and the other crime. *There is no one to assume the crime and the validity of crime apart from Antigone*'.[13] Just when Lacan insists that the function of the ethical act is precisely to demonstrate that the sociosymbolic order – the Other – fails to institute the norms we ourselves attribute to it, and that, in consequence, anything, including in particular the impossible, can happen, Butler falls back on her stubborn and unwarranted premise that the Other is a consistent structure imbued with powers of sexual and moral determination; that the Other has ultimate authority when it comes to the creation and recognition of all the legitimate forms of life.

The presence of a field of objective, yet unacknowledged, transgression in any social formation is what Lacan wants to argue when he develops the idea that Antigone is the defender of the legitimacy of crime. In short, Lacan's Antigone is an advocate for the sacrificial victim burnt at the stake in a doomed attempt to establish the coherence of a social system, to create a world in which the law could legislate effectively against all exceptions. The paradox, of course, is that the law's violation is a premise of the act through which its legislative power is meant to be expressed. Recently, Žižek has emphasised the properly symbolic effectivity of both Antigone's act in particular, and *l'acte psychanalytique* in general. If complicity with the exercise of power is conditioned by an unrecognised violation of the law with which this power is allied, then the symbolisation of crime, that is to say the interposition – *creation* – of a signifier in the place where before there was only power's secret and obscene enjoyment, has the potential and authentically subversive effect of both dismantling, and tenuously reconstituting, the entire sociosymbolic field.

When, in his ethics seminar, he associates crime with what he calls the discourse of the father – that is to say, with the incestuous criminality of Oedipus – Lacan is *not* effectively attributing to the paternal function a smooth patriarchal command over the social world. As we've seen, this is the idea Butler attributes to the normative influence of a putative Lacanian structuralism. Rather, Lacan's statement acknowledges that the father is always redoubled: the reassuring father who gives protection from maternal jouissance and indexes language's mediation of sociality – the father in his imaginary and symbolic guises – is always haunted by the obscene father of 'primal', traumatic enjoyment, the real father who inserts a distressing gap between the hardly hidden imperfections of actual or concrete paternity and the symbolic paternal function as such. In this light, Creon's crime consists in his failure to do what Oedipus does at the end of the road, so to speak, when he discovers the truth of his incestuous desire, rips out his eyes, and wishes never to have been born.

Lacan's Antigone is therefore the figure of his mid-career teaching with which he makes precisely the same move Butler's discourse makes at its most challenging moments. For both thinkers, thought must move beyond the political discourse of hegemony and its implied framework of competing interests struggling for recognition or articulation. Both thinkers develop a more radical argument, one that aims to spell out the logic by which criminal unintelligibility is constituted in the first instance. This disclosure creates a space in which it becomes possible to discover new directions for thought and action, directions made unthinkable before the struggle for hegemony even began. In other words, Antigone is a name for the subject who refuses to accept the terms of life as they are constituted in any social status quo. Refusing to give up on her desire, this subject accepts the consequences that come with the occupation of a zone of death and impossibility in the 'mad', seemingly suicidal hope that a different and better future might come.

Hardly coincidentally, the radicalism of Antigone's act also poses a crucial challenge to today's sociosymbolic universe of queer theory in crisis. The present-day queer political horizon is, on the one hand (even when it says it isn't), deeply entrenched in liberal ideology and its rhetorical apparatus of rights and freedoms – what does sexual freedom ultimately mean if not the freedom to elect not to wear a condom, knowingly to infect my partner? – and, on the other, limited by a negative minoritarianism conditioned by a relation of pure non-dialectical opposition to its 'heteronormative' other.

In such circumstances, the most politically consequential move, the one that would truly constitute an act in the Lacanian sense, might be precisely its self-obliteration – the thoroughgoing dissolution of the field of intelligibility of queer thought and activism in the Western world. Minimally, this would mean rendering the category of sexual orientation meaningless without the addition of socioeconomic qualifications; without an analysis of the production of sexual identities not by 'discourse', but rather by the capitalist mode of production. More radically, it would mean dispensing with the whole apparatus of the politics of sexuality altogether. The new assumption here is that the fight against sexual violence and homophobia doesn't in fact depend on either the positing of sexual identities, both essential and strategic, or their complicated and ultimately pointless deconstruction.

It's perhaps necessary to specify that the point of such a gesture is not to cease working towards the most concrete goals of what has generally flown under the rubric of gay and lesbian politics. Some of these goals – the legal recognition of same-sex partnerships, the extension of marriage and adoption privileges to same-sex partners – have in fact been questioned, and sometimes clamorously denounced as complicit and normative in some activist formations. Others, such as the further development of anti-discrimination legislation and, most crucially, the integration of responsible anti-homophobic sex education[14] into public school curricula, are less controversial, and quite comfortably span the theoretical and generational chasm that separates the gays and lesbians from the queers.

The point, rather, is to acknowledge two fundamental truths. First, the 'concrete goals' of gay/lesbian or queer politics mentioned earlier aren't as dependent on identity-predicated iterations of homosexuality, or their deconstruction, as we've been led to think. Nor does the merely theoretical subversion of these identities necessarily provide any tangible advantage in their pursuit. In other words, you don't have to presuppose the existence of homosexuals, or else obsessively analyse the politics of their discursive construction, in order to argue against the expression and effects of homophobia. As Lacan implied about the Woman existing only in masculine fantasy, there's a good case to be made that the homosexual exists only in *homophobic* fantasy, as both the traumatically passive male who reminds the man of his latent erotic receptivity, and the pornographically archetypal lesbian couple who make visible a spectacle of feminine jouissance for a masculine look. Second, even in its most post-liberal strains, queer theory has been overwhelmingly confined within a narrow political horizon which fails to recognise how sexual rights and freedoms, not to mention the critique of this discourse of rights and freedoms, never appear at the top of the list of priorities of the most concretely disenfranchised the world over, queer and straight and everything in between.

With striking generality, patriarchal despotisms function in tandem with an apparatus of sexual repression designed to stifle all forms of erotic expression except for the standard male heterosexual one. But it's also true that when you're starving and jobless; when you know that a band of drugged-out soldiers is waiting for night to fall to attack your village and rape you; or when you're a glorified indentured servant at a militarised *maquilladora* patrolled by union-bashing private paramilitary units, it isn't likely that you'll choose to have your desire for emancipation pivot around either the discourse of sexual identity or its theoretical subversion.

Unjust and subtly devastating though it can surely be, the kind of homophobia queer theory talks about is a quite refined form of oppression – one that develops in comparatively benign social formations, from which the more physical forms of sexualised violence, from rape to excision to the proliferating forms of torture, have ceased to police and deform sexual relations in the widest sense.[15] Meanwhile, in other parts of the world, homophobia becomes part and parcel of a more generalised masculine sexual violence, which perverts the entire field of sexual relations, targeting primarily the sexual expression of women. Here, in Salafist Islam for example, it's less a question of the direct oppressive targeting of homosexuality, however prominently this features in the programme, than a masculine-perverse protest against the very libidinal conditions of human life as such.

The Queer Big Other Doesn't Exist

This broadening of queer theory's typically bourgeois and Euro-American horizons has the highly desirable consequence of shifting the focus back towards more conventionally materialist political concerns. At the end of the day, what could be more bourgeois than the conference circuit or cocktail hour subversion of sexual convention? In this light, Žižek's polemic against Laclau, his radical democratic followers, and by extension their allies in the queer theory camp, acquires its sharp and refreshing bite.

The 'radical' in radical democracy disturbingly signals the finality of its abandonment of classical Marxism's denunciation of the material and cultural devastations of capital. In historical terms, radical democracy is simply the Menshevik reformism of today. There is indeed a quite bitter irony in the fact that the concept of radical democracy for classical Marxism referred not to the fullest possible extension of the progressive potential of bourgeois liberalism (classical Marxism was of course also in favour of this, in principle if not in strategy), but rather to the dictatorship of the proletariat – in other words, to the only apparently paradoxical truth that true democracy is possible only after the destruction of the democratic institution as it has taken form through the centuries in the tradition of constitutional parliamentarianism.

While the dictatorship of the proletariat, for basic historical reasons, is no longer desirable or even possible in the mode Marx himself imagined, one fundamental point remains: it's imperative to affirm the possibility of a truly alternative democracy, one that would transform in their totality the conditions of material production. Quite necessarily, this alternative must emerge today under the sign of democracy's denial or negation. Not all so-called totalitarianisms, in other words, are created equal.

It's important to add that, in the new social order, sexual politics must be tied essentially and decisively to an analysis of basic economic conditions, or more precisely to an interrogation of the impact of the organisation of production, as well as wealth and resource distribution, on the lived experience of sexuality. Even more crucially, the properly libidinal essence of politics must be pushed to the forefront: what unconscious desires and fantasies undergird social programmes, both transformative and conservative? Queer theory must proceed to its auto-critique, to the traversal of its most intimate liberal fantasies, especially within those poststructuralist tendencies where it explicitly posits itself as post- or anti-liberal.

In Lacanian terms, the subservience of queer theory to today's dominant but increasingly fragile reformist ethos on the political left is defined by a transferential relation to what we could call the queer big Other. This big Other, I'd like to suggest, takes two typical forms. First, there's the liberal version characterised by positive transference, by a belief in a potentially benevolent Other: if only we are properly included in the spectacle of popular culture, if only we succeed in constructing adequate representations of our diversity, then we would finally experience ourselves as a strong community, as a fully legitimate network of citizens unambiguously recognised by, and integrated with, the social system.

Second, there's the more fashionable, self-consciously subversive or transgressive, post- or anti-liberal variation, which rests on a negative transference vis-à-vis an oppressive figure of authority: if you, big Other, think you can force your patriarchal heteronormativity on me, then you're sadly mistaken, because I'm going to transgress, in concert with my radical friends, all the socially re/productive values you hold dear.

These seemingly contrary and politically irreconcilable structures can be qualified as transferential in that they address themselves to an idealised symbolic authority presumed either to harbour the power to grant or withhold recognition, or else to uphold a disciplinary regime of heteronormative desire. That it's not strictly speaking possible for non-heterosexual subjects to be socialised in the absence of an often acute and painful sense of difference and exclusion, renders this fantasy in both its guises – a sanctioned queer social home; a secret transgressive paradise of limitless sexual freedom – all the more irresistible.

No doubt this line of analysis goes some way towards explaining why there has always been an uneasy undercurrent, a sometimes desperate and exclusionary conformism, in the various post-gay queer movements; an elitist and cliquey, paradoxically normative force, which belies their outward rhetoric of diversity and inclusiveness. Is it possible that it's only from the perspective that, despite our quite manifest sexual differences, *we're all the same*, that it becomes possible to cope with radical, genuine difference? The disturbing, uncanny difference that pulls the rug out from under my identity, even when this identity is defined as impossible, unsustainable and necessarily exclusionary?

The traversal of queer theory's latent transferential fantasy requires us to acknowledge that the idealised queer big Other, who would bestow consistency and legitimacy on the various non-heterosexual communities, is increasingly the middle-class or upper-middle-class, elite-educated, savvy consumer, almost always located in the global North, or else the 'securitised' enclaves of the megalopolises of what we used to call the third world. The visibility of the hypercontemporary queer subject conceals a mass of other 'queer' subjects (many have probably never heard the term and many others would no doubt reject it) very differently positioned with respect to both geopolitics and the mode of production. The objective interests of these non-heterosexual masses may not fit too neatly within the hegemonic framework of queer theory.

For example, consider the circumstances of a 'badly' educated, working-class lesbian toiling away at several part-time jobs to support her family. Or those of a young, crypto-gay Iranian man contemplating a sex-change operation so he can envision a sexual relationship without either violating religious principles he may in fact hold dear, or risk execution at the hands of the state. That either of these subjects should experience a spontaneous frisson of solidarity with a bourgeois and staunchly secularist queer movement is not nearly as obvious a contention as we might wish to think.

The experience of the nonexistence of the queer big Other might serve to subvert the libidinal logic of ersatz solidarity between subjects and constituencies who identify as sharing the same sexual orientation (or simply the same set of assumptions about sexuality), redistributing their political awareness along different, more concretely socioeconomic, lines. Additionally, it might finally expose the secret complicity of the discourses of sexual transgression and anti-generative asociality with the normative or disciplinary power it so clamorously claims to subvert.

To return to the anecdote with which I began, it becomes apparent that there's a subtle but insidious blackmail at work in that political pamphlet handed to me in Christopher Street that day years ago. This blackmail is conveyed through the assumption that my concern with my putative sexual rights should trump all other concerns; that a candidate's voting history on gay issues should take precedence over her record on poverty or welfare, for instance. It's in this precise sense that sexual orientation is a bourgeois concept. The time has come to anticipate a new kind of Marxian unity of theory and practice, which would frame its internal impossibility as that species of insipid pseudo-political literature that greeted me that day in Greenwich Village.

This urban enclave's gentrifying trajectory over the past half-century, paired with its ideological centrality to the modern (Western) gay movements, might now serve – why not? – as a signifier for the queer-theoretical project, which should now finally step aside to create space for a genuinely radical and universal alternative.

3

Is There a Queer Marxism?

Missed Encounter

It's been over 20 years now since Teresa de Lauretis chose to give the title *Queer Theory* to a special issue of the journal *differences* on poststructuralist approaches to sexuality studies. A quarter century has passed since the publication of the book that in many ways started the whole thing, Eve Kosofsky Sedgwick's *Epistemology of the Closet*.

What has happened since then? Quite a bit. By now, there are numerous book-length introductions to queer theory addressed primarily to undergraduates; a panoply of popular trade paperbacks on queer culture featuring watered-down paraphrases of the major theorists; and regular conferences around the Euro-American world that call for papers on queer theory or from a queer theory perspective. From time to time, you may even find the occasional advertisement that will name queer theory as a desirable field of competence for permanent positions in the academy – almost always, however, alongside a more general (literary theory or cultural theory, social or political theory) or traditionally defined (eighteenth-century English literature, the sociology of sexuality) subfield. Indeed, most humanities and social science clusters in major Anglo-American universities today feature at least one faculty member on whose webpage an interest in queer theory will be proclaimed.

In short, what's happened in the past quarter century is that queer theory has become institutionalised. Especially remarkable, despite its no doubt imperfect and scattered qualities, is the fact that this institutionalisation has occurred in tandem with a widespread, and much lamented, decline of the humanities and social science disciplines in the university writ large. These disciplines carry negligible institutional weight in comparison to other, more pragmatic and economically justifiable units, which bring in significant revenue from the private sector.

Viewed in this light, the queer theory phenomenon poses intriguing questions. Why now? Or, more precisely: why have queer theory and queer scholarship in general gained ascendancy in the university at the present historical moment? Or again, posed in a more materialist way: what features of university life today – its various social, economic and political determinants – have allowed for the entrance of this seemingly untoward object of study into the hallowed halls of the academy? After all, this academy historically has defined itself as the preserver of cultural tradition and defender of the social status quo. Further, this tradition has never, until very recently, thought of organising the study of culture and society from the point of view of sexuality.

Beginning in the 1960s with the birth of cultural studies in the Birmingham school, and the publication of the first French texts that would be grouped under the post/structuralism rubric, cultural studies rebelled against a past it newly conceived as staid, stuffy and conservative – in short, as resistant to the very social and political realities that created, in the form of feminism and the gay movement, the conditions of possibility for the vulnerable emergence of women's, gender and sexuality studies.

Less commonly acknowledged in such exercises in casual historicisation, however, are the voices of dissidence and resistance. These voices tried to make themselves heard in a context dominated by the mutually reinforcing influence of, on the one hand, the New Left social movements that accompanied the unprecedented expansion of the university sector in the 1960s and 1970s, and, on the other, elite theoretical and philosophical discourses, in particular Derrida's deconstruction and Foucault's new historicism, which provided theoretical frameworks for the new scholarly approaches. These latter discourses were the ones that most directly fed into the queer theory project. Like the figures who inspired it, queer scholars sought to break with the more directly politicised sociohistorical approaches characteristic of the work of numerous gay and lesbian studies pioneers of the 1970s and 1980s.[1]

Viewed in this light, it's impossible to deny that queer theory played a major role in the emergence of the ludic motif in postmodernity that Teresa Ebert mercilessly criticised in the mid-1990s from her historical materialist perspective. For Ebert, the poststructuralist feminist current with which dominant queer theory was allied participated in a general theoretical regression away from concrete socioeconomic analysis, and towards a politically retrograde concern for the vagaries of language, discourse or signification.[2]

The significance of Ebert's book for my purposes is that it reminds us how mature queer studies – by which I simply mean to signal the body of work that has placed itself under this rubric over the last couple of decades – has repressed the historical memory of the inaugural break with the Marxist tradition, by means of which the discourses from which it draws came into being. The difficulty of linking queer theory up with the Marxist tradition is the direct result of this phenomenon; it's to Ebert's tremendous credit that her work brings this repression to our attention.

In general terms, queer theory has shown reluctance to historicise itself. More precisely, it has failed to question retrospectively the political stakes involved in the game-changing theoretical move away from Marxism and materialist analysis that accounts for its very existence. In other words, queer theory's paradigmatic interest in the link between sexuality and questions of identity and meaning not only displaced the previous generation's tendency to consider sexuality in the same context as the social organisation of production. Additionally, it worked to erase the very traces of this move, in some cases going so far as to portray materialist methods as detrimental to the expression of its own, more properly cultural, concerns.

Even in the best cases, for instance in Judith Butler's influential analysis of drag performance among poor African-American youth, interest in the impact of socioeconomic determinants is characteristically reduced to the occasional mention of class.[3] Indeed, as is the case in poststructuralism more generally, class in queer studies is routinely refigured as merely another aspect of the cultural work effected by the play of signification and power. Such a gesture leaves the material determinants of culture, that is to say culture's production in and by a properly capitalist system, entirely out of the equation.

To be sure, there are very few places one can go in the repertoire of queer discourse to find critical assessments of this unspoken shift from economics to discourse, from history to performativity. Even more egregiously, queer theory has failed to entertain the possibility that its appearance at the present historical moment is a symptom of capitalist social relations in their most recent, supermobile and globalised phase. This phase is characterised by the shift of material production from the historical locations of industrial production in Europe, North America and Japan, to the global South. Concurrently, the forms of labour in the global North have become increasingly virtual-immaterial, 'cognitive', transient and precarious.

In such a context, it becomes positively crucial to examine the few key exceptions to the non-engagement of queer theory, including its pre-queer antecedents, with the Marxist tradition. Through such an initiative, we can gain a broader perspective on the political significance of the transformations of sexuality studies over the past half-century than can be established from within the horizons of dominant queer discourse itself.

Foremost among these transformations, in fact the very hallmark of queer theory, is surely the undermining of the long-standing premise that sexuality has been liberated through (at least the appearance of) the relaxation of taboos and prejudices against the expression of feminine and non-heterosexual sexualities. If my own classroom experience with young students in Canada is any indication, this smugly unhistorical premise is shared virtually universally by today's generation of university-age youth. The later work of Michel Foucault was instrumental in calling into question the assumption that we've emancipated sexuality from repression. Much less commonly acknowledged, however, is the fact that Foucault's decisive turn away from the Marxist tradition before he undertook his *History of Sexuality* project is significantly responsible for queer theory's general allergy to materialist analysis. Indeed, I would suggest that Foucault's conception of sexuality as discourse/power in that book assumes a rejection of influential Marxian theories of ideology, in particular Althusser's, which had previously had tremendous impact on that generation of thinkers. For these reasons, it will be helpful now to consider exactly how the massive impact of Foucault's work on sexuality has rendered the prospects of a contemporary queer Marxism remarkably, even irremediably, dim.

Few today would dare to question that Foucault was correct to argue in the late 1970s that sexuality is an invention of late modernity – the mid-nineteenth to late nineteenth century, to be precise. This was the time when sexuality became an object for science. The purpose of this shift was to inaugurate a form of knowledge of a properly sexual kind, and to tie this new quest for knowledge to an ambition of truth which, for Foucault, shifted the agency of power from its previously constricting and repressive force to a new, productive logic of biopower.

In light of this thesis, it would appear uncontroversial to claim that the queer theory phenomenon brings to its logical conclusion the 'incitement to discourse' that Foucault brilliantly traced back to the birth of sexology and, even further, to the institution of the confession in Christianity.[4] Queer theory brings this logic to its endpoint with the argument that sexuality discourse is a productive and disciplinary instrument of biopower. Indeed, if the 'old', sovereign form of power gained ascendancy by virtue of the crown or the state's authority to mete out the death penalty, then sexuality is the emblem of Foucaultian biopower – that is to say, the very incarnation of its authority to regulate not the destruction, but rather the production, of human life as such. For Foucault, modern science's epistemological thrust into sexuality was a fundamental component of the shift towards a new social logic of bureaucracy and management. This new logic functions by instrumentalising the forms of knowledge as a means of producing and disciplining human life.

Rereading *The History of Sexuality*'s introductory volume today, at a time when its main theses have already completed their drip through the grains of elite queer theory, I'm left with an indelible sense of Foucault's dismay at what we can retrospectively call the sexological turn: that epochal shift that transformed sex from a matter of acts and behaviours to a question of desires and identities, of what Foucault called the truth of the self.

If we accept Foucault's premise that sexuality discourse is essentially an elaborate ruse designed to have us chatter endlessly about sex, all the while further tethering ourselves to the omnipotent forces of power, then clearly the conclusion is warranted that the very existence of queer theory can be read as a demonstration of this ruse's spectacular success.

No doubt there is a cutting irony here, and it comes at queer theory's expense. That elite queer theory has shown itself to be hyperaware of the trap to which the coupling of sex and truth inevitably leads, has not evidently led it to abandon the project of a discourse about sex.

This is indeed the inescapable paradox of the sex-as-discourse premise common to later-period Foucault and the mainstream of elite queer theory. If sex is coterminous with a discourse/power tandem complicit with a disciplinary regime of truth, then one can only succeed in furthering one's disciplinary subjection as one tries to expose the effects of the discourse, the workings of the regime. Those who depart from Foucault's enigmatic reference to 'the claims of bodies, pleasures, and knowledges, in their multiplicity and their possibility of resistance' (157) at *The History of Sexuality*'s conclusion, fare little better. Inevitably, they can only produce yet another discourse on the body, another discourse on pleasure, which inevitably will be subject to the same old accusations with respect to their hopeless complicity with power. The concept of power attains such grandiose heights of abstraction in late-period Foucault that any neo-materialist attempt to reconnect power with capital becomes the very emblem of retrograde theoretical naïvety.

Yet, it can't be denied that Foucault's association of sexuality discourse with the design of power effected a paradigm shift that changed the very nature of the inquiry into sex. The difficult but necessary *'what is sexuality, and how does it intersect with politics?'* questions gave way to the more manageable, but less consequential, *'why have we now decided to pose that question?'* Foucault's work provided, or at least appeared to provide, a persuasive answer: power made us ask it. That this answer was ever deemed capable of explaining much of anything is the aspect of queer theory's history that remains difficult to explain.

In retrospect, it's now possible to say that this answer provided a reactionary alibi for the treasonous abandonment of the Marxist tradition of ideology critique. As I've argued elsewhere, what is so undesirable about Foucault's idea of power is that it prevents us from linking its exercise to concrete sociopolitical and economic interests, however conscious or unconscious these might be.[5] There can be little doubt that for the queer theory generation, Foucault's strange and paranoid notion of power effectively replaced the old Marxist idea of ideology, going so far as to imply that all the crucial work the latter concept made possible relied on an obsolete, sovereign understanding of the exercise of social control. In my view, cultural theory has yet to come to grips fully with the complicity of, on the one hand, this wide-scale retreat from ideological analysis and, on the other, the collapse of not only so-called actually existing socialism, but also (and more importantly) the very credibility of the idea of communism and the entire anti-capitalist project.

The dominant narrative of socialism's collapse in the last decades of the twentieth century forgets what was perhaps Marx's most basic lesson: people make history. To which a Freudian is obliged to add: *but they don't know what they're doing.* The now-familiar complaint on the left is that this dominant narrative assumes that we moved away from ideology critique in response to, and in order better to take account of, the putatively objective failure of socialism during the final decades of the last century. As if, that is to say, we had no role to play in that failure, as if we didn't sabotage the project ourselves.

Cultural theory has failed to come to terms with the extraordinary convenience of the fact that, at the precise moment when power was being reconceptualised as diffuse and all-pervasive, as *intentional* but *non-subjective*, the political and economic mechanisms that used to provide some protection from the unshackled ravages of capital were being systematically dismantled in front of our very eyes. Even the old-fashioned idealist assumptions of intellectual history are more instructive here: the material structures inspired by socialism collapsed for no other reason than because we chose to discredit the idea; because we agreed to allow the master signifier 'capitalism', with its indelible tie to Marxist economic historicisation, to be replaced by another, insidiously naturalising, term: 'the market'. We have allowed this signifier to impose itself as an objective description of a natural law, one that conveys a direct knowledge of the economic real as such.

Certainly, there's nothing novel today in asserting a link between the proliferation of sexual identities during the twentieth century and the expansion and globalisation of capitalist relations. Indeed, Deleuze and Guattari did precisely this when they wrote their magnum opus *Capitalism and Schizophrenia* in the early 1970s, not coincidentally the time that brought the period of creative and experimental efflorescence of the last century to a dramatic close. I'll have much more to say about Deleuze and Guattari, and more specifically their important proto-queer disciple Guy Hocquenghem, in the following chapter. However, here I'll simply remark that the anti-oedipal argument, as Deleuze and Guattari develop it, forms, disciplinarily speaking, a kind of underground current in queer theory. Since the heady early days of this discourse, numerous critics have come to the conclusion that this current provides a preferable alternative to what they consider the residual, difference-eradicating and perniciously universalising Hegelianism of Judith Butler's work, for instance.[6]

In contrast to Foucault, whose late work severs any link his thought may once have had to the Marxist tradition, Deleuze and Guattari, on the level of their enunciation at any rate, retain a properly Marxian ambition to develop tools for the undoing of the repressive or exploitative side of capital, even if capital *as such* for them remains an immanently utopian deterritorialising force. Too infrequently acknowledged in the ever-expanding 'D and G universe', however, is the fact that even their thesis was hardly a new one.

As they well knew, Marxist thinkers before them, not to mention Marx himself, had already linked capitalism's obliteration of old social forms – not only the rigid systems of obligation in feudalism, but also the bourgeois world of industrial production and the nuclear family – to what Herbert Marcuse, for one, previously and famously referred to as the 'repressive desublimation' of sexuality – that is to say, the absorption by consumer society or fascist ideology of libidinal satisfaction.[7] Indeed, fascism for the Frankfurt School was a paradigmatic example of the way in which enjoyment on a general social scale can work in tandem not with emancipation, but rather with ideologies of domination and oppression.

Lacan's intervention into the complicated legacy of Freud's superego concept has led to the relatively recent development of a Lacanian version of the repressive desublimation argument, which runs roughly as follows. In bourgeois Vienna at the dawn of the last century, the price paid for the stability of the social link was the proliferation of what Freud in 1908 called 'modern nervous illness', which in his view resulted from the imposition of the constraints of 'sexual morality'.[8] Although it's also possible to find in Freud's texts the grounds for a more structural version of this argument, according to which the neurotic symptom would rather be an inevitable facet of psychic life as such, it remains the case that Freud explicitly argued for the more sociological version on more than one occasion.

By the time he addressed the crypto-Maoist student rebels who made their disruptive presence felt in his seminar around 1969–1970, however, Lacan was arguing that a new, superegoic injunction to enjoy had begun to permeate social life. Further, the predominant affect of shame, which had previously accompanied the experience of enjoyment, had now been replaced, in the context of the 'sexual revolution', by a generalised ethos of impudence. Whereas previously, in other words, social shame accompanied the admission in polite company of an inappropriate sexual dalliance, today shame accrues if one admits to *not* being interested in sexual (and back then, political) transgression; if one confesses that one's sexual experience has never quite extended to flavours beyond vanilla.

The shift from the old to the new politics – from the politics of sovereign power to biopower, to refer to Foucault's original idea, later influentially taken up by Giorgio Agamben as well as Michael Hardt and Antonio Negri – emerges when we consider that for both the Frankfurt School and Lacan, desublimation and the injunction to enjoy are properly critical concepts. Marcuse thought that desublimation worked hand in hand with the fascist phenomenon; Lacan chastised the crypto-Maoists for playing into the hands of the decrepit French educational bureaucracy.

For Deleuze and Guattari, in contrast, the de-Oedipalisation resulting from late capitalism's dissolution of the old feudal, bourgeois and nuclear-familial ties that bind is desirable because it creates possibilities for new 'deterritorialised intensities', 'bodies without organs', 'lines of flight' and other such themes, the concrete political implications of which have never to my mind been made clear. What separates Deleuze and Guattari from what I would call the mainstream of the Marxian tradition is their profound belief that what requires liberation is not human labour from capitalism, but rather capitalism from its own external hindrances – that is, the forces of stasis or immobility that prevent it from reaching its full transformative potential. That such a theory should come to prominence at a time when the obscenely destructive forces of capitalism have been allowed to appear in ways unseen since the industrial revolution is surely a sign that the fashions of cultural theory are as beholden to ideology as any other aspect of human activity.

With the benefit of hindsight, the Deleuzo-Guattarian anti-oedipal thesis appears as perhaps the most wildly and naïvely utopian gesture of the poststructuralist moment; the strongest, least ambivalent statement in support of the claim that there need not be a contradiction between, on the one hand, emancipation from the constraints of gender and sexuality and, on the other, the de-alienation of human labour. The deep simpatico between Deleuze and Guattari's desiring-productive utopianism, and the sexual vanguardism that queer theory inherited from the 1960s sexual liberation ethos and the Stonewall moment, seems clear enough when viewed in this light. The agency of capital in all this sexual deregulation is rarely discussed in queer appropriations of *Anti-Oedipus*.

Instead, queer theory tends to enlist Deleuze and Guattari in support of the argument that a defining feature of the contemporary period is a perhaps unprecedented opportunity to supplant all existing impediments to the full expression of sexuality and gender identities. Or rather, perhaps more accurately, what is unprecedented is the investment in, or aspiration towards, such a liberation – in other words, the articulation in thought of the notion that sexuality's entanglement with what Lacan calls 'the defiles of the signifier' is merely a historical contingency.

For other, 'stodgier', writers on the cultural-theoretical left, however, the new sexual utopianism went hand in hand with a large-scale retreat from reformist and revolutionary ideologies, which were sharply critical of the neoliberal impetus to unshackle the forces of capital from the tenuous mid-century constraints that held it back. Today, any critical intersection between this tradition, which maintains its fidelity to the original Frankfurt School insight about the complicity of libidinal spontaneity with ideology or political domination, and the various queer developments in sexuality theory of the last two decades, is decidedly difficult to discern. Examples of such work, therefore, are of paramount interest.

The remainder of this chapter (and the following one as well) will explore the work of the few writers who have bravely engaged in this obscure project of talking about politics and sexuality, sexuality and politics, from within the Marxian horizon. Is there, then, a *queer*

Marxism? The answer, disappointing in its vagueness, can only be: 'sort of, not really'.

In their attempts to shift the course of queer theory in a more politically radical direction, the authors of concern have been required to forget about sex, to occlude desire. In so doing, they've committed the fateful error of heeding the bad advice Jung famously offered to Freud on their 1912 sea voyage to the United States. They've had to gloss over the importance of sexuality as psychoanalysis theorises it in order to secure its compatibility with hegemonic understandings of culture, politics and history.

Varieties of Totality

Among the few recent attempts to develop a Marxist alternative for queer theory, Kevin Floyd's *The Reification of Desire* stands out for its scope, novelty and theoretical rigour. Drawing on the writing of strange bedfellows Georg Lukács and Michel Foucault, Floyd bases his argument on the notion that both queer theory and Marxism are forms of what he calls totality thinking. Despite the tremendous contribution Floyd's book makes to the project of connecting queer theory to Marxism, however, its main premise errs where it mistakenly reads as potentially complementary two distinct ideas of totality based on vastly different assumptions about political power.

In what follows, I'll also suggest that whatever value the Lukácsian reference might have in promoting the reintroduction of historicised class analysis, or an updated version of it, to the study of sexuality, Floyd's discussion falls prey to a paradigmatic, and ultimately self-defeating, assumption about the purchase of 'heteronormativity'. As we've seen in previous chapters, this assumption creates a false enemy, one that, in this context, a considerable theoretical artillery is deployed in order to destroy. For psychoanalysis, desire can hardly be described as heteronormative. Yet, this statement doesn't imply that there's no such thing as homophobia. Despite its professed queerness, in the final analysis Floyd's challenging discussion is conspicuously devoid of sex. It will be necessary, however, to delve into certain of its details in order to discern not only where exactly sex is missed, but also the consequences of this miss for how we think about the problematic (non-)relation of queer theory to Marxism.

Floyd's discussion fails adequately to address the fact that its Lukácsian, and properly Marxist, investment in the idea of a totality of social relations determined by capital can't be reconciled with the Foucault-derived notion of knowledge as power, by means of which Floyd conceptualises the process of social differentiation. The hallmark of Lukács's work, for Floyd, is the way it insists on considering society as a historical whole, every part of which is shaped by the social organisation of production. The consequence of this is that no social phenomenon can be legitimately considered in isolation from any other. Further, capitalist relations leave their mark on every one.

For its part, the queer studies discipline distinguishes itself by what Floyd calls 'a refusal of sexual particularization, a refusal of sexuality's routine epistemological dissociation from other horizons of social reality'.[9] The slippage in Floyd's totality thinking emerges here. As far as the force of determination goes, we move from a properly materialist concept of social production in the Lukácsian version of totality, to a politicised (implicitly Foucaultian) epistemological framework in queer theory. From the Marxist perspective, the imperative isn't simply to avoid considering homophobia, let's say, in isolation from evangelical Christianity. Rather, the methodological obligation is to consider both as part and parcel of a social totality, of which the capitalist mode of production is the dominant organising principle. Going missing in the transition from Lukács to queer studies is the classical Marxist conviction that knowledge of social reality is deeply connected not to an abstract discourse/power tandem, but rather to the position in the mode of production from which one sets out to know. Left to its own devices, for example, as a tenured professor my knowledge of the conditions of academic labour will be very different from that of the precariously employed contract instructor. The whole point of Marxist education, of course, is precisely to eliminate this difference.

This same point can be made in a more contextually salient way by examining how Floyd's queer Marxism approaches the specific problem of sexuality. Succinctly put, sexuality features in Floyd's argument as one among many 'social and historical horizons' (8), which together make up his particular understanding of the social totality. With this gesture, Floyd effectively places sexuality on the same level as all the 'other axes of hierarchized social differentiation'

(8), by which he understands the familiar left cultural-theoretical list including race, gender, nation and of course class.

Under these parameters, the task of queer Marxism becomes the 'critique of various forms of heteronormative assumption' embedded within these various knowledge systems. Importantly, for Floyd, this critique can then annex itself to the critique of capital, since all of these critical initiatives converge on the level of their 'common critique of epistemological particularization', which in turn is based on an 'impulse of generalization' shared by all (9). In simpler terms, Floyd wants to update Lukács's insistence that no social phenomenon can be isolated from the shaping influence of capital. He does this by adding to 'class' more recently acknowledged categories of social difference, most importantly sexuality.

Considered in these terms, the strategy of queer Marxism must be to introduce the critique of heteronormativity, alongside the other pernicious flatteners of difference targeted since the advent of the New Left, into the critique of capital. Because, under the assumptions of Floyd's totality thinking, every social difference is horizontally connected to all the others in a sort of rhizomatic whole, the critic can, and therefore must, move freely from one to the other without concerning herself with the outmoded orthodox methodological question of the primacy of determination.

Some examples: Floyd's queer Marxist might choose to link HIV policy in India to the struggle against so-called Islamic fundamentalism; or else, the death sentences issued against homosexuals in Iran to this nation's position in the global petroleum market. (These are my examples, by the way, deliberately chosen to contrast against Floyd's decidedly US-centric ones.) Epistemologically speaking, the enemy for Floyd is 'particularisation', by which he means the consideration of any axis of social difference – class let's say – in isolation from any other: here, sexuality. As a self-professed Marxist, Floyd places the emphasis on global relations of capital. Under the general assumption of a social totality, these relations have an effect of determination on all the other forms of social difference, which themselves then impact back upon capitalist relations, forming a complex network of multidirectional influence and impact.

It must be said, however, that no major Marxist current before the 1960s, even and including the work of Gramsci, ever indulged in such a thoroughgoing relativisation of social determination. Clearly, Floyd shares with Gramsci a desire to loosen the causal knot with which orthodox Marxism ties economic production to social and cultural phenomena. Unlike Floyd, however, Gramsci never questioned the assumption that social production lay at the base, as it were, of the ideological struggle for hegemony. The Gramscian totality remains divided, although less distinctly than in classical Marxism, between economic and cultural factors in such a way that the former retains a modicum of priority over the latter. In Floyd, however, the relations of production threaten to become merely another form of social 'knowledge', like Danish neo-fascism or lipstick lesbianism. In stark contrast, classical Marxism disparages as revisionism, reformism, or social democracy any concession to methods of analysis that deprioritise the power of the mode of production (capitalism) to create a form of social differentiation (class) which overdetermines, or transects, all the others in however complex a fashion.

To his credit, Floyd shows an awareness of this issue from the outset. Indeed, he introduces his book with an anecdote about the apparently infamous 1996 appearance of Judith Butler at a *Rethinking Marxism* conference – the most significant multidisciplinary gathering of Marxist scholars in the United States. At this conference, Butler delivered her noteworthy 'Merely Cultural' paper[10] which, unsurprisingly, was attacked by the more orthodox (or faithful) attendees for effecting precisely the move of epistemological relativisation that Floyd wants to set alongside Marxism under the premise that both traditions, the queer-theoretical and the Marxist, base themselves on the idea of a social totality of seamless interconnection.

As Floyd acknowledges, this 'Butler among the Marxists' affair made manifest 'a schism between Marxism and queer theory' (2) at its own mid-1990s theoretical moment. On his reading of the development of queer theory since that time, however, this schism has become less pronounced, and Floyd clearly wants to position his project as one that aims to bring the two camps even closer together.

In my view, however, Floyd aims to effect this reconciliation of queer theory and Marxism with a gesture that merely reiterates the standard feminist, gay and postcolonial objections to Marxist discourse already fully articulated in New Left doctrine almost a half-century ago. To summarise what I've paraphrased of his discussion thus far, the relation between Marxism and queer theory for Floyd features points of divergence and convergence. They converge in their common ambition to analyse social relations as a field in which every phenomenon permeates every other. But they diverge in the particular way they conceptualise that totality, with Marxism, of course, classically positing the mode of economic production as the 'ultimately determining instance' of social phenomena.

On this basis, Floyd frames his contribution to the debate as an exploration of how it becomes possible to 'see this divergence' between Marxism and queer theory 'in a different light' – that is, to depart from queer theory's alternative conception of totality to identify 'the limitations of Marxian categories' (9). Here he provides his own illuminating specification of what this might mean for the study of sexuality. 'What if', Floyd asks, Marxism 'tried to account for insights produced within queer theory rather than always framing sexual questions in classically Marxian terms, assuming that capital mediates sexuality in terms of traditional understandings of privatization and commodification, for example?' (9). Floyd's mediating response to the dispute between Butler and the 'non-cultural' Marxists is ultimately a rather banal 'you're both right!', which glosses over an underlying theoretical incompatibility. How, we might ask, could Marxism itself be asked to account for sexuality other than in 'classically Marxian terms' without betraying its methodological commitment to the determining power of the social organisation of production? Even more importantly, from the psychoanalytic perspective, Floyd's argument fails to consider how Freud's idea of the unconscious throws a wrench in the theoretical machine that isolates economics from sexuality in the first place.[11]

Floyd also draws from Lukács's work a further basic strategy for realigning queer studies with Marxism. *The Reification of Desire* takes not only the aspiration to an understanding of social relations as a unique totality, but also the key notion of epistemological privilege, from Lukács's 1923 classic *History and Class Consciousness*. Floyd conveys the idea's significance with a reference to Fredric Jameson's influential endorsement of the centrality of Lukács's text to the Marxist tradition of cultural analysis. According to Floyd's paraphrase of Jameson, this centrality consists in how it creates a new way to think about 'the epistemological priority of the experience of various groups or collectivities' (10), specifically those that Marxism has associated in a variety of internally controversial ways with the working class or proletariat. As might be expected, Floyd aims to position heteronormativity's victims among those groups. That is, he claims that by virtue of their socially marginal position, non-heterosexuals acquire a variety of social knowledge that will deliver potentially subversive insights about the mechanisms of domination in society as a whole.

As we've already considered, Foucault strongly argued in the 1970s that the creation of sexological science in the nineteenth century helped to consolidate a sort of paradigm shift by means of which non-heterosexual erotic activity was transformed from a set of performable actions into a panoply of psychological identities. The act of sodomy, for instance, previously performable by anyone succumbing to temptation, became embodied in the person of the sodomite. To be sure, it's impossible to overstate the formidable extent to which elite queer theory, with respect to what it has argued concerning both gender and sexuality, has defined itself, through the enlistment of such notions as the performative, for example, as the attempt to subvert the relation of both terms to notions of psychological identity – to what Foucault called the 'truth of the self'.

In light of the historical invention of the homosexual, then, Floyd's argument implies that the sexological turn initiated a form of epistemological *deprivileging*, which Lukácsian methodology can then reprivilege. It's easy to see how the notion of a homosexual knowledge, for instance, is only conceivable once there's an identifiable group of persons in whom that knowledge might be embodied. According to Floyd, homosexual knowledge, privileged by virtue of its subaltern position in the social totality, can then be articulated, presumably in tandem with sexuality's other non-heterosexual forms, in a way that calls into question the social order as such.

Yet, we've seen on a number of occasions already in this book that queer effects a decisive and universalising exit from the regime of sexual identity. In this perspective, the link to epistemological privilege then becomes illegitimate, seeing as we've assumed that everyone is (potentially) queer. As a result, queer knowledge becomes indistinct from any other variety of social knowledge. Floyd's idea of queer epistemological privilege therefore rests on an underlying ambivalence concerning the relation of this knowledge to the historicity of the homosexual identity.

This insight brings to bear a related, but more concrete, question. Above and beyond the problem of sexuality's historicity, to what extent is it even legitimate to characterise queer knowledge today as an example of what Lukács calls the proletarian standpoint? Lukács assumes that the subordinated social position of the proletarian determines a perception of the social world fundamentally different from the perception held by its more privileged counterparts. In short, the proletarian's knowledge is more likely to generate accurate ideas about the social totality's organisation, simply because its subordinate position *in the mode of production* means that it directly confronts the concrete effects of capitalist social relations. That is, the proletariat has a vested interest in learning how the system works simply because the system mercilessly exploits it. By contrast, it's in the interests of the bourgeoisie to dream up inspirational odes to rights and freedoms as a means of masking that same exploitation from both the workers and itself.

The difficulty with the place of sexuality in this logic now, quite glaringly, appears: how exactly does sexuality correlate to social position in the organisation of production? Short answer: it doesn't. Longer answer: this correlation, especially in the indigenous geopolitical locale of queer theory, varies tremendously. At any rate, as we've already seen, the correlation doesn't even apply to the period before the modern invention of sexual categorisations and the identities they produced. Before this invention took place, it simply wouldn't have been possible to think about how social privilege might vary in accordance with a sexual identity that had yet to see the light of day.

Further, Floyd's Luckácsian argument hardly becomes more convincing even once we acknowledge the appearance of the modern homosexual on the historical scene. Is there any consistent empirical evidence to show that self-identified homosexuals have been concretely marginalised in properly socioeconomic terms? How, in any case, would we figure into the equation all those extremely numerous persons widely scattered across the globe who engage in same-sex activity, but who, for whatever reason, don't identify as homosexual, let alone as queer? Even today, many of these persons live in cultural contexts in which such an identification is either discursively or socially impossible. The entire set of assumptions concerning how homophobia maintains a regime of the closet is simply ethnocentric, not to mention unhistorical. Indeed, 'coming out of the closet' requires acceptance of a narrative of sexuality that is both culturally and historically specific. In my view, it also implies tacit acceptance of the mainstream commercial gay-queer culture to which any queer Marxism worthy of the name should stand opposed. Quite literally, not everyone can afford to come out.

Without question, the liberal and post-industrial global North is the habitus of queer studies. Far from being subjected to systematic socioeconomic disadvantage, the evidence suggests that self-identified homosexuals and queers in these regions demonstrate average earnings significantly above the norm. Indeed, it's hardly possible to consider the queer phenomenon broadly understood without taking into account how capital has increasingly, over the last few decades, identified the various non-heterosexual communities in the 'advanced economies' as privileged markets for the most highly profit-generating commodities.

Moreover, at least on the level of its cultural visibility, homosexuality prior to its late modern forms shows a strong link with the aristocracy and, later, the upper bourgeoisie. Think, for instance, of the numerous European royals known to have been homosexually inclined; or Proust at the moment of the European aristocracy's historical collapse. In this light, it hardly makes sense to link homosexuals or homosexuality in any general way with the Marxian notion of the proletariat. Further, there's every reason to think that the appeal of Western queer discourse in the global South would largely be limited to groups already thoroughly 'Westernised', or at least favourably positioned with respect to the international relations of capital.

To summarise, Floyd's analysis makes two main errors. First, the analogy it formulates between, on the one hand, the mode of production or structure of social relations and, on the other, the realm of sexuality, is a false one from Marxism's perspective. The analogy is false because it obfuscates, or simply discards, the causal relation between the two. It's hardly necessary to defend the ultraorthodox view that the economy single-handedly determines everything in the social and cultural spheres to recognise that Floyd's analogy de-emphasises the epistemological or methodological centrality of economic organisation in a way that only reiterates the signature post-Marxist move that the Gramscian work of Ernesto Laclau and Chantal Mouffe, for example, accomplished in the 1980s.[12] In short, there's nothing more 'Marxist' about Floyd's set of assumptions than those that have generally informed the work of the left-liberal post-structuralist contingent of cultural theorists since that time.

Second, Floyd's contention that queer critique is universal or totalising because 'heteronormativity' shares these characteristics is indefensible in the most basic logical terms. Indeed, if heterosexism totally saturated the social field with its normative command, there would be no queer perspective from which this heterosexism might be questioned. As the more convincing psychoanalytic accounts consistently stress, what lies at the root of heteronormative power – or more properly of the resistance to homosexuality, of *homophobia* – is already a displaced, repressed form of homosexual desire itself.

Finally, there's a glaring lack of evidence to show that the queer phenomenon, in concrete class terms, is anything but bourgeois. The fact that there's no direct correlation between sexuality and social privilege should force us to admit that whatever social knowledge we might consider to result from the homosexual or queer experience isn't likely to deliver helpful general insights about how the workings of global capital enforce relations of domination and exploitation.

Queer Historical Materialism, Actually Existing!

Readers who go along with my argument that Floyd's work fails to provide an alternative to the reformist or left-liberal tenets of the 'post-Marxism' of the past few decades might be interested to know, if they don't already, that an alternative queer Marxism exists: one whose main purpose, it's not an exaggeration to say, is precisely to return the analysis of sexuality to the orthodox – or vulgar, some will say – Marxist emphasis on the mode of production's primacy.

One of the few places to go to find such a classically Marxist alternative in queer theory and sexuality studies is to the work of Donald Morton, comrade-in-arms of the previously mentioned Teresa Ebert. In 1996, Morton published an invaluable anthology entitled *The Material Queer*, for which he wrote an uncompromising introductory essay. This invaluable piece systematically denounces the wide panoply of post-Saussurean semiotic or semiological paradigms in cultural theory. These are the methods that substitute language-premised methods of cultural study for traditional materialist approaches, which work with a Marxian understanding of the underlying socioeconomic organisation of production.

Morton and his allies offered their refreshing (and under-read) anthology as a self-consciously historical materialist alternative to the anthologies on poststructuralist sexuality studies then proliferating, such as Routledge's *The Gay and Lesbian Studies Reader*, published three years earlier in 1993.[13] The underlying premise of Morton's argument is that the political inadequacy of the contemporary study of sexuality can be boiled down to two main incorrect assumptions: first, that sexuality should be methodologically 'primary' in cultural analysis; and second, that desire is 'autonomous', that is 'unregulated and unencumbered'.[14]

My own argument in this section will be that although Morton's first criticism is justified, the second is well intentioned but unfortunately faulty, although for decidedly unpostmodernist reasons for which he might have some sympathy. To set up my intervention, it will be necessary first to bring out the details of Morton's against-the-grain discussion.

For Morton, queer theory is a fundamentally flawed subspecies of postmodernism, that goes off the rails where it gives sexuality methodological primacy and adopts a faulty, that is to say bourgeois, understanding of desire. Let's take the former point first. In his presentation of the postmodernist current for which he wishes to offer an alternative, Morton names some of the central figures of late twentieth-century cultural theory – Eve Sedgwick, Deleuze and Guattari, Roland Barthes. Taking it as one of the foundational texts of queer theory, Morton attacks Sedgwick's *Epistemology of the Closet* for setting the stage not only for queer theory's monumental overvaluation of the general political significance of sex, but also for the way it transforms sexuality into a methodological fetish in cultural analysis. 'An understanding of virtually any aspect of modern Western culture must be, not merely incomplete, but damaged in its central substance', Sedgwick memorably wrote on *Epistemology*'s first page, 'to the degree that it does not incorporate a critical analysis of modern homo/heterosexual definition'.[15]

Although this statement was declaimed well before queer theory or sexuality studies had accumulated any significant amount of academic capital, it's difficult not to read it with the benefit of hindsight as a hubristic instance of disciplinary self-privileging; as a performative utterance designed to secure a position within the academy for a particular kind of cultural study. More significantly, however, this institutional ambition was shot through with a particular ideological conception of sexuality, premised on a suturing of sexual knowledge to identity. In other words, the goal of Sedgwick's project wasn't to explore in general terms the possibility or nature of sexual knowledge, but rather to inaugurate, and effectively sanctify, a new form of homosexual knowledge for which the homosexual identity, however (ambivalently) problematised, could serve as the ground.

In Morton's view, Sedgwick's manifesto-like introduction to the book mistakenly singles sexuality out, thereby isolating it from other methodological concerns – most especially those, like the 'old-fashioned' idea of class, that relate directly to the socioeconomic realm. To be sure, this feature of Morton's discussion anticipates Floyd's argument against epistemological particularisation in *The Reification of Desire*. Sedgwick's work continues in the long feminist tradition of politicising sexuality when, as I argue in a variety of ways throughout this book, we should rather move to sexualise the political – that is, inquire into the ways in which political questions and controversies are shot through with libidinal interest and the vicissitudes of unconscious desire. In this precise sense, Morton's argument against Sedgwick that *Epistemology*'s political error lies in its foregrounding of sexuality *as such* misses the point.

I based my major criticisms of Floyd's project on the tenets of Marxism itself, concluding that it remains complicit with the general culturalising reaction against Marxism, which took place during the last few decades of the past century. By contrast, my concerns with Morton's argument aren't political in nature. They stem, rather, from my investment in psychoanalysis. Ultimately, we disagree about what we might call the nature of the human predicament.

As I'll develop in detail, the weakness of Morton's approach lies in its assumption that politics can be separated out from sexuality. However counterintuitive it may sound, however, Morton is justified in arguing against Sedgwick that to take sexuality as the primary and exclusive focus of cultural analysis is already to depoliticise it. This is so because the gesture of directly politicising sexuality has the paradoxical effect of desexualising politics, of effectively reneging on our responsibility to consider the impact of the unconscious on the negotiation of political antagonisms; to consider, that is, the unconscious of the social formation as such. Again, the mistaken assumption is that politics and sexuality are separable; that the very arena of politics itself is not already shot through with sexuality.

To do the argument justice, however, we'll need to consider in detail how Morton qualifies his position against the prioritisation of sexuality in cultural studies. Morton cites Deleuze and Guattari as the main proponents in postmodernity of what he calls the 'deregulation of desire', a thematic that assumes, he specifies, that sexual desire is 'autonomous, unregulated, and unencumbered' (1), particularly in relation to the material constraints imposed by labour time and the radically unequal quality of its remuneration. Morton's historical materialism stands opposed to the structuralist-poststructuralist paradigm according to which it's the signifier, not the mode of production, that shapes, distorts or represses sexual desire. In this vein, Morton goes on to condemn the later work of Roland Barthes for introducing into the study of culture a preoccupation with jouissance or enjoyment – that is, with the way in which sexuality's excessive stimulation of the body disrupts the stability or coherence of meaning in language, in the texts of culture.

To support his contention, Morton cites *The Pleasure of the Text* (1973), a book widely read by first-generation Anglo-American post-structuralists. In this book, Barthes influentially evokes what he calls the 'grain' of the voice in cinema by referring to 'the fleshiness', 'the breath, the gutturals' of the lips 'in their materiality, their sensuality', for example (2). This Barthesian concern for the body, this ambition to capture the experience of embodied being in thought, in language, is without question one of the central preoccupations of cultural theory in the twentieth century's last few decades – the same ones that witnessed the emergence of queer theory. The philosophy of Descartes, or rather a simplified and misleading obfuscation of the Cartesian project (see the notorious 'mind/body split'), was, for this tremendously broad current, enemy number one. The resurgence of phenomenology, as well as the continued impact of the work of Deleuze, are surely symptoms of this effort – not only anti-Cartesian, but surely also anti-Marxist – to 'think through the body', as Jane Gallop influentially put it at the time.

Now, we should acknowledge that the Marxist tradition is not without its puritanical aspect. Indeed, a deep suspicion of embodied experience can from time to time be found there insofar as it might compromise, or so it was feared, those (allegedly) supreme Marxian values of productivity and utility. As Julia Kristeva was prone to point out in the 1980s, the resurgence of psychoanalysis and the body in French thought was in many ways an attack on a (perceived) hyper-rationalism in the Marxist tradition.

To be sure, Marx and Engels engaged in decidedly unscientific commentary on the topic of homosexuality in their correspondence, and both were arguably also guilty of an idealisation of the heterosexual bond in post-revolutionary society. Still, I want to argue that it's a mistake to associate Morton's invective against jouissance with the Marxian neurosis. Morton's discussion makes clear that it isn't concerned with pleasure or desire as such (leaving aside for now the complication of these terms in psychoanalysis), but rather with the particular conceptualisation of these ideas in postmodernity as he construes it. In his own words, Morton's target is 'the primariness of sexuality/libidinality, the autonomy of desire, and the freedom of the sexual subject from all constraints' (2).

Indeed, it's easy to imagine how the argument against Morton's opposition to postmodernity's concern with jouissance might proceed by dismissing it as mere envy or *ressentiment*. From this point of view, for which psychoanalysis could certainly be enlisted for support, Morton's commitment to historical materialism does indeed require a sacrifice – a renunciation – of enjoyment, and the truth of this commitment would be the condition that everyone else must do the same. Hence, the story might continue, the inability to tolerate the obscene pleasure Barthes, for instance, takes in his text. Morton's reader might sense that there is indeed, for him, something obscene about the idea of so many young, carefree, Ivy League-educated bourgeois American academics sitting back in their comfortable office chairs, gazing out at bucolic campus surroundings, sipping their organic green tea, taking a break for a few yoga poses, and musing irresponsibly about sex in a way that has nothing to do with the world's more unpleasant realities.

However problematic the psychodynamic determination of this sort of fantasy may be, it carries a core political salience nonetheless. To an alarmingly significant extent, queer theory is a symptom of the radical disjunction that separates the (relatively) comfortable material conditions of academic life in the industrialised world from the very different conditions that define the lives of the vast majority of the world's population. Sex is surely a universal concern: no subject, no matter how materially deprived, can truthfully profess to be unperturbed by the conundrum it poses. Yet, it's doubtful that one tends actually to worry much about its concept if one isn't sure where one's next meal is coming from. It's in this precise sense that the methodological foregrounding of sexuality is objectively bourgeois.

The second theoretical objection Morton raises against postmodern theories of sexuality targets the notion that desire is, or can be, free of constraint; that it carries an irreducible autonomy with respect to all those extraneous forces that would determine it. Against the idealism inherent in such accounts of desire, Morton invokes a contrasting materialist interest in how desire is conditioned; how it emerges, that is, as a properly historical phenomenon shaped by social, political and economic forces.

In accordance with this contextualist definition of desire, Morton limits the formulation of his anthology's project to his own American context. As he puts it, the book aims

> to place these two traditions [the idealist and the materialist] against one another in order to reveal that the social injustices that persist today are not due to the moral failures resulting from 'bad attitudes' or 'prejudicial opinions' but are related to the operations of ideology in U.S. society that occlude questions of *need* by promoting an obsession with *desire*. (3, my emphasis)

In other words, sexuality must be recontextualised not as a utopian instrument of subjective liberation or deterritorialisation – as the royal road to a non-complicit or revolutionary psychic structure – but rather as yet another vehicle of ideology, a further ideological state apparatus, to use the now old-fashioned expression of Althusser. The ideology of desire dissimulates the deep connection between the way we experience our sexual needs and the social organisation of production.

To demonstrate how foreign this argument is to contemporary queer theory, we can cite as an example the Marxian theory of Victorian homophobia outlined in a Canadian-authored collective pamphlet featured in *The Material Queer*.[16] British industrial-age homophobia emerged not as a symptom of the generalised prudishness Foucault famously debunked in *The History of Sexuality*, but rather from purely material concerns.

In short, homosexuality threatened the nineteenth-century bourgeoisie because the prospect of sexual enjoyment outside the confines of the heterosexual family unit threatened to sabotage the bourgeois state's project to assign responsibility for the provision of social services to the private sphere, organised around the unstable institution of the patriarchal nuclear family. The Victorian working-class man had no choice but to adopt the protestant work ethic because he had a wife and family to take care of at home, knowing full well that the state would decline to take over responsibility for the family should he prove unwilling or unable to do so himself. Bluntly, if the father is busy cruising men at the public toilets, it's not clear who's going to be bringing home the bacon. Properly socialist pressure on the state to provide public services then threatens to emerge.

Despite his concern for tying sexuality to what, in his view, are its exclusively material conditions, Morton shares not only with psychoanalysis, but also with the anti-Marxist work of the later Foucault, the ambition to wrest sex from psychology. Both Morton and Foucault reject as a bourgeois illusion the claim that there's any truth of the self to be discovered in sex. But, there's a fundamental difference distinguishing their arguments from one another. Whereas Foucault relegates sex to the abstractly conceived productive forces of discourse and power, Morton instead wants to show how the convoluted and intellectualist musings of queer theory are significantly conditioned by the comfortable material circumstances of its proponents. He goes on to argue, for example, that queer discourse's 1990s move towards themes such as the virtual and the technological (cyborgs and cybersex) only underscores its constitutional aversion to the nitty-gritty of material life, in particular as it features in such contexts where its necessities are in penury.

Judith Butler, say, can view desire as something more, or other, than what is contained at the level of basest material need, only because the conditions of her own existence ensure that her material necessities are already properly taken care of. For Morton, all the essential tenets of queer theory are based on specific assumptions about sexuality, which only those persons with the required leisure time and income level will develop. Later, I'll argue that this view is incorrect. It's impossible to deny, however, that there's a substantial grain of truth in Morton's discussion, however glibly it might come across. For this reason, it will prove helpful to delve into its theoretical substance as a means of leading up to my own critique of Morton's position.

The work of two icons of 1970s- and 1980s-era French theory, Jean Baudrillard and Jean-François Lyotard, emblematises for Morton a turn in the Marxian tradition that effectively betrayed its political project. This betrayal, writes Morton, put into place 'the displacement of the economic account of need by the linguistic account of desire' (4). This concise formulation encapsulates the immanent antagonism that any theoretical project working in the wake of Marx and Freud must inevitably confront. Morton's reading of Baudrillard and Lyotard targets the analogy their work develops between the Marxist realm of political economy and the structuralist-cum-poststructuralist, semiotic-linguistic terrain of the *sciences humaines*. The classical Marxist distinction between exchange value and use value is famously compared to Saussure's differentiation of the signifier from the signified: exchange value is to the signifier as use value is to the signified. A detailed look at a substantial chunk of Morton's text, which quotes from Baudrillard's influential *For a Critique of the Political Economy of the Sign* (1972), is in order:

> Capitalism, which needs exchangeability or equivalence between commodities, is founded on exchange value and is driven by the need to produce from exchange value a surplus value that is itself responsible for the difference of class. Overcoming capitalism would involve a return to the more fundamental level of addressing human need, represented by use value, and a consequent cancellation of all those (needless) desires produced by capitalist commodity fetishism at the level of exchange-become-surplus-value. But, against Marx, Baudrillard argues that 'use value is [also] an abstraction. It is an abstraction of the system of needs cloaked in the false evidence of a concrete destination and purpose, an intrinsic finality of goods

and products' and thus that both 'use value and exchange value' are 'regulated by an identical abstract logic of equivalence'. (4)

In short, the so-called linguistic turn of semiotics and structuralism, for Morton, is a symptom of critical theory's regression back from historical materialist analysis. The growing emphasis on language in twentieth-century thought, on the construction and deconstruction of signification or meaning, is to be understood as part and parcel of the increasing hegemony and widening globalisation of capitalist logic. Capital superimposes an obfuscating but profit-generating cloak of empty value on the material conditions of production. Analogously, linguistic, textual and discursive modes of analysis introduce a distracting emphasis on rhetoric and representation into the more concrete political and historical problem of human need's satisfaction.

For a critic of my generation unsatisfyingly acculturated into the postmodern academy, at a time when historical materialist analysis was an activity performed only by those hopelessly out of touch, Morton's argument is a seductive one. Undeniably, for the majority of the human population today, and even for many in the most 'advanced' post-industrial societies, the satisfaction of basic needs is still *the* primary problem of day-to-day life. And generally speaking, the cultural theory of the last few decades is not the sort of place where one might expect to be confronted with this difficult truth. Morton's theory communicates the noble wish to theorise away our ridiculous fascination with impossible desires and ineffable exchange values, finally focusing squarely on the satisfaction of our most basic species needs.

But there's a problem. As much as I want to agree with Morton, I have to grant Baudrillard his argument, albeit while distancing myself from the consequences he draws from it. Over a century of psychoanalytic experience provides inconvenient but overwhelming evidence that even at its basest or barest, human life can only fail to limit itself to the dimension of biological or physiological need. The argument that psychoanalytic experience shows this because it's only the bourgeoisie who ever get analysed fails, unfortunately, to convince.

Here is the basic lesson of Freud's *Beyond the Pleasure Principle* (1922): the essence of human life is its own excess over itself; an inhuman and immortal drive which, zombie-like, persists beyond mere biological death.[17] Similarly, as Lacan argued in the aftermath of the sociopolitical tumult of the late 1960s, surplus value, which he translated into the neologism *plus-de-jouir* (surplus enjoyment), survives the socialist revolution. As impractical and politically irritating as the statement surely is, Baudrillard is entirely correct to argue that use value is an abstraction. Objects of experience never appear to the sexuate human subject in purely practical or utilitarian terms, unsullied by a stain of excessive and unconscious libidinal interest. Use value can never be reconciled with the immaterial vicissitudes of human desire.

For psychoanalysis, desire is indeed useless and pointless. Utopian socialism – that is, the socialism that posits a return to a natural balance of need after capitalism's fall – would be a feasible project only if we, as speaking human subjects, were satisfied by the satisfaction of our needs. As everyone knows, the infant can go on wailing even after he's changed and fed. The sobering psychoanalytic lesson is that the baby's cry indexes every human's constitutively denatured essence, or being-towards-death. In fact, there's something in the prospect of satisfaction that repels us. This is the sense in which desire is essentially perverse: constitutively out of balance with both the environment and the organism itself. What we desire, in fact, is *non*-satisfaction; satisfaction's indefinite postponement. Simply put, the purpose of desire is to ensure that we are never definitively satisfied; that every object presented to us to satisfy our needs is finally deemed insufficient, unsatisfactory.

To the psychoanalytic claim about desire, which we could call a truth of human nature if desire wasn't precisely what separates us off from nature, the historical materialist will offer the rejoinder that Freud only made it because he was a product of the Viennese bourgeoisie, of European capitalism at the height of its imperialist phase. Yet, the psychoanalytic claim about desire isn't historical. Because it's ultimately devoid of content, because its essence is in effect correlative to every object's failure to extinguish it, desire as such can't be historicised. As far as queer theory is concerned, the necessary corollary of this is the truth that homosexual desire can manifest itself when there is no discourse to support it; nothing on the level of concrete historical actuality – social formations, institutions, identities, writings – through which it might, as it were, be given body.

With respect to Marxism's political ambitions, the claim that the essence of desire isn't historical shouldn't be taken to mean that the implementation of a social alternative to capitalism is impossible in any a priori way. It only indicates that if we were someday to eradicate capitalism, whatever that might mean exactly, it doesn't follow that we would suddenly cease to be creatures of desire. Again, the human subject will always remain unreconciled with its basic animal needs.

This being said, Morton is correct to argue that the paradigmatic shift Baudrillard's work helped to effect in cultural theory – from mode of production to mode of signification – is politically unfortunate, by virtue of its participation in the disturbingly wide-ranging abandonment of the critique of surplus value in the post-1968 period. It's one thing to claim that desire is inextinguishable; it's quite another to conclude from this that nothing can be done about the tyranny of exchange value.

Who could deny that we've allowed increasingly complex and speculative systems of value not only to obfuscate, and therefore legitimate, ever more scandalous social inequalities, but also to determine our very collective material destinies? Even the day-to-day realities of university life in both the private *and* public sectors – student loans and faculty research funds; student–instructor ratios; the availability of digital and paper-based forums for publication, 'research dissemination' and 'knowledge mobilisation'; even, and especially, course content – are in the most intimate way intertwined with the wildly unpredictable vicissitudes of global capital. It's almost superfluous to add that the increasingly stressful world of academia, or at least those parts of it that show resistance to its instrumentalisation by the demands of capital, is the very same environment that right-wing pundits routinely lambaste as hopelessly out of touch with real-world economic 'realities'.

Who's Afraid of Transsexual Marxism?

Both Floyd's uncomfortably poststructuralist Lukácsian Marxism and Morton's orthodox historical materialism suffer from their unwillingness, or inability, to take account of the contribution of psychoanalysis to our appreciation of human desire. Indeed, from the psychoanalytic perspective, there's nothing at all queer in either theory, if we understand by that term how Lacan described the sexual drive as irreconcilable with discourse and meaning.

It's probably not coincidental that we must step outside the Anglo-American world to find examples of anti-homophobic Marxian theoretical initiatives that find in psychoanalysis not an obstacle, but rather a tool. The two most important such examples are the writings of Guy Hocquenghem (to whom the next chapter is dedicated), and Mario Mieli. Intriguingly, these remarkable, and certainly under-read, efforts to acquaint Marxism with an anti-homophobic critical project date back to a time well before queer theory's pioneers even appeared on the scene.

A central figure of Italian gay politics in the 1970s and self-described 'outrageous queen', Mieli founded the *Fronte Unitario Omosessuale Rivoluzionario Italiano* (United Italian Revolutionary Homosexual Front) in 1972. In 1977, he published an important book adapted from a dissertation he wrote for a doctorate in moral philosophy (of all things), translated into English in 1980 as *Homosexuality and Liberation: Elements of a Gay Critique*. Ignored even by most self-professed queer Marxist critics writing in English, this text without doubt figures among the most important works ever to address either the significance of homosexuality for Marxism, or the implications of Marxism for the gay movement and its subsequent offshoots.

The Mieli story is a heroic but tragic one. He committed suicide in 1983 at the young age of 30, apparently unsettled by the negative reception he anticipated for the autobiographical work, *Il risveglio dei faraoni*, he had just finished writing. We can reasonably speculate that the reactionary Stalinist 'family values' ethos of post-war European institutional communism played a significant role in Mieli's demise. More certain is that no work on queer Marxism can afford either to ignore the immense contribution of Mieli's singular text, or to wonder about, and speculate on, the future directions his work might have taken had his provocative writing career not come to such a premature end.

Because the text is too long and significant to broach in general terms in the present context, I've chosen to focus on the element that most directly invokes Marxism and the Marxist tradition. From this angle, the most important aspect of *Homosexuality and Liberation* is its insistence on linking homophobia to the relations of capital. Therein lies Mieli's undeniable significance for my own project. Read retrospectively from over three decades on, his book glaringly exposes dominant queer theory's failure to establish this link, or even to acknowledge that it had ever previously been made. Even worse, in this perspective the queer project gains the patina of a patent regression, for homophobia's implication in the logic of capital is already the starting point of Mieli's discussion – indeed, its most central framing assumption.

To be sure, we should take this fact today as evidence of the remarkable extent to which Marxist critical assumptions have disappeared from the discourse on sexuality since Mieli wrote his text. Although *Homosexuality and Liberation* puts forth arguments both explicit and implicit to support the capital–homophobia link, the text's mode of address and ensemble of references together convey a reality that has become decidedly unfamiliar. At the time of the book's publication, there existed a group of activist and academic readers in Italy and the UK (Mieli was also active in London's revolutionary left gay scene), however small or marginal, for whom it went without saying that the liberation of homosexual desire must necessarily go hand in hand with a radical transformation of the capitalist status quo.

In the contemporary situation of queer studies, Mieli's text gains even further in value by virtue of its extraordinarily prescient acknowledgment of the startling efficiency with which capital capitalises (there is no more perfect word) on the new sexual phenomena that came into increasing visibility in a newly sexually permissive society. By the mid-1970s, it had already become abundantly clear to Mieli's keen critical eye that this society 'makes very good use of the "perversions"' which, he affirms, are 'sold both wholesale and retail'; are 'studied, classified, valued, marketed, accepted, discussed'.[18]

Knowingly, Mieli writes in the wake of both the naïve sexual liberationism of Norman O. Brown and the more politicised doctrine of repressive desublimation influentially advanced by Herbert Marcuse, whose work *Homosexuality and Liberation* quotes in some detail. The reference to Marcuse's book makes abundantly clear that Mieli had already gained the famous insight that Michel Foucault would much more conspicuously develop in *The History of Sexuality*, the first volume of which was published the very same year as *Homosexuality and Liberation*. Be it by virtue of the material effects of capital or the amorphous forces of power, both texts posit the same result: the impulse behind sexual liberationism had been decisively deformed and co-opted, and its effects of disalienation or subjective emancipation fully attenuated and renormalised. For both Mieli and Foucault, the rhetoric of sexuality's liberation had, by the late 1970s, become a tired and toothless cliché.

Mieli's deft handling of the classic Freudo-Marxist problem of the relation between, on the one hand, the demands of a civilisation that must organise production in order to survive and, on the other, the realities of a disruptive and impractical human sexuality, displays a remarkable subtlety. To be sure, Mieli's approach puts paid to the hopeful notion that impactful social change can result from the expression of taboo sexualities. Nonetheless, Mieli consistently resists proceeding to the resigned conclusion that no form of sexual advocacy or practice will ever have any effect on the negotiation of sex roles and social relations.

Central to Mieli's take on the tricky Marx-Freud conundrum is the notion of labour which, to risk an understatement, has failed to figure prominently in academic queer discourse. In essence, Mieli cleverly adds to the doctrine of commodity fetishism famously developed by Marx in the first volume of *Capital* the idea that it's not just labour which is alienated in the commodity, but sexuality as well. Or rather, it's more accurate perhaps to say that Mieli, clearly under the influence of Freud here, implicitly reformulates Marx's complex understanding of labour to foreground the agency of Eros in it. For Mieli, that is to say, the specifically human energy or life force that goes into any process of social production is the very same energy at work in sexuality. More concretely, the worker on that Fiat assembly line makes the same sort of expenditure of effort attaching a part to his car engine that he would make making love to his partner. And for Mieli at least (psychoanalysis isn't so sure), it's clear that this worker would much rather engage in the latter form of expenditure than the former.

In Mieli's view, the liberation of homosexual desire requires the emancipation of sexuality from both patriarchal sex roles and capital. This liberation depends first and foremost on our recognition of the fact that capitalism has already learned how to prey upon dissident desires, transforming them into what he calls 'the squalid fetishes of sex marketed by the system' (209). The enemy constituency here for Mieli includes all those reactionary souls who derive apparent satisfaction from the mediocre titillations such fetishes provide. It's quite clear from Mieli's discussion that numerous gay men and other sexual dissidents figure prominently among them.

Mieli's argument draws on Marx's *Grundrisse* (1858, published 1939) to make two main assertions. First, humanity will not be emancipated until human labour, and therefore sexuality for Mieli, ceases to be alienated in the production of falsely liberated perverse commodities. Second, technological advancements have created a historically unprecedented opportunity for emancipation.

This last point is explained through reference to two phenomena. What Marx called the 'surplus labour of the mass' is no longer needed for general human well-being; and intellectual labour, heretofore restricted to the privileged classes, has made itself available to the worker, whose time is no longer monopolised by the exigencies of the (manual) working day. For Mieli, this means that the many revolutions in production that had taken place since Marx's day only underscore how 'it is even less necessary to channel all libidinal energies into reproduction' (211) and, indeed, how 'sexual repression is obsolete' (212).

For Marx, the dramatic reduction in socially necessary labour already discernible when he wrote – the time, that is, we collectively spend making what we need to survive – frees us up to pursue scientific and artistic endeavours, freely associating with one another to achieve our full collective creative potential. For Mieli, by contrast, these same improvements emancipate us from all sexual constraints: everything from reproduction to conventional gender roles; from patriarchy to the exhausting demands of the working day.

All of this suggests an immensely preferable alternative to contemporary hegemonic queer theory. But as a product of its time, Mieli's argument is marred by several significant limitations. In particular, Mieli's fidelity to the classical Marxist line sees him fail to address certain key problems, which have only become more urgent in the decades since he wrote. The most obvious of these can be formulated as a question. Despite the emancipation from conventional industrial material production of a wide swathe of humanity across the global North and South, why do we remain basically as chained in our labour to our computers and wireless devices as any worker ever was to the production line? In many ways, the Blackberry-iPhone invasion of non-labour time is as insidious as the pre-trade union extended work day.

To give him due credit, Mieli provides an answer to this question, and here again he remains faithful to the Marxist view. For Mieli as for Marx, the alienation and exploitation of labour continue long after humanity has ceased being obliged to work all day to ensure its survival. This can be explained by capital's dependence on the surplus value extracted from surplus labour, which is another way of saying that the relations of capital are based on human desires, not human needs. Hence Mieli's focus on perverse commodity fetishism and the Marcusean critique of desublimation, but also his cutting invective against the 'homocops': all those reactionary queers 'who are better adapted to the [capitalist] system', and 'who find ideological arguments to justify their position as contented slaves' (194). Being faithful to Mieli's line of argument requires us to align most of mainstream queer theory with these homocops.

These details highlight how Mieli's discussion hinges on a crucial distinction he outlines between, first, those expressions of non-normative sexuality that remain complicit with capitalism's colonisation of the perverse libido, and second, an alternative expression of homosexual desire, which would undo in a liberating way sexuality's repressive sublimations in commodities. More simply, Mieli distinguishes between 'the reified pages of Vogue' (198) and what he calls the transsexual potential of human sexuality. In his invaluable introduction to an Italian-language edition of *Homosexuality and Liberation*, Christopher Lane helpfully summarises the salience of Mieli's notion. His 'transsexual aesthetic doesn't enable men to pass unnoticed among women, leaving heterosexuality untouched', Lane writes. Rather, 'it defamiliarizes all social understanding of gender, destroying heterosexuality's status, leaving us all to begin, as it were, from scratch'.[19]

In this way, Mieli's idiosyncratic understanding of transsexuality fully anticipates the 'deconstruction' of the gender binary and the critique of the 'heterosexual matrix' in queer theory. The crucial difference, however, is that Mieli traces a direct path from the work of deconstruction and critique to the subversion of not only patriarchy and heterosexism, but capitalism as well. In this sense, Mieli's work could serve as a crucial missing link which, in today's context, could potentially connect poststructuralist feminism and queer theory with the critique of capitalist social relations. As you may recall, this was precisely Floyd's ambition, and one senses that Mieli would have proven more valuable than Lukács to his project.

But how exactly does Mieli support his point concerning the properly material implications of a 'queering' of gender and sexuality, a trope which today has become entirely familiar? Shouldn't poststructuralist queer theory's failure to engage with Marxian concerns inspire sharp scepticism about Mieli's thesis? In my own view, these material implications are inadequately developed in *Homosexuality and Liberation*. What Mieli does indeed say, however, is that the liberation of non-normative sexuality can be complicit with capitalism because the sexuality concerned remains in a repressed and sublimated form, which reinforces the ethos of discipline and productivity upon which capital depends. But the discussion is based on vague understandings of repression and sublimation, and fails to delve into the complexities and ambiguities of these concepts as developed originally in Freud's writing.[20] Further, it's not at all clear that the relations of capital today depend on a prohibition of enjoyment. On the contrary, the paradox of contemporary capitalism is the apparent symbiosis of a hypercompetitive and individualistic work ethic with a hedonistic and consumerist injunction to 'enjoy!'[21]

Read with the benefit of hindsight, Mieli's discussion leaves today's readership with two options. First, we can congratulate Mieli, as well we should, for his awesomely prescient diagnosis of capitalism's spectacular colonisation of the gains of feminism and the gay movements, all the while insisting that it still makes sense to claim that certain non-reified expressions of homosexual desire offer 'a fertile potential for revolutionary subversion' (212). Alternatively, we can take the contemporaneity of gay liberation and the queer phenomenon with the neoliberal era's unprecedented unshackling of capital as evidence that, *pace* Mieli, the whole notion of a specifically sexual emancipation in all its possible forms is simply incompatible with anticapitalist politics, that is to say with politics properly speaking.

Leaving aside for a moment the complicated question, pregnant with significance for theory, of how we understand the term in Freud's wake, we might unabashedly and in a spirit of realism acknowledge that a certain degree of sexual repression is a precondition of radical political organisation and action. If an ethos of hyperpermissiveness does indeed characterise contemporary capitalism, then a certain degree of old-fashioned inhibition or self-abnegation might in fact carry forward new initiatives for politics, including even those that fight against homophobia. Despite the weighty historical evidence to the contrary, we might add that there is nothing *necessarily* homophobic, patriarchal or even 'sex-negative' about the thematics of discipline and auto-critique in the tradition. In any case, if, as I argue in detail in the following chapter, Lacan's Freud is right, and repression results from language rather than 'civilisation', no social transformation, no matter how radical or anti-capitalist, will ever succeed in undoing it.

In the end, the most salient feature of Mieli's work for the contemporary critique of queer theory is its conviction that being or identifying as homosexual doesn't in itself pose any necessary challenge to the ideological status quo. By insisting on inserting class conflict among the queers, Mieli implicitly upholds the fundamental Marxian principle that the capitalist mode of production creates a *diagonal* social difference – one that cuts across all the other, less materially significant, differences of race, religion and ethnicity, for instance (with the exception of sexual difference which, for psychoanalysis at least, is a diagonal difference of a precisely analogous kind). Like the symptom which, according to Freud, takes advantage of pre-existing physical problems to express itself in its encoded way, class antagonism colonises other varieties of difference in a manner that obfuscates how religious and racial conflicts, for example, are often subtly displaced socioeconomic conflicts at the same time.

What has changed significantly since Mieli's historical moment is the fact that capitalism's colonisation of homosexuality now extends well beyond the conformist, 'straight-acting' constituencies he identifies as the enemies of his transsexual aesthetic (although these of course continue, problematically to be sure, to exist). On the contrary, it would seem today that the most cutting-edge queers – those who refuse sexual identification and monogamy; those who dismiss 'vanilla' sexual activity and marriage as hopelessly complicit – are the ones best adapted, with their transient lifestyles and antipathy for attachment, to capital in its current, hypermobile phase. Surely it has become impossible to pretend that unfettered capital and 'traditional family values' are mutually enforcing social forces, even if populist conservative ideology functions to prevent this antagonism from manifesting itself politically – that is, as an explicit and self-conscious contestation of dominant social and economic models. The radical queer millionaire Internet pornographer who organises 'sex-positive' sex toy parties in his spare time (the new Tupperware?) has become one of the best emblems of contemporary capitalism.

Capital Enjoyments

So, then, what are the consequences of all of this for the search for a Marxist alternative to queer theory? To get us started, we can return to Morton's critique of Baudrillard, more specifically to his dismissal of postmodernism's reinterpretation of exchange value as the hegemony of the signifier's subversive play over the concrete meaning of the signified. I claimed that Baudrillard was correct, and in agreement with psychoanalysis, to deny the possibility that the human subject can content itself with the satisfaction of need. Need, like use value, is in this specific sense an illusory abstraction. What the postmodernist analysis lacks, however, is the fundamental psychoanalytic corollary that the impossible excess of desire, and by extension the sexy phantom of exchange value, is a mechanism of defence designed to shield the subject's ego from the dangerous eruption of enjoyment.

In other words, psychoanalysis adds to the classic Marxist analysis of the commodity form the key notion that exchange value is correlative to the defence against, the repression of, enjoyment. Where enjoyment is concerned, there is no surplus value, no Lacanian *plus-de-jouir*. And yet, by this last statement I would appear to contradict myself. After all, did I not claim just a few paragraphs back that Lacan articulates his criticism of utopian Marxism by denying that any manner of social transformation, no matter how radical, can succeed in extinguishing surplus enjoyment, in reconciling the human subject's desire to the object of need?

For Lacan, we attribute surplus value to an object – we perceive in the object an ineffable 'x' that can potentially extinguish desire – as a result of our unwillingness, buttressed by our ego investments, to derive libidinal satisfaction from it. Although psychoanalysis argues that neurosis – the defence against jouissance – can never be eliminated in any final, once-and-for-all fashion, clinical practice is premised on the notion, properly utopian in this precise sense, that by confronting our dissimulated enjoyment we can attenuate the seductive and inhibiting power of the ideals that prop up our self-image. In this way, it's possible at least to begin to see through the false promise of the idealised, full satisfaction issued by the surplus value of exchange. This unlimited, perfect satisfaction, psychoanalysis teaches us, is one we desire to experience simultaneously with our self-apprehension; without the expropriation of selfhood, the subjective destitution, to use Lacan's suggestive phrase, that inevitably accompanies authentic drive satisfaction.

In this precise sense, then, the commodity form in Marx's political economy is structurally correlative to the ideals (ideal ego and ego ideal) of which Freud speaks in the presentation of his concept of narcissism. The commodity's seductions are premised on the idealisation, and therefore the repression, of the enjoyment against which they defend the ego's investments. As Lacan argued relentlessly in his early teaching, these investments always adapt with supreme efficiency to the demands of the 'American way of life' and 'the service of goods' – the smooth functioning, to Marxianise Lacan's idiom, of capitalist social relations. Despite the changes in emphasis that modulate his teaching over time, Lacan was unwavering in imparting the lesson, initially targeted at the ideology of ego psychology, that the aim of analysis must be to attenuate the lure of the ego so as to make manifest the enjoyment dissimulated by the symptom. If this is indeed the ultimate kernel of truth in the Freudian project writ large, then psychoanalysis should make a similar promise, however impossible or 'interminable', as concerns the enticing lure that surplus value and the commodity form unfurl.

On this assumption, Marx's critique of surplus value does precisely the same work as Freud's critique of the ego on the level of what we might call the structure of their respective speculative systems. Marx's critique uncovers the obfuscating idealisation of exploitative production relations, which make up the disavowed truth of surplus value (i.e. *reification*: commodities in capitalism make nasty qualitative relations between persons appear as innocuous quantitative relations between sexified things). Analogously, Freudianism unearths the enjoyments that, dissimulated by identification, hold together our alluring ego structure, the very same structure that provides the commodity with its enticing libidinal appeal.

If the point of psychoanalysis is to teach us to wrest ourselves from the force of the inhibitory ideals through which we develop a sense of ourselves, then the goal of ideological critique is an uncannily similar one: to diminish our dependence on those social forms that dissimulate the bitter truth of unjust relations of production. Psychoanalytically put, Marxist critique decodes the unconscious satisfactions, the multiple forms of consumerist jouissance, that bind us to market ideology. These are the formidable forces that see us purchase that bottle of perfume or cologne despite the fact that we know better, that we're not quite sure we even enjoy the scent. If the old project of so-called Freudo-Marxism ever had a point to make, it was perhaps that the two agendas, viewed on this level, are one and the same.

Taking the literary cue from Freud, Lacan tied the destiny of the desiring subject to the vicissitudes of the tragic genre, from the desire of the destitute Oedipus 'never to have been born', through Antigone's uncompromising perseverance at the limits of *atè*, to Sygne de Coûfontaine's pathetic and suicidal facial tic. This tic indexes a pure negativity, an absolute 'no', whose possibility is carved out by the signifier, according to Lacan, in Paul Claudel's dramaturgical trilogy. But, as Alenka Zupančič insightfully argues, desire also belongs to the realm of comedy, here understood as the generic mode that exposes the difference between the lofty and otherworldly ambitions of desire and the inadequate objects that fail to satisfy it.[22] This is the desire not to desire; the desire whose aim is to sabotage its own realisation, whose modus operandi is precisely to repress the knowledge of its own impossibility.

This desire is to be distinguished from what Lacan called desire's real – the drive, that is – which does in fact deliver satisfaction. But we can only experience this satisfaction at the ego's expense, as a consequence of the ego's fleeting collapse. This explains why we must distinguish the play of desire, its endless substitution of inadequate objects, from enjoyment or jouissance which, despite its impossibility, happens nonetheless, whether we care to know about it or not. Desire is to the play of signifying substitutions as jouissance is to a resolutely non-signifying, meaningless satisfaction. With unrelenting seriousness, this satisfaction remains in unconscious form as the neurotic symptom, banished from conscious knowledge to allow for the ego's construction. Similarly, the pleasure we derive from our ego structure is to be contrasted with the Freudian 'beyond' of pleasure, the traumatic satisfaction we derive, as it were, from the drive.

Lacan's notion of enjoyment, as the beyond of the pleasure principle, also allows for a psychoanalytic reformulation of Marx's old concept of use value. Earlier, I agreed with Baudrillard's qualification of use value as an abstraction, as a Marxist illusion. But this agreement holds only to the extent that use value is held to be separable from its coupling with the ideal of exchange value; to the doubtless debatable extent, in other words, that the Marxist critique of the commodity form ultimately leads towards a sort of egalitarian utilitarianism, that it is held to insinuate that the utopian defeat of capitalism will reconcile humanity with the value of use as a realisable *summum bonum* or general social good.

But what if we posit instead that it's really Marx's idea of *use value* that should be connected to Lacan's concept of enjoyment – that self-expropriating experience of embodiment which dispenses, for a time at least, with the protective barrier the ego erects in defence against it? That is, should we not hold that when Lacan coined the term *plus-de-jouir* to connect psychoanalysis to Marx's discourse on the commodity form, he really meant to say that it's use value, not exchange value, that corresponds to the always imperfect and fleeting satisfactions the castrated subject of the unconscious is only able to access? This compromised satisfaction must then be distinguished from the phantom promise of '*more!*' enjoyment. This is the excessive enjoyment that both fascinates and repels us in the Other; the surplus jouissance we can never manage to experience for ourselves.

Psychoanalysis surely argues that there can be no definitive exorcism of exchange value, no once-and-for-all cure for our chronic collective overvaluation of the commodity-objects that capitalism displays to lure the insatiable appetites of desire. But psychoanalysis can also teach Marxism the lesson that the resistance-breaking assumption of our imperfect and shameful enjoyments, on the one had, and the desire-causing power of the commodity, on the other, are inversely proportional. The more we acknowledge our jouissance – the more bravely we come to terms with its 'base', and properly perverse, libidinal origins – the more independence we gain with respect to the dictates of commodity relations. In short, tarrying with the drive and its inhuman insistence can insulate us from the temptations of sacrifice, postponement and compromise by which we tether our destinies to the imperatives of capital. Freud rigorously defined the analyst's task as impossible, its practice interminable. Yet, he doggedly persisted in its performance, with obviously remarkable results. No doubt we must conclude that, in conformity with Lacanian ethics, the impossibility of the ultimate completion of the critique of the commodity form is the very reason for which its practice presents itself to us as an absolute duty.

It's probably no coincidence that in these last considerations of Lacan's intervention in Marx's labour theory of value, queer theory has seemingly disappeared from view. What does this mean? As I argue in detail in the next chapter, Freud's definition of sexuality, or more precisely of the drive, paradoxically implies that sexuality is *a*sexual. Indifferent to gender, it remains unmoved by every positive quality of the object.

To the extent, then, that we identify queer theory with the thematics of endless discursive production concerning the construction and undoing of gender and sexual identities in and through the multiform and conflicting forces of power, this theory is simply irrelevant to the psychoanalytic critique of capital whose very general parameters I've just sketched out. What happens to queer theory, by contrast, when it confronts jouissance and its constitutive deadlock, the dogged persistence of Lacan's *plus-de-jouir*? The critical project that targets and demystifies the lure of surplus value is indifferent to sexual categorisations, and in this sense carries a universal relevance and address. Everyone is queer, therefore no one is queer, let's move on.

4

Capitalism and Schizoanalysis

Against Queer Theory, *Avant La Lettre*

In 1972, nearly two decades before the emergence of what we know today as queer theory, Guy Hocquenghem published his singular text *Homosexual Desire*. Despite its relatively marginal status within current debates on politics and sexuality, this book precociously broaches a number of central topics that anti-homophobic critics still raise today: the psychodynamics of homophobia; desire's role in the exercise of power; and strategies for the facilitation, if I can put it this way, of the experience of homosexual desire.

Hocquenghem's book is an unacknowledged forerunner of contemporary queer theory. Indeed, although queer theory is barely aware of it, it helped set the stage for its most fundamental debates. Most importantly for my concerns, *Homosexual Desire* represents one of the most consequential attempts to think about homosexuality and homophobia in acknowledgment of both psychoanalytic and Marxist insights.

Hocquenghem's book was first translated into English in 1978, and then conspicuously reprinted by a major American university press in 1993. So, why does it remain an obscure anomaly in English-language queer discourse? The answer might lie in part in the book's French intellectual cultural origins during the immediate post-1968 period – a culture whose investments, both political and theoretical, now contrast sharply with those that animate contemporary gay and queer politics in the global North. We can account for the relative non-reception of Hocquenghem in Anglo-American sexuality theory today by citing the contrasting historical locations, theoretical assumption, and political ideologies that separate Hocquenghem's moment of writing from contemporary queer theory.[1]

In this light, one of this chapter's aims will be to engage in an exercise of translation between the various discourses concerned – Freudian and Lacanian psychoanalysis, Gilles Deleuze and Félix Guattari's schizoanalysis, and Anglo-American poststructuralist queer theory[2] – not in order to reconcile their conflicting contentions, but rather to force a productive encounter. My wager is that this encounter will help to identify the political and theoretical stakes of sexuality theory in general and, more specifically, to call into question the most basic tenets of contemporary queer theory.

Homosexual Desire predates by four years Foucault's monumentally influential engagement with the repressive hypothesis in his introduction to his book series *The History of Sexuality*. As we've considered in previous chapters, Foucault overturns in that text what was perhaps the most pervasive assumption about sexuality in the twentieth century: that it struggles for expression against oppressively normative social forces; that its force goes against the current of power. Foucault countered that power rather works in tandem with sexuality – indeed, that the discourse of sexuality is itself a subjectivity-producing mechanism of power.

Reading Hocquenghem today, we recognise retrospectively the tremendous debt Foucault's text owes to what is perhaps, in comparison with *Homosexual Desire*, the more consequential attempt to do battle with the 'French Freud', namely *Anti-Oedipus*, the first volume of Deleuze and Guattari's *Capitalism and Schizophrenia*. Hocquenghem's book shows the influence of *Anti-Oedipus* on every page. Despite its tremendous impact on cultural theory in general, however, this text has had a comparatively minor, although latterly increasing, impact on hegemonic queer theory's development.

In his reading of Freud, Lacan unwaveringly insisted on the inseparability of desire from, indeed its causation by, an irreparable lack in both the subject and its sociosymbolic Other. Against this emphasis, Deleuze and Guattari offer an alternative account of desire as self-generating production. This production is immanent to a field of forces that thwarts the 'territorialising' ambitions of meaning and representation – the Oedipus complex, that is, which is the familial form these latter take in psychoanalytic theory, according to Deleuze and Guattari. It's easy to discern the imprint of the anti-oedipal concept of desire's positivity on Foucault's contention that social repression produces, rather than inhibits, desire. For his part, Hocquenghem directly lifts his vocabulary of desiring-machines and deterritoriali-sation from the pages of *Anti-Oedipus*, whose publication the same fateful year as *Homosexual Desire* is perhaps merely the most contingent aspect of their consequential intertextual relations.

But surely there are other reasons, theoretical and political in nature, that explain why so much Anglo-American poststructuralist queer theory has failed to engage with Hocquenghem's argument about homosexual desire. Three such reasons immediately come to mind. First, Hocquenghem subscribes to the Deleuzo-Guattarian thesis that Freud 'discovered' what Hocquenghem calls 'the mechanisms of desire', defining the latter term as an 'abstract general force at work in sexual life'.[3] In light of Hocquenghem's attribution of this thesis to *Anti-Oedipus*, we can extrapolate from the qualification of desire as abstract that desire is something other than what it tends to be in queer poststructuralism, namely a determinate (and in this sense 'concrete') effect of particular conditions of discursive or historical possibility. More simply put, Hocquenghem could not subscribe to the Foucault-derived queer assumption that one can only desire what discourse or history has already made it possible to desire.

Hocquenghem's consequential distinction between 'homosexuality' and what he alternatively calls 'homosexual desire' provides a salutary illustration. Homosexuality belongs to the 'molar' (another Deleuze and Guattari term) level of modern sexuality discourse. According to Hocquenghem, this discourse bestows a normative identity on the subject on the basis of its sexual behaviour, effectively circumscribing this subject within the parameters of a pathologising and guilt-inducing regime of knowledge. By contrast, homosexual desire corresponds to the disruptive 'molecular' level of desiring production. This level escapes the imperative of representation enforced by discourse. As a result, it has the capacity to thwart the power of sexual knowledges to define, and therefore normalise, the subjects about whom they seek to know.

Hocquenghem sees the absurdity to which any attempt at defining his concept will lead. '"Homosexual desire" – the expression is meaningless', he writes. 'There is no subdivision of desire into homosexuality and heterosexuality' (49). Impersonal, non-subjective and even non-human, for Hocquenghem desire designates a faculty of production, which need not pass through a signifying function to have its effects. Desire is therefore resistant to, and unexpressed by, historical discourses – that is, by the available knowledges that attempt to take account of it at any particular moment in time.

I'll have occasion shortly to look further into this notion of a desire liberated, as it were, from the constraints of history, or at least history conceived along Foucaultian lines as the set of conditions of possibility, embedded in thought and language, for knowledge. For the moment, however, it will prove helpful to retain that whereas homosexuality, for Hocquenghem as well as for Deleuze and Guattari, is part and parcel of a specific historical social formation, namely capitalism, *desire as such is not a historical concept*. Desire persists beneath the molar agencies of meaning, knowledge and power, and for this reason it can't be described as conditioned by them.

Although rarely acknowledged in the secondary sources, this separation of desire out from discourse is an act of thought that Deleuze and Guattari attribute explicitly to Freud. It's also what Foucault effectively dismantles in his reformulation of the repressive hypothesis. This reformulation has proven decisive in both the institutionalisation of sexuality studies over the last decades, and the development of queer discourse. To sum up what I've argued thus far, the first reason for Hocquenghem's minimal impact on queer theory relates to his endorsement of the 'abstract' (non-discursive and non-historical), properly Freudian view of desire. Through its enlistment of Foucault's historicist conception of sexuality as discourse-power, queer theory has shown itself bent on opposing this view.

Not unrelated to the first, the next factor impeding the assimilation of *Homosexual Desire* into queer theory *doxa* is its resolutely universalising reach. With reference to the classificatory zeal of mid-twentieth-century American researcher Alfred Kinsey's sexual identity surveys, Hocquenghem asks rhetorically: 'Was it really necessary to send out so many questionnaires and investigations in order to establish that everyone is more or less homosexual?' (52).

It's crucial to note that the universal referent of Hocquenghem's 'everyone' isn't the same, strictly speaking, as the one queer theory wants to acknowledge. Once more, we can take one of the foundational texts of poststructuralist queer theory as an example. Eve Kosofsky Sedgwick famously identified two contradictions in modern sexuality discourse. One of these contradictions occurs between a 'minoritizing' and a 'universalizing' view of what she terms 'homo/heterosexual definition'.[4] The former view proceeds from the assumption that the classificatory apparatus of sexual orientation is relevant only to a restricted group of people. Not everyone, that is, will feel that the question 'am I gay or straight?' applies to them. By contrast, the latter view assumes that it does indeed concern everyone; no one can avoid asking themselves whether their desire targets same- or other-sex objects, or perhaps both. The importance of Sedgwick's presentation of the question lies in the fact that the object to which each view of sexuality refers is different from the one implied by what Hocquenghem calls homosexual desire. The content of the idea of sexuality featuring universal and minoritarian versions is equivalent to what Freud refers to as 'object choice' – the relation, that is, between our own biological sex and the sex of the persons to whom our desire is addressed.

Hocquenghem would have had to dismiss Sedgwick's outline of the means of formulating the possibilities for sexuality in late modernity, because it remains shaped by the molar categories of personhood and sex identity, the very sedimented, territorialised parameters against which he pitches his alternative concept of homosexual desire. An important consequence follows. In response to Sedgwick's exhortation first to underline the 'incoherence of definition' inherent in the discourse on sexuality, and then to identify 'discursive power' as the 'rhetorical leverage' required to 'set' its terms (11), Hocquenghem would likely reply that the entire definitional apparatus of sexuality simply fails to recognise the disruptive force, indeed the essence, of desire. In a thoroughly Freudian vein, Hocquenghem insists that desire cannot be defined because it resists, by its very nature, all efforts at identification and classification. Simply put, desire can't be expressed in any of the codes – semiotic, discursive, social, political, historical, however you may wish to name them – with which one might consider it amenable to articulation.

Sedgwick's implicit understanding of universality expresses one of two possible ways of qualifying the purchase of sexual definition on the subjects this definition defines. By contrast, Hocquenghem offers a stronger, less familiar and intuitive, formulation of the universal as the attribute of an *an*oedipal desire. This desire is not only logically prior to its reactive personalisation in sexuality discourse. Much more radically, it also undermines the very premise that desire is a function of a human individual. Desire's impersonality throws a spanner in the works of the vocabularies of object choice and sexual orientation – that structure of sexuality discourse around which Sedgwick's thinking, and most of queer theory's, pivots.

This remains the case not only when queer theory insists, as Sedgwick does, on the underlying incoherence of the object choice concept, but also when it aims to 'deconstruct' this concept's presumptive identity foundations by asserting that sexuality subverts the sex and gender binaries on which the rhetoric depends. In Hocquenghem's view, I can't say for sure if I'm homosexual or heterosexual not because my desire is indifferent to sexual difference (although it is that too for Deleuze and Guattari), but rather because this desire isn't ultimately directed at an individual person. Desire, for Hocquenghem, harbours an inhuman or mechanical quality, which effectively lifts sexuality above the psychological realm of human attributes and qualities. Further, that desire is transindividual and can't be articulated isn't merely a feature of a particular discourse – the modern, post-sexological discourse of sexuality, for example. Desire, as it were, always remains indifferent to history.

Although I endorse both its universal purchase and the pressure it puts on contemporary ideas of object choice and sexual orientation, I'll have occasion later on to question the understanding of desire Hocquenghem takes from *Capitalism and Schizophrenia*. Indeed, the very qualification of desire as unnameable already alerts us to language's dependence on negation to evoke it, and therefore sits uncomfortably alongside what Deleuze and Guattari protest is desire's inherently positive, or more precisely productive, work. For now, however, we can move on to the third and last prong of Hocquenghem's queer theory-challenging argument.

What I have in mind is his contention, also inspired by *Anti-Oedipus*, that the modern homosexual identity, unlike homosexual desire in Hocquenghem's specific sense, is indeed a historical phenomenon. We've already seen how poststructuralist queer theory typically links the historicity of homosexuality to a 'modernity' figured as merely discursive – in contrast, for instance, to more conventional Marxian materialist conceptions of history, viewed as the succession in time of the modes of production. Instead, Hocquenghem views modernity's obsessive encoding of desire as a reaction against the radically transformative socioeconomic impact of capitalism. For Hocquenghem, the discourse of sexuality is therefore a reactive product of a particular historical mode of production. In queer theory, by contrast, the relation of modern sexuality to underlying economic structures remains essentially unexamined.

No doubt, here again, political context sheds some light on these contrasting assumptions about how we should conceive of the forces shaping modern ideas of sexuality. As Bill Marshall notes, the Anglo-American post-Stonewall gay movement reflected a political field shaped by the ideologies of 'liberal individualism and self-invention',[5] which gave rise to social formations anchored in ethnic and other identities. With few exceptions, these identities' agendas were restricted to an ambition of inclusion within the capitalist mode of production and the liberal-democratic state apparatus.

Marshall goes on to argue that the French revolutionary republican tradition, with its hallmark stress on the virtues of abstract citizenship, has tended to discourage the emergence of identity-predicated interest groups. Confronting the abstractly defined republican citizen with the state structure without the mediating influence of a strong civil society (this tension was more evident 40 or 50 years ago than it is today), this system proved more conducive to the emergence of politically radical projects, which sought the overthrow of the entire bourgeois state structure. Evidently, this state of affairs has no close equivalent in the US. This brand of 'hard left' politics has had a comparatively marginal impact on not only the historical US-based gay and lesbian movements, but their more contemporary offshoots as well.

To be sure, the subject of the late 1960s revolutionary project was defined primarily not by cultural and sexual identities, but rather by socioeconomic class. It's certainly true that the students in the *soixante-huitard* political alliance thought of their status along class lines. This would explain why, in the immediate post-1968 period, the various groups campaigning for the liberation of homosexuals, notably including the FHAR (Front homosexuel d'action révolution-naire) with which Hocquenghem was at one time affiliated, tended to emerge out of, and on occasion in association with, Trotskyist groups and parties of the far left.

These groups reacted against widely recognised sexist and homophobic currents within the French Communist Party (PCF) which, in the 1950s and early 1960s, was still wilfully blinding itself to both the abhorrent crimes of Stalinism and the tenacious but disintegrating structures of French colonialism. Although the association of the French homosexual movements with left politics would deteriorate throughout the 1970s, in the late 1960s the problems of sexual regulation and homophobia were widely considered inseparable from the analysis of class formations and the logic of capital, in general accordance with the classic lines of Marxist thought.

The sociopolitical context goes a long way towards explaining the relative tardiness and initial political radicalism of the emergent homosexual movement in France. Yet, it can't on its own account for the properly theoretical argument developed by Hocquenghem after Deleuze and Guattari. Indeed, Hocquenghem asserts that the appearance of the familiar modern homosexual identity is a determinate consequence of, and also reaction against, the social deterritorialisations effected by capital with increasing intensity in late modernity. According to this thesis, mounting social upheaval, dislocation and fragmentation are the consequences of the commodification of wage labour and the expansion of markets. These social phenomena work to disperse the centripetal energies of the kinship group and scatter libidinal energy more widely across the social field. At the same time, however, reactive and proprietary forces of control attempt to contain capital's explosive social energies. As Hocquenghem sums up in full-on 'D and G mode', 'capitalism decodes the fluxes of desire and immediately circumscribes them within privatisation' (142).

But a fundamental ambiguity clouds *Capitalism and Schizophrenia*'s theoretical horizon. Forces linked to capital are held to account for *both* the crumbling of the social and symbolic structures that codify and normalise desire *and* the reactive, indeed reactionary, resignification of desire in the bourgeois interpretative matrix of Freud's Oedipus complex. To be sure, this ambiguity leaves its mark on Hocquenghem's estimation of homosexual desire's properly political implications. As I'll explore further at the conclusion of this chapter, schizoanalysis' belief in the availability of a non-signifying desiring production – a mode of desire, that is, emancipated from the signifier, from the constraints of language – sees Hocquenghem wax rapturously on the topic of a sexual liberation modestly confined to the limits of capitalist modernity. Like its distant queer-theoretical cousins, Hocquenghem's anti-oedipal desiring utopia turns out to have disappointing, and entirely questionable, political implications.

The Redoubling of the World, and What to Do About it

Queer theory's general embrace of the later Foucault's psychoanalytic scepticism has caused the complex relation between Hocquenghem's anti-oedipal influence and the wider French psychoanalytic field, particularly the Lacanian one, to go largely unexamined. Undoubtedly, the intertextual link that joins both *Homosexual Desire* and *Anti-Oedipus* to Lacan's reading of Freud has an uncanny or spectral dimension, one which bespeaks a significant but buried influence belying the paucity of explicit references. Yet, just when Deleuze and Guattari's revolt against Oedipus promises to rejoin the Lacanian concept of the drive on some elusive theoretical horizon, we're reminded anew that the two discourses finally talk past one another, anchored as they are by irreconcilable assumptions about fundamental philosophical issues, such as being, knowledge and language.

Anti-Oedipus does in fact get around to crediting Lacan for severing the link more decisively than Freud between the faculty of desire and its entanglement with signifying representations, and therefore, at least potentially, with meaning. Now, Deleuze and Guattari repeatedly condemn meaning as a wellspring of guilt, which destructively reflects the productive force of desire back upon itself. In Lacan, by contrast, meaning, or rather truth, has an ineradicable, however illusory, significance for the subject of the unconscious. For his part, Hocquenghem refers to Lacan only once in *Homosexual Desire* in a none too nuanced gloss on the mirror stage. Nonetheless, it's clear enough that Hocquenghem takes on board Deleuze and Guattari's rejection of Lacan's major thesis about the subject, namely that this subject is *subject to* the signifier. This subjection carves out a primary ontological lack, which no representation will fully succeed in filling out. Because Hocquenghem's reading of psychoanalysis is so clearly mediated by Deleuze and Guattari's work, and because, despite the many buried references, *Anti-Oedipus* in an important sense is a critical assessment of, and also polemical attack against, Lacanian psychoanalysis, it will be helpful to explore in more precise terms how the two theoretical lines ultimately deviate quite dramatically from one another.

Deleuze and Guattari's reading of Lacan in *Anti-Oedipus* is comparable in its fundamentals to the critique of Freud developed by Hocquenghem in *Homosexual Desire*. As we've already considered, Freud's work for Hocquenghem manages to identify a disruptive, non-historical and uncontainable desiring function in the psyche, only to harness it, at moments of theoretical regression, to the meaning horizon of the bourgeois family. Not dissimilarly, Deleuze and Guattari first sing the praises of Lacan's *objet petit a* – his term for the immaterial 'lost' object that causes desire – as the concept that wrests the libido from its allegedly forced canalisation towards privileged and normative bodily organs. However, they then accuse Lacan of reintroducing through the back door a stifling signifying function in the form of what he calls the Other – that is, the 'locus of speech' that indexes desire's dependence on language, on social discourses. According to Deleuze and Guattari, Lacan's theory of the object liberates desire from 'any idea of need and any idea of fantasy'.[6] However idiosyncratically (for Lacan, the object is always and necessarily an object of unconscious fantasy), they find in Lacan's teaching an anticipation of their qualification of desire as both immediately productive and unconditioned by lack or absence, even the kind of lack (of nourishment, for example) that triggers a biophysiological need like hunger.

For Deleuze and Guattari, no fantasy comes between desire and what they call 'the conditions of objective existence'; no mediation between production, or the activity of desire, and what is produced, which they call 'the real' (27n). Production may indeed be bound by certain conditions, be they social, historical, political or psychical. But if these conditions are without limit, if they exclude no possibility, then production simply names the infinite faculty of desire as such. Desire is immanent to a network of forces and flows at once material and kinetic, natural and social. Thus, no obstacle opposes desire either within itself or without. More precisely, there is neither a *something* that concretely impedes the satisfaction of desire, nor a *nothing* – a self-difference in the object, as Lacan in fact argued – that effectively subverts satisfaction from within.

Lacan's theory works to estrange desire from itself, to prevent desire from encountering itself in the object that causes it. For Deleuze and Guattari, by contrast, the Lacanian reference to fantasy and 'the symbolic' are reactive symptoms of a mechanism of repression to which the molar agencies of meaning and interpretation give rise. The repression of desire creates the illusion that desire depends on lack. Indeed, the main target of Deleuze and Guattari's polemic against psychoanalysis is the premise that a lack sustains desire; that desire is set in motion by, and addresses itself to, a nothing. Lacan's definition of desire posits instead an internal dialectic whereby desire sustains itself by sabotaging its own fulfilment. By contrast, Deleuze and Guattari attribute to desire a potentially unlimited creative function hindered only by an alien oedipal force of normalisation imposed by language, by the signifier, from without.

The anti-oedipal argument against psychoanalysis in general, and Lacan in particular, can be quite straightforwardly articulated and has become relatively familiar, if rarely grasped on the level of its consequences. What interests me here, however, are the comparatively unexplored implications of the motivation, as it were, for Deleuze and Guattari's antipathy for lack and negation. These implications have the tremendous benefit of acquainting us not only with the error that causes them to view lack as something from which desire requires emancipation, but also with the problematic, and concretely political, consequences of their alternative desiring production framework. This line of inquiry gains in significance for my argument in this chapter because it sheds valuable light on Hocquenghem's view of the political importance of the modern homosexual social movements at the time he wrote *Homosexual Desire*. Along the way, I'll also be interested in identifying – surprisingly, perhaps – the common ground that Lacan and his anti-oedipal critics share, namely a desire to place the subjective or productive function as decisively as possible in the sociopolitical here-and-now.

A wide swathe of contemporary cultural theory has allowed the intuitive appeal of Deleuze and Guattari's association of lack with guilt and repression, indeed with all that thwarts the productivity of desire, to prevent us from asking a seemingly naïve question. So let's ask it here: what exactly *is* the problem with Lacan's idea of a desire predicated on a lacking, in the sense of immaterial, object – an object whose objective absence nevertheless fails to prevent it from causing the appearance of the subject who desires it? More simply, how does the anti-oedipal camp view lack, in its relation to the force of repression?

One of the ways in which Deleuze and Guattari argue against the ontology of lack in psychoanalysis is by drawing an analogy, as I've already suggested, between desire and need. *Capitalism and Schizophrenia* insinuates a relation of dependence between the organism and something it apprehends as existing outside itself, and therefore as potentially antagonistic. The authors have in their crosshairs the psychoanalytic deduction of the concept of desire from biophysiological need. They argue that both functions introduce a dimension of negativity into an operation they prefer to conceptualise in exclusively positive terms. Just as need places the organism in an antagonistic relation with the surroundings from which it must draw its sustenance, so desire for psychoanalysis relegates the subject to the 'passive syntheses' (26) of external conditions. Similarly, these syntheses place the subject under the determinations of the environment by effectively cutting it off from them. The assumption, in other words, is that the object of desire, from the subject's point of view, remains foreign or outside.

None of this appears to be controversial at first glance. Yet, we can point out in response to Deleuze and Guattari that if they're perturbed by the notion of a desire determined by need, then it's emphatically not psychoanalysis that should worry them. Indeed, Lacan produced a helpful formula for the Freudian concept when he defined desire as the result of the *subtraction* of need from demand.[7] If desire is what's left over once you've eliminated need, in other words, then the latter may hardly be said to determine the former. Further, the subject in this psychoanalytic scenario becomes something other than an entity shaped by ambient forces, an actualisation of social or environmental norms. That subject is the misleading schizoanalytic caricature of the psychoanalytic subject of desire.

Anti-Oedipus makes explicit the instructive political context of this unfortunate misinterpretation of desire in psychoanalysis in the following assessment, quoted from Clément Rosset's book *Logique du pire* (1970). This key passage succinctly summarises the anti-oedipal view of the implications of the (Lacanian) notion of a desire caused by an empirically or materially missing object. In psychoanalysis, so the allegation goes,

> the world acquires as its double some other sort of world, in accordance with the following line of argument: there is an object that desire feels the lack of; hence the world does not contain each and every object that exists; there is at least one object missing, the one that desire feels the lack of; hence there exists some other place that contains the key to desire (missing in this world). (26)

Deleuze and Guattari incorporate this misconstrual of the psychoanalytic argument to support their contention that the premise of a lacking object that causes desire is complicit with an ideologically suspect otherworldliness. In other words, Lacanian psychoanalysis gives rise to an obfuscating, almost religious, spiritualism, which diverts desire's attention away from the everyday world and towards a mystical, unattainable beyond.

We've already seen that the schizoanalytic alternative is to fill out, as it were, the empty space of desire by locating both its conditions and the products of its action on the same level of materially available immanence. Simply put, both the cause and the effect of desire occupy the same 'lackless' space. Clearly, Deleuze and Guattari interpret the empty psychoanalytic object of desire as a break, conceptually speaking, with the Marxist tradition's injunction to focus attention on material reality and the here-and-now. Yet, despite his suspicions about political Marxism, Freud himself viewed the analytic cure as a rigorously analogous project to shift libidinal energy away from its neurotic entanglement with fantasy's possible worlds and towards an investment in what Freud also called reality. In Freud's view, this reality happily includes the 'normal' – that is, imperfect – pleasures and satisfactions that everyday engagement with the immediate environment is prone to yield.

To present schizoanalysis as a politically desirable alternative to Freudianism, *Capitalism and Schizophrenia* needs to give a misleading account of the very nature of the psychoanalytic project. If the subject of the unconscious is indeed marked by its dependence on an impossible object, then the aim of analysis must be to train this subject to access as directly as possible the satisfactions made available through the objects of ordinary experience. Freud's text abounds with statements that frame the analytic process as one aiming to enable the neurotic to carve out simpler, more direct routes to satisfaction. Indeed, this is what neurosis *is* for Freud: a barrier against a disruptively intense enjoyment in which our ego would prefer not to take part. The problem, of course, is that over a century of clinical experience bears compelling witness to the difficulty of overcoming this barrier.

In this light, the anti-oedipal critique of psychoanalysis mistakenly takes its non-political thesis – derived from clinical observation of a neurotic subject who resists satisfaction – for an ideological endorsement of this subject's symptom. Deleuze and Guattari's argument can't take account of the fact that, for psychoanalysis, the dreamy redoubling of the world that results from a neurotic relation to desire is effectively a sort of ideological misrecognition, the dismantling of which is the very aim of the analytic process. The objective of analysis is precisely to minimise the effects on the subject of the symptom as well as its underlying fantasy support.

There's a complication, however. This positive clinical outcome is possible only to the extent that we acknowledge the impossibility of the symptom's complete and once-and-for-all eradication. For psychoanalysis, there's no possibility of a direct apprehension of the material here-and-now. Indeed, with Lacan's radicalisation of Freud, we come to the idea that the best way of attenuating the symptom's neurotic power is paradoxically to identify with it, to claim it as the truth or essence of our being. The symptom becomes the fragile cordon that separates us from the otherwise all-consuming force of jouissance. Contrary to the anti-oedipalists' contentions, then, a reference to reality (or more properly, for Lacan, to the real), along with an associated demystification of the seductions of an illusory beyond of this paltry and disappointing world, are the two features that Freudian psychoanalysis shares with its revisionist schizoanalytic critics.

The incompatibility between psychoanalysis and anti-oedipal discourse is therefore ontological rather than ideological in nature. Indeed, we should resist succumbing to the misleading emphasis *Anti-Oedipus* places on the allegedly stifling consequences of the psychoanalytic description of a subject shaped by fantasy and an unconscious signifying function. Instead, both Lacan, and Deleuze and Guattari, belong to the same tradition – inaugurated by Marx and Freud – that attempts to theorise what I would call *the critical sovereignty of desire*. This tradition aims to think possibilities for subjective or productive agency that defy their own conditions of historical possibility. In other words, desire is what calls into question the very limits of what can be entertained in thought in a given discourse at a given time.

The fundamental antagonism between the two systems therefore relates to their respective conceptions of desire. *Capitalism and Schizophrenia* qualifies the subject's involvement in the signifying function as an obstacle, which must be overcome in order to found a new political order of desiring production. By contrast, psychoanalysis qualifies this implication as an objective, indeed transcendental, condition unamenable to historical alteration. This condition, however, *always fails* to normalise the subject's desire. Occasionally, new things can emerge in the order of the signifier, as Lacan himself admitted in his early teaching. Nonetheless, the condition of our subjection to this order isn't amenable to historical remediation.

The schizoanalytic argument errs where it decides to read the transcendental conditionality of desire – that is, that there is no desire without fantasy and the lack that causes it – as political *in itself*. In other words, Deleuze and Guattari mistakenly situate politics on the level of desire's supposed significations, and then theorise as compensation an alternative world of desire liberated, as it were, from their normalising agency. Rarely, if ever, put forth in appraisals of their work is the psychoanalytic rejoinder to this intuitively very attractive alternative scenario. Indeed, I now want to argue that psychoanalysis forces us to qualify Deleuze and Guattari's recourse to an alternative faculty of desiring production as a symptom of the very worrisome redoubling of the world with which they reproach Freud and Lacan. And talking of production, the most productive way of exploring this unfortunate feature of the anti-oedipal argument is to examine the form it takes in Hocquenghem's appraisal of Freud's vexatious notions of paranoia and narcissism. More specifically, we'll focus in on how these notions help to shape Freud's controversial, and somewhat confused, theory of male homosexuality.

Repression, Idealisation, Sublimation

Earlier, I considered how Hocquenghem wants to wrest homosexual desire from repression, an agency he associates with an oppressive force of psychosocial normalisation. Hocquenghem is noticeably upset by the link Freud makes, notoriously, between sexuality's homosexual element and the so-called social instincts, which range in Freud's writing from the benign fraternal altruism of humanitarian feeling (*esprit de corps*), to the severe hallucinations of persecutory anxiety, or even psychosis. For example, Hocquenghem draws out how Freud describes the delusions of Senatspräsident Schreber, that paradigmatic psychotic of psychoanalysis, as sublimations that draw on improperly repressed homoerotic libidinal investments.

Understandably, *Homosexual Desire* worries about what, to all appearances, is Freud's condemnation of the homosexual libido to the twin abject destinies of repression and sublimation. In the repression scenario, homosexuality is shoved down into the murky depths of the unconscious, where it foments obsessive guilt feelings and straitjackets creative initiative when it doesn't conjure up wrenching psychotic delusions. In the hardly more attractive case of sublimation, homosexuality is rebranded as the identificatory ideals of masculine narcissism – army general or sports hero, for example. In Hocquenghem's reading of Freud's text, these ideals acquire creepy Foucaultian powers of inescapable discipline and all-seeing surveillance.

Four years prior to the publication of *The History of Sexuality*'s first volume, Hocquenghem shows a remarkable degree of prescience with regard to what would become one of queer theory's central tenets:

> The homosexuality which [society] represses and sublimates keeps springing from every pore of the social body. It delves all the more violently into the private lives of individuals, although it knows that what goes on there exposes society itself and slips out of reach of the law-courts. (61)

In Hocquenghem's view, Freud's territorialisation of homosexual desire fuels the energies of social regulation, including most notably the pernicious power of homophobia. By refusing to recognise itself, homosexuality exacerbates the masochistic severity of its self-monitoring. This has the devastating effect of sanctioning a hypocritical complicity between official prohibitions on sexual enjoyment and the pursuit of forbidden pleasures. In this way, the repressive sublimations of homosexuality simultaneously produce and normalise a murky, subterranean world of paradoxically transgressive ecstasies, which only gain in intensity from the intuitions of guilt with which they come, as it were, pre-packaged.

It's easy to see, in this inauspicious light, why Hocquenghem decides to attack Freud's insight that secondary narcissism – that is, the subject's attachment to its ego ideal – feeds off of a deflected homosexual libido. The psyche's investment in the father, which would otherwise take on a directly sexual tenor, is transformed into the energy that sustains the precarious structure of identification. In no uncertain terms, Freud qualifies the psychosocial function by which the normative male or masculine subject appears worthy to itself as an object of properly, if unconsciously, homoerotic interest. It's readily apparent why this premise brings Hocquenghem to the conclusion that the way to escape from homosexuality's complicity in repressive idealisation and guilty self-surveillance is through *de*sublimation – the conversion, that is, of disguised homoerotic investments into conscious homosexual desires and actions.

With this move, Hocquenghem shows that he has equated Freud's idea of sublimation with repression, the latter understood in rather vague energetic terms as the transformation of sexual libido into a nonsexual identification with the father figure. The consequence for Hocquenghem is not only that the homosocial instincts of fraternal feeling inevitably exacerbate the superego's lacerating accusations. Also, any 'work' performed on the homosexual libido that deflects it away from direct satisfaction is going to lead down the same masochistic path. On this level, Hocquenghem's argument reveals a close affinity with the writing of post-Freudian anti-psychiatric sexual liberationists such as Wilhelm Reich and R. D. Laing. As Hocquenghem was surely aware, these figures, hardly coincidentally, had a decisive impact on the theories and experimental clinical practice of Félix Guattari.[8] In its response to this sort of neo-Freudian revisionism, the Frankfurt School, looking for a way to theorise the libidinal appeal of fascism, qualified desublimation not as antagonistic to, but rather as complicit with, the force of repression. Summarily put, the argument here is that the desublimation of sexual interest short-circuits the critical faculty of consciousness, thereby increasing our vulnerability to ideology by making enjoyment support the forces of social control.[9]

For his part, Hocquenghem uses the loaded term 'desublimation' to refer specifically to a withdrawal of sexuality's investment in the social ideals that funnel desire through the psyche's oedipal representations. In this view, desublimation is a condition of possibility for the liberated, deterritorialised and non-signifying desire for which Hocquenghem wishes to advocate. Because it inhibits the expression of same-sex desire, the oedipal structures sublimate the libidinal forces that buttress not only the cohesiveness and internal discipline of the nuclear family, but also the reactive privatisation of desiring production in capitalism. 'Narcissism and homosexuality', Hocquenghem concludes, 'supply the field of sublimation with its preferential object, to the point where we can truthfully say that sublimation is simply homosexuality in its historical family truth' (81). Sublimation, for Hocquenghem, is the agency that converts the free expression of same-sex eroticism into the inward accusations of the superego and the delusions of psychotic paranoia. In this light, it would seem logical to conclude that desublimation is indeed the royal road to desire's anti-normative and productive emancipation.

It's certainly true that Freud, in numerous places, qualifies the sexuality inherent in our relation to the oedipal ego ideal as homosexual in nature. In this sense, Hocquenghem is certainly correct to complain that psychoanalysis can only envision actual homosexual sex – sex acts between men, I mean – as resulting from the dismantling of this narcissistic relation as well as the sublimation on which it's viewed to depend. Evidently, this is the line of thought that sees Hocquenghem link the activity of sublimation *as such* to the whole Freudian apparatus of the Oedipus complex. As we recall, Hocquenghem understands this last complex to refer to a normative sociosymbolic order which, for Deleuze and Guattari as well, imposes a guilty regime of desire on those on whom it exercises its disciplinary force.

From this point of view, psychoanalysis simply denies the possibility of a form of libidinal expression that would escape from the oppressively familialist triangle composed of 'daddy, mommy and me', as Deleuze and Guattari sarcastically write. Psychoanalysis is perceived to offer no recourse to the self-identified and sexually active homosexual, whose existence could only be accounted for by an alternative theory that shrugs off the weight of the oedipal system, with its rigid regime of sexual difference and retrograde obsession with lack. For Hocquenghem, homosexual desire as he wishes to think of it is simply inconceivable within the bounds of the framework of signification upheld, in this view, by Oedipus. Indeed, in this landscape, homosexual desire can only move towards an unhappy – paranoid, guilty, masochistic, psychotic – end.

It seems from all this that Freud's theory of homosexuality is ill equipped to think through the expression of homosexual desire in the contemporary and ordinary sense of the phrase. Freud's contention that a specifically homosexual libido maintains the social ideals anchoring masculine identity holds forth little promise for the consideration of homosexual *sex*. You could even go so far as to say that there's no sex in Freudian homosexuality: on the level of theory, male homosexuality can only figure as the repressed and disavowed foundation of the social world, or rather, more specifically, the social world of men.

Yet, as unpromising as Freudian discourse might seem, we shouldn't fail to notice how Hocquenghem's intuitively compelling discussion sidesteps two key questions. First, *what precisely is homosexual* in the libido at work in Freud's description of narcissism's ego ideal? As the question hints, is it possible that 'homosexuality' in Freud, at least in the contexts I've considered here, bears only the most tenuous of connections to the historical constant of (male) same-sex sexual behaviour? Second, even more crucially as regards my purposes in this chapter, what are we to make of Freud's sketchy attempt to *distinguish* sublimation from both idealisation and repression? How, more precisely, might this distinction critically inform Hocquenghem's recourse to a problematic anti-psychiatric and liberationist paradigm for desublimation?

As far as the first question is concerned, it's important to note that Freud's manifestly sex-neutral discussion of his ego ideal concept has a latent masculine specificity. The homosexuality in narcissism describes the phallic or paternal identification of a 'normal' (read: heterosexual) male subject with a masculine and superegoic sociosymbolic ideal. This is the subject whose castration is underwritten, if I can put it this way, by the father. Freud's treatment of masculine narcissism contrasts starkly with his efforts at evoking the comparatively impenetrable, seemingly self-satisfied narcissism of women, in whom Freud famously failed to find the masochistic permutations of conscience he connects to the masculine ego ideal. It would perhaps only bring to the surface a buried coherence in Freud to propose that the homosexual libido idealised in masculine narcissism – on both its repressed-but-socialised and liberated-but-paranoid poles – bears no relation to the psychic life of the contemporary self-identified gay man.

Indeed, as I argue in detail in the next chapter, the theory of male homosexuality in psychoanalysis is condemned to repeat phobic and nonsensical clichés to the extent that it turns a blind eye to what I call cross-sexuation. This phenomenon remains unthinkable under the assumption, explicitly contradicted by Freud, that all biological males undergo the castration associated with the person Freud called 'the boy'. This latter, masculine form of castration can lead to the sort of oedipal identification that places the male subject under a power of self-surveillance, which threatens to strengthen to paranoid extremes. Despite these dangers, Freud considers this form of identification, at least on the manifest level of his discussion, the ideal outcome of the oedipal conflict's male version. By contrast, Lacan associates this outcome with sexual inhibition and neurosis, choosing instead to underline the clinical value of castration itself.

What's significant about my conjecture concerning cross-sexuation is that it indexes a structure of male homosexuality aligned with the castration of the Freudian girl who, unlike the boy, doesn't identify with the phallus at the end of the phallic stage, and therefore doesn't require the prohibition whose precariousness exacerbates the dynamic of idealisation and paranoia looming ominously over masculine psychosexuality in Freud's account. In other words, I'm suggesting that the putatively homosexual quality of the libido at work in Freud's discussion of masculine narcissism may, in fact, refer only to the repression of same-sex eroticism necessary to achieve the 'normal', more or less heterosexual, masculine subject.

In this context, Freudian homosexuality is simply the unconscious homosexuality of the straight man; a homosexuality that manifests itself symptomally – in hazing rituals and homophobic violence, for instance – as the male concerned struggles to assume his castration. Under this alternative hypothesis, Hocquenghem's legitimate worries cease to be concerning. Why? Because the portentous homosexual libido of Freudian narcissism proves to be unrelated to homosexual desire properly speaking – neither in Hocquenghem's schizoanalytic, nor in the psychoanalytic sense of an 'assumed' object choice: that is, of a roughly determinate, if neurotic, libidinal tendency.

Now, the issues raised by my second question focus in on the set of assumptions Hocquenghem brings to his reading of homosexual desire's unpromising development in Freud's work. Here it will be helpful to inquire after the pressure psychoanalysis can exert back on Hocquenghem's very concept of homosexual desire. More specifically, what happens to this concept when we take seriously Freud's insistence that the idealisation of an instinct is not the same thing as its sublimation? And what about the corollary that sublimation is to be distinguished from repression or, perhaps more rigorously, that sublimation provides an *alternative* to neurosis? In other words, are there moments in Freud's text that allow us to rescue the concept of sublimation from its tragic implication in social repression? My answer to this last question will be 'yes'. Indeed, it's possible to tease out of Freud's writing a version of his concept of sublimation that's not only fully compatible with what we might call actually existing homosexual sex, but also, and by definition, anti-normative in a way that responds to Hocquenghem's entirely legitimate concerns.

It's important to acknowledge at this juncture that the discussion may have reached unpalatable, and seemingly apolitical, levels of theoretical abstraction. In this light, it will be wise to stress that what's at stake is the very need for an alternative to psychoanalysis to theorise a non-oppressive and properly political concept of desiring production. I'm in the process of arguing that Freud's text already signposts an idea of sublimation that conforms not only to the aspirations of Hocquenghem, and Deleuze and Guattari. Additionally, this idea has the merit of avoiding what I'll describe in the final section of this chapter as the latently isolationist and politically problematic anti-representationalism of these writers; that is, their revolt against the logic of the signifier as Lacan systematically developed it in his teaching.

Freud's clear but undeveloped contention about sublimation is that it's an *alternative* to repression's neurotic effects. To develop Freud's claim, we'll need more clearly to distinguish sublimation's action from the compulsive admonishments of the ego ideal or superego. Since the sublimation question has proven to be one of the most controversial and tortured aspects of Freud's legacy, we should begin by posing some very basic questions. Of what precisely does the force of repression consist, according to Freud? And crucially, how are we to conceive of the object on which this force acts?

I've already considered how Hocquenghem views repression in Freud as a force of symbolic meaning attribution, which operates directly and normatively on desire's production. If we look carefully at his text, however, we see that Freud makes a different contention. Repression operates instead on what he calls 'ideational representatives' (*Vorstellungsrepräsentanzen*) – ideas, that is, which represent the drive's libidinal pressure to the psyche. Freud argues that repression's force exerts itself on representations, not on the libido itself, however we might choose to conceive of it. Freud's definition of repression's object is crystal clear: 'an idea [*Vorstellung*] or group of ideas which is cathected with a definite quota of energy (libido or interest) coming from an instinct'.[10] The idea of a repressed instinct or libido, therefore, isn't authentically Freudian (or Lacanian, for that matter). Homosexual desire in Hocquenghem's specific sense of the term can't be an object of repression. *Only representations* – signifiers, in Lacan's vocabulary – *can be repressed.*

Moreover, we should note that, as is the case with many of Freud's concepts, repression comes in two varieties. There is first of all primal repression, 'which consists in the psychical (ideational) representative of the instinct being denied entrance into the conscious' (148). Secondary repression, or what Freud also calls 'repression proper', refers to the process whereby 'mental derivatives of the repressed representative', in other words derivatives of the object of primal repression, are similarly pushed into the unconscious on account of their 'associative connection' with this repressed representative (148). Freud underlines that this latter, primally repressed representative is subject to fixation: it stays irretrievably caught in the unconscious, where it persists 'unaltered'; and the instinct, Freud continues, remains forever 'attached' to it (148). In this primary sense, then, the libido is always-already repressed; always-already deformed or denatured by its attachment to an unreachable unconscious representation, a 'representative of representation' (*représentant de la représentation*), as Lacan will say in his teaching.

The subtraction of this key signifier from consciousness is a necessary condition of the unconscious for Freud, and therefore of consciousness as psychoanalysis conceives of it in its imperfect, split form. The secondary form of repression is the agency responsible for our neurotic symptoms. Aspects of our everyday sociosymbolic world succumb to this primally repressed representative's forces of attraction if they become associated with it through the classic Freudian mechanisms of condensation and displacement, as originally described in *The Interpretation of Dreams* (1900). We are far, in Freud's semiology of the unconscious, from the vulgar post-Freudian world of repressed libidinal energies thwarted by moralistic social conventions that foment dreams of transgressive liberation.

The schizoanalysts' sociologising misreading of Freud is all the more unfortunate, if not inexcusable, given that Freud himself provides valuable insights into the means by which repression works in tandem with idealisation. Indeed, Freud goes so far as to describe the mechanism of primal repression as fetishistic in nature. When a signifier (or idea – *Vorstellung* – if you prefer Freud's term) is repressed from consciousness in the very process of this latter's constitution, part of this signifier splits off, so it appears, and then undergoes idealisation to form the ego ideal. The irretrievably repressed signifier in the unconscious has a counterpart in consciousness, Freud holds. This counterpart is the point of symbolic identification from which the subject can look upon himself with narcissistic satisfaction. However, it's also from the point of view of the ego ideal that the subject will berate himself for his inevitable inadequacies. 'In this connection', Freud adds,

> we can understand how it is that the objects to which men give most preference, their ideals, proceed from the same perceptions and experiences as the objects which they most abhor, and that they were originally only distinguished from one another through slight modifications. (150)

These modifications are the signifying distortions performed by the unconscious as a means of breaking through the barriers of censorship and repression. Repression is therefore the flipside of idealisation. Only a thinly disguised instance of condensation or displacement

– a jokey pun or play on words – mask from us the truth that these two apparently conflicting agencies derive from the same abject and obscene unconscious object.

Having described this dissimulated connection between repression and idealisation, we're now in a position to shed more light on the question I posed earlier about what Freud really means to say when he qualifies narcissism's libido as homosexual. The acquisition of 'normal' masculinity requires the idealisation of a representation whose counterpart is the signifier of a repressed homosexual attachment.

Simply put, to acquire a masculine identity, according to Freud, you have to repress the homosexual libido on which this identity depends. I would only add that Freud doesn't intend to imply that all men are 'really' homosexual, even if his analysis does indeed posit a secret homosexual essence to normative masculinity. The point is subtler and more radical: originally bisexual, we're nonetheless forced by the signifier to aspire to a sexual identity.

But the deep logic of Freud's writing on sexual difference also implies that this identity can never be secured; that it will forever be undermined by the symptomatic emergence of incompatible and inappropriate desires, regardless of how we choose to define our sexual orientation. This entirely orthodox reading of Freud is infinitely more subversive and weighty with implication than either queer theory's deconstruction of a putative heterosexual matrix, or the sci-fi schizoanalytic utopia of an infinite quantity of sexes and genders.

Freud's revelation of masculinity's dependence on the simultaneous repression and idealisation of the libido's homosexual tendency also goes a long way towards explaining the frustrating intractability of homophobia, not to mention the actual but disavowed homosexual relations, often of a clearly abusive nature, that seem to run rampant in male homosocial institutions. The seeming timelessness of these phenomena already signals how unsatisfactory are the competing historicist accounts that cite specific discourses of sexuality.

Psychoanalysis suggests a more convincing, consequential and indeed more troubling explanation: the exclusion of explicit and acknowledged homoeroticism (of course, it's everywhere present in barely disguised form) is the very condition of male sociality, of the capacity of (heterosexual) men to function normally within predominantly male social institutions. Indeed, we can look to the contemporary Hollywood buddy-flick comedy to discern how this reality can be managed through humour. Homophobic violence between men can be avoided by the non-repressive sublimation (discussed below) of the straight man's homosexual latencies, on the condition that they're openly acknowledged, however ironically, or in however politically incorrect a fashion.

To his tremendous credit, Hocquenghem readily sees how psychoanalysis theorises – somewhat against itself, to be sure – the link between the normative male subject's fragile castration and the dynamics of homophobia. Indeed, he recognises the implicit anti-homophobic ramifications of Freud's narcissism theory, and even castigates post-psychoanalytic psychiatry for transforming this theory into a crude pathology, which links homosexuality in an essential way to paranoia and psychosis.

In my view, Hocquenghem's misreading of psychoanalysis lies elsewhere – namely, where he equates Freud's concept of sublimation with narcissism's tendency to fuel the accusatory fires of the superego. If sublimation, as Hocquenghem contends, can only mean our normative, masochistic identification with the ideals of social morality, then we can hardly blame him for casting psychoanalysis aside to find alternative means of thinking about human creative potential. Yet, it can't be denied that Freud's pithy, properly theoretical definition of the sublimation concept belies the notoriously repressive conservatism of his decidedly bourgeois examples. In the last analysis, Freud defines sublimation as an alternative to idealisation, one that clears a path for libidinal satisfaction by averting the usual pitfalls of repression and neurosis.

A detailed consideration of Freud's contentions about sublimation is therefore in order. We've already observed that the ego ideal emerges when we select from the representations in our psychical environment an object from whose perspective we can look upon ourselves in a pleasing light. Idealisation is the process whereby the apparent libidinal value of this object is inflated. In order for this to occur, the aspect of this same object that produces a disturbing and excessive libidinal excitation has to be repressed. By contrast, sublimation 'concerns object-*libido*', as Freud puts it. Sublimation therefore acts not on the object per se, but rather on what Freud calls the *Trieb*, the drive. Sublimation directs the drive towards an aim 'other than, and remote from, sexual satisfaction', as Freud famously contends.[11] This last qualification is the one that has so puzzled commentators wishing to lend some precision to Freud's sublimation concept. If sublimation is to be distinguished from secondary narcissism because it doesn't idealise the object, and therefore fails to produce a neurotic symptom, one would tend to think that sublimation does indeed produce satisfaction, and that this satisfaction would have to be sexual in nature.

Indeed, the relation between a properly sexual satisfaction and the activity of sublimation remains muddled in Freud's formulations. Emerging with greater clarity, however, is the contention that sublimation successfully lessens the intensity of the narcissistic identification that supports repression. 'The formation of an ideal', Freud asserts, 'heightens the demands of the ego and is the most powerful factor favouring repression; sublimation is a way out, a way by which those demands can be met *without involving repression*' (95, my emphasis). The exclusion of sexuality from sublimation becomes quite baffling in this light.

Freud's somewhat clumsy attempt to distinguish sublimation from idealisation hinges on the proposition that satisfaction is absent of the quality he calls 'sexual'. However, given the kinship of Freud's more concrete descriptions of sublimation with his earlier qualification of the drive in the *Three Essays on the Theory of Sexuality* as generically perverse, there is evidence to suggest that 'sexual' is here to be understood alongside Freud's evocations of happy love, fully achieved genital maturity, or the synthesised instincts – those normative ideals that correspond, according to Freud's deeper logic, to precisely nothing in human experience.[12]

Consequently, 'sexual' in this sense would refer to a mythically direct brand of satisfaction, a pure experience of the libido entirely cleansed of its implication in the ego, as well as the signifying or symbolic representations on which it depends. In this precise sense, the sexual in Freud is a prototype for the utopianism characteristic of both Deleuze and Guattari's notion of desiring production, and Hocquenghem's idea of homosexual desire. In this view, the term refers precisely to the merely logical possibility of an experience of sexuality emancipated from what Lacan calls the defiles of the signifier.

The confusing details finally fail to cloud the clarity of Freud's basic point about sublimation, namely that it's an alternative to the kind of repression that creates symptoms; a more direct route to satisfaction than the one that passes through the endless detours of neurosis. Less straightforward, of course, is Freud's choice not to restrict sublimation to the libido itself. On the one hand, Freud claims that sublimation acts on the drive properly speaking rather than its object. On the other, however, he claims that sublimation is involved in the construction and buttressing of the ego ideal – that is to say, the structure of narcissism that functions to *impede* sexual satisfaction. This tension, or outright contradiction, is so deeply embedded in Freud's fragmentary comments on sublimation that it's impossible simply to iron it out.

The most helpful approach to this difficulty is the one I've just outlined. As speaking subjects, we're barred from the experience of a 'pure' sexuality, of a full and uncompromised enjoyment. In Lacanian terms, a part of jouissance is forever unattainable, forbiddingly sequestered in the alien place of the Other. We lose this unattainable *plus-de-jouir* in consequence of our subjection to language. In consequence, every possible experience of sexuality, no matter how uninhibited or 'raw', is minimally sublimated. This is to say that the experience is made possible by a significant, but temporary and partial, lessening of the ego's repressive hold. In sum, sublimation refers to the human capacity to access satisfaction, to experience enjoyment, without entirely obliterating the fragile fantasy structure that sustains desire. The fantasy accomplishes this by standing between us and the annihilating force of an unbridled and unlimited, and therefore impossible, jouissance.

We can further illuminate the distinction between idealisation and sublimation in Freud's theory with reference to Lacan's analogous distinction between desire and drive. The reference is instructive only if we keep in mind that each concept, for Lacan, refers to one of the two sides of a Möbius strip, which counterintuitively blend into one another. Desire and drive, in other words, are never met in their pure form. Or, perhaps more accurately, 'pure desire' – a phrase Lacan uses in the context of his analysis of Antigone, for example – corresponds to an experience of the drive, and vice versa.

Idealisation describes the process through which the object of identification is split into competing representations, one of which is invested with narcissistic libido and the other thrust down into the unconscious. The result of idealisation is a self-alienated and self-thwarting desire: we don't really want what we think we want; satisfaction can only be experienced as its opposite – the symptom's inconvenient or painful excitations. By contrast, the drive takes the form of a perverse, meaningless, autoerotic loop: it achieves satisfaction by circling around an object from which libido has in fact been withdrawn. The drive becomes its own object, such that the qualities of that around which it circulates become indifferent, as Freud in fact suggests at the end of his sexuality essays.

The element of Lacan that Hocquenghem, via Deleuze and Guattari, finds most attractive is the psychoanalyst's reformulation of Freud's *Trieb* as *pulsion*. As a result, when Deleuze and Guattari write about a specifically *desiring* production, and Hocquenghem then introduces his derivative notion of homosexual *desire*, in Lacanian terms they're describing the acephalous libidinal force of the *drive* – impersonal or transpersonal, anoedipal, satisfying, devoid of a proper or even qualifiable object because it is deflected in its essence from any normative or reproductive aim. Further, and crucially, the drive is unmarked by the phallic signifier's failed attempt to represent the difference between the sexes.

From the Lacanian perspective, however, Hocquenghem follows Deleuze and Guattari as they effect what can only be called a reidealisation of the drive. The gesture inevitably participates in the retrograde liberationist fantasy of escape from a repressive world of civilised morality, in fact the very same fantasy against which Foucault railed when he subjected the repressive hypothesis to brilliant scrutiny in *The History of Sexuality*.

The relation between sublimation and the pleasure yielded from sexual practice is fundamentally indeterminate. If a properly 'sexual' relation is impossible, as my interpretation of Freud's theory suggests, then sexual practice is, always-already as it were, sublimated. There's no general qualitative or quantitative distinction to be drawn between the satisfaction derived from sexual activity properly speaking (let's assume momentarily the ordinary meaning of the phrase) and the activity of sublimation, which ranges from Freud's too respectable example of men's club membership to Lacan's more *terre-à-terre* example of matchbox collection. This is surely the sense in which we should understand psychoanalytic 'pansexualism' – that notorious Jungian substantive intended as a discrediting criticism of Freud.

Lacan couldn't be accused of circumlocution when, presenting the drive concept in his seminar, he said: 'For the moment, I am not fucking, I am talking to you. Well! I can have exactly the same satisfaction as if I were fucking'.[13] The casually provocative tone of Lacan's pronouncement shouldn't detract from its serious theoretical implications. First, any properly conceptual distinction between sexual and non-sexual drive satisfaction is untenable. Second, there is no satisfaction available to us other than the earthy, idiotic, non-cognitive or paracognitive satisfaction of the drive. Further, we can only fail to integrate this satisfaction into our self-concept. For this reason, we always experience this satisfaction as incomplete or compromised; as less satisfying than the fascinating jouissance we locate in the body of the Other.

In short, the ideals that mediate our identificatory relation to the symbolic order and the dislocating intensities of drive satisfaction are incommensurable. All promises of a fuller, less problematic satisfaction, be they hygienic, revolutionary, bourgeois, intellectual, nationalist, utopian or otherworldly, bear witness to the obfuscating idealisations of neurotic fantasy, and will therefore remain forever unfulfilled. *There's no externally imposed, social or political, obstacle to enjoyment from which we require liberation.* The only effective impediments to all possible satisfactions are the neurotic ideals we insist on imposing upon ourselves.

And yet these ideals, these Freudian *Vorstellungen*, prove resistant to eradication. Indeed, they make up the tenuous and unreliable barrier that shields us from psychosis, preventing us from succumbing to the trauma aroused in us by fantasies of the Other's jouissance. The promise of Freudian analysis has never been utopian, in the precise sense that it has never claimed the possibility of completely wiping out neurosis once and for all. At the deepest, most troubling level, the symptom is ineradicable. This is the sense in which analysis is interminable, which doesn't mean, however, that the patient forever remains on the couch. What it does mean is that there's a horizon in analytic experience where the seductive pull of fantasy fails, although the fantasy structure as such remains intact and psychically operative.

Here, the clinical aspect of the Lacanian rejoinder to schizoanalysis emerges. Full-on, 'triggered' psychosis or 'schizophrenia' is experientially intolerable, unsustainable. Psychotics like the paradigmatic Schreber manage to construct a workable psychic life for themselves by producing neurotic symptoms – in other words, by telling an Other (in this instance embodied by an anonymous readership) about their 'nervous illness'. In this important sense, neurosis is an escape from psychosis. The relation psychoanalysis theorises between the neurotic world of desire – with its unending object substitutions and eternally deferred satisfactions – and the non-repressive experience of the drive – with its satisfying, but also traumatic and non-cognitive, enjoyment – is therefore properly dialectical. This means that it's conflicted, foundational and resistant to any final synthesis or pseudo-Hegelian *Aufhebung* ('sublation').

Sublimation is the psychoanalytic name for the human capacity creatively to manage this tension, to (fail to) work out a compromise. It's not coincidental that Deleuze's entire philosophical system is, in an important sense, an attack against dialectical thought from Plato to Hegel, from Marx to Lacan. Neither is it by chance that Deleuze and Guattari premise their idea of desiring production on a properly non-dialectical ontology, on the purely positive virtuality of an infinite vista of becoming. The ideology of becoming contrasts sharply with the psychoanalytic insistence on repetition – that is, on the insurmountable, but also potentially creative, way in which we fail, over and over again, to encounter our own being; to integrate our being, that is, with our social identity.

Within the Lacanian framework, then, the subject seeks relief from desire's unceasing frustrations in drive satisfaction. But equally, we retreat to neurotic fantasy to find shelter or distance from jouissance when it becomes, as it inevitably will, excessive: invasive, claustrophobic, smothering. In this light, we can define sublimation not as the experience of drive satisfaction as such, but rather as the 'impossible' eruption of the drive within consciousness, within the order of social relations. When satisfaction breaks out in our everyday sociosymbolic world, this world's proper functioning – its coherence, its very 'impression of reality', as the old film theorists used to say – momentarily breaks down, revealing in the process its essential contingency and lack of foundational meaning.

In order to avoid Deleuze and Guattari's retrograde idealisation of the drive as desiring production, we must specify that sublimation is the experience of drive satisfaction from within the imperfect order of the signifying function. Sublimation exposes the limits of this function, confronting us in the process with the inconsistency and inadequacy of the world, but also with its perplexing and potentially exciting openness, its ambiguous susceptibility to change.

Beyond the Revolutionary Libido

Alongside all those pragmatic queer critics who draw their concepts willy-nilly from multiple theoretical discourses, you might wonder why such a seemingly arcane effort to distinguish between psychoanalysis and the anti-oedipus discourse even matters. To help spell this out, we can return to Hocquenghem by way of conclusion to consider the concrete political endorsements he outlines in *Homosexual Desire*.

Despite his political education among dissident Trotskyist groups objecting to the Stalinist ossification of the French Communist Party, Hocquenghem took membership in the libertarian, anti-authoritarian element of the 1968 generation. For Hocquenghem, the historical significance of the then-emergent gay movement consisted in its membership of the emblematic new social movements, including feminism and environmentalism, of the time. According to Hocquenghem, these movements distinguished themselves by premising their political project not on any determinate concept or theory, such as human rights or the class struggle for example, but rather on what he calls 'a particular desiring situation' (142): 'particular' as opposed to Marxism's universalising narrative of the proletariat's glorious historical destiny; 'situation', in its existential or sociological concreteness, as opposed to the concepts of political theories, including Marxism, which insist on the possibility of abstracting subjectivity from its grounding in determinate social identities.

Writing in the early 1970s, Hocquenghem attributes tremendous significance to the widespread popular struggle against US involvement in Vietnam. In his view, this struggle saw a novel association of progressive forces, which successfully rallied 'against sexism, the cult of masculinity and the American version of war as a kind of "manly game"' (142). With Hocquenghem, it becomes clear, we're very much in the New Left 'rainbow coalition' ethos of the time. This time corresponds to the period of socialism's 'return of the repressed', when all those constituencies who felt marginalised by (pseudo-)orthodox Marxist economism began to make their voices loudly heard.

These informative contextual details notwithstanding, it's rather Hocquenghem's theoretical take on the new social movements that concerns me here. The historical gay movement puts into operation what Hocquenghem calls 'a crude sexualisation of the social field' (144). That is, this movement effects a direct libidinal investment, which sidesteps the normative-repressive representationalism of democratic political processes as conceived, presumably, by both communist party vanguardism and the liberal parliamentary tradition. As Hocquenghem describes, 'the political system operates on the relation between signifier and signified, on the pyramidal relation between representative and masses' (145).

Decentred, amorphous and anarchic, this new libidinal politics dispenses not only with the need for centralised planning, strategy and organisation, but also with the entire 'phallic' (147) hierarchy that's supposed to be required to implement them. Indeed, Hocquenghem dismisses outright the entire framework of representation as 'the reign of the political' (146) when he qualifies anyone who claims to speak on behalf of the masses as both necessarily complicit in a repressive regime of signification, and supportive of a system that menacingly dwarfs the persons of which it is comprised. Here again, Hocquenghem supports his argument with a reference to *Anti-Oedipus*, more precisely to Deleuze and Guattari's distinction between a subjected and a subject group:

> A revolutionary group remains, as far as the pre-conscious is concerned, a *subjected group*, even when winning power and for as long as that power itself reflects a form of mastery which continues to enslave and crush desiring production ... A *subject group*, on the contrary, is one whose libidinal investments are in themselves revolutionary; it introduces desire into the social field. (147)

This passage demonstrates how, in emblematic anarcho-libertarian fashion, Hocquenghem's brand of anti-representationalist politics provides an alibi to the would-be revolutionary subject. This alibi threatens to rationalise quietism: it suffices that one's libidinal investments be revolutionary (whatever that means), and the rest, so it would appear, will take care of itself. Distressingly, this political cop-out devolves from a classic banality of vulgar postmodernism, which advances the doctrine of a relativism of political narratives and theories which are, Hocquenghem concurs, 'all equally true whatever the bearer' (142). The assumption is this: since everyone can weave a post-Marxist yarn in which his or her identity – ethnic, sexual, religious, whatever – can play a starring role, the entire project of theory to think through the practical means of effecting thoroughgoing social change becomes simply superfluous.

Far from offering an alternative to an insipid politics of identity, as many who have chosen to follow in this tradition now claim, the politics of desiring production, at least in the mode offered by Hocquenghem, exhibits the traits of a dubious humanistic voluntarism. In the unceasing flux of desire, I can access 'n' genders, 'n' sexes, 'n' identities. Such a politics simply reconfigures the conceptual apparatus of identitarian humanism by multiplying it. Liberal multiculturalism paints a rainbow of ethnic identities premised on an unmarked (white and 'Western', of course) exception, from whose point of view cultural diversity is offered for display. In an analogous way, the anti-oedipal discourse sets up an unwitting hierarchical structure in which the unfixed desiring nomads can look down upon all those other benighted subjects still reactively sutured to their markers of sociological and sexual identity.

By refreshing contrast, psychoanalysis suggests a different political configuration, in which identity is marked as both necessary and necessarily failed. The subject of politics, also by definition a subject of the unconscious, 'is represented, undoubtedly, but also it is not represented',[14] to quote Lacan. This can be taken to mean in the present context that the unconscious subject is socially indeterminate, ultimately empty. A compatible Marxism adds to Lacan's contention that the subject is also subject to the real of socioeconomic antagonism, the rift that cross-cuts the entire social field, diagonally bisecting all possible configurations of social identity. Instead, Hocquenghem's practical politics offers little more than an apolitical narcissism of becoming in which the political meaning of my libidinal investments appears transparently, undistorted by the jouissance of an unconscious knowledge from which I remain irremediably separated. In classic 'bad utopian' fashion, Hocquenghem's argument further sidesteps the problem of the symbolic order, of the big Other and its mediation of political organisation. Planning, structure, reasoning, decision-making processes remain necessities that refuse to disappear in the aftermath of the overthrow of a bourgeois parliamentary regime.

In sum, the Deleuzo-Guattarian anti-oedipalism in which Hocquenghem's politics takes shape is in the end a heroic, but hopelessly idealised, libertarian and ultraliberal anarcho-capitalist utopianism. This discourse associates the agency of reaction to emancipatory social change not with the violent and concretely dispossessing deterritori- alisations of a capitalist system seeking profit through the exploitative extraction of profit from labour, but rather with the *resistance* to such deterritorialisations – that is, with the very effort to limit or eliminate capital's addictive cult of economic growth, as well as the sociopolitical schizophrenia it instils as a result.

'The sexualization of the world heralded by the gay movement', Hocquenghem writes, 'pushes capitalist decoding to the limit and corresponds to the dissolution of the human' (145). But what if the exact opposite is true? What if the gay movement idealised by Hocquenghem fully participated in capital's repressive eroticisation of commodity relations, effectively turning us away from what Freud began to describe as the paradoxically asexual and world- shattering satisfaction of the drive? Rereading Hocquenghem today should remind us of the importance of formulating an alternative post-humanism, which both reidentifies the self-thwarting limit of capital, and reasserts the importance of a politics recognising both the necessity and necessary failure of representation.

5

The Sameness of Sexual Difference

This chapter's basic assumption is that, in addition to its strictly clinical value, psychoanalytic case literature can be read as an argument against *the direct politicisation of sexuality*. The terrain here is tricky, however, since this doesn't mean that the literature is immune from bias or ideology, particularly as concerns the interpretative framing of desires that appear to deviate from what is understood as heterosexuality. Indeed, in the consideration of Lacanian clinical discourse I undertake below, I identify precisely this kind of failure.

Although they often throw the baby out with the bathwater, queer and pre-queer critics have admirably expended significant energy undoing the heterosexist assumptions that have marred too much clinical literature since Freud. *Yet the unconscious as such resists overt politicisation.* This remains true whether one views the unconscious as content or form. While the former assumes a murky reservoir of erotic fantasies or impulses barred from consciousness, the latter foregrounds the Freudian tradition's more rigorous concept of a properly semiotic logic. This is the logic by means of which unconscious thoughts are distorted in order to evade censorship imposed by the ego. From this perspective, the political appears as the *refusal to analyse*, as the resistance to the exercise of will required to unbundle the symptom's dissimulated enjoyment, whether this enjoyment takes the form of an addiction to bourgeois real estate websites, or the phobic and misogynist violence of the various and proliferating religious fundamentalisms.

Lacan's famous claim that Marx invented the symptom explicitly links the psychoanalytic project to the properly materialist demy-thologisation of surplus value. For Lacan, the dissimulation, the *reification* of exploitative relations of production in the commodity's sexy phantasmagoria, is the particular historical form taken by the symptom in the capitalist social formation. In this way, Lacan's thesis explicitly sexualises the commodity relation, reminding us that the most 'scientific' iteration of political economy ultimately rests on the identification, and attempted dismantling, of an illusion or misrecognition buttressed by the ego's libidinal resistance to the unconscious.

In short, our denial of the unconscious tethers us all the more tightly to the exalted and abstract world of capitalist valuation. We are returned thereby to the imperative to sexualise the political; to link our resistance to a politics of emancipation to our refusal to tarry with the scandal of a sexuality that refuses to conform to any norm. But a detailed consideration of the assumptions that frame the clinical approach to sexuality and sexual difference will be required to show not only how psychoanalysis evades the trap of a more vulgar kind of politicisation, but also sometimes fails to live up to its own rigorous ethical imperative.

Psychoanalysis and Queer Theory: Same Difference?

Among the numerous efforts of Anglo-American queer theorists to grapple psychoanalytically with the phenomenon of homosexuality, an antinomy has arisen in connection with ideas of sameness and difference. Influential queer theorists, such as Judith Butler, have argued against the psychoanalytic concept of sexual difference. For its part, Lacanian theory reasserts Freud's original pronouncement that for psychoanalysis, sexual difference is of an order other than the cultural and the biological. For Lacan, sexual difference is neither symbolic nor imaginary, but rather real. In opposition to this view, queer theory considers the psychoanalytic emphasis on sexual difference an imposture that circumscribes sexuality's diverse manifestations within a normative (read: phallocentric, patriarchal and heterosexist) sociosymbolic framework.[1] Implicit in such discourses is the notion that if a difference qualified as sexual invariably pathologises homosexuality, then it's by reclaiming an idea of sameness – 'same-sex desire' – that sexuality theory is to consider homosexuality.

Two observations can be made at this early juncture. First, the post-structuralist current of cultural theory affiliated with queer discourse characteristically holds that the proliferation of sexual differences beyond the conventional male–female binary is in itself of political value. Gilles Deleuze and Félix Guattari's idea of a deterritorialised multiplicity of 'n' sexes is emblematic of this view. Against this backdrop, the recourse to an idea of a *sameness in desire* claimed *as a difference* presents as logically awkward. That the difference against which the sameness of sex desire is contrasted is itself formulated as a concept of difference, namely sexual difference, only adds a further layer of fog to an already misty theoretical landscape.

Second, the queer-theoretical protest against sexual difference takes aim at the psychoanalytic assumption that sexual difference stubbornly remains the same, in the precise sense that it doesn't vary in accordance with the vicissitudes of cultural and historical discourses. Moreover, queer theory has proven hostile to the psychoanalytic premise that this same sexual difference remains psychically operative for all subjects, regardless of what Freud called their small differences ('race' and language group, for instance), and is therefore a difference which is, as it were, different from the other varieties of difference.

There's a manifest difficulty at work in the discourse on sexuality that calls out for 'deconstruction'. The queer-theoretical notion of a sameness in sex desire depends on the assumption of its difference from a sexual difference which, so it holds, can only produce hetero-sexuality. And, the sexual difference on which psychoanalysis insists rests on the idea of a sameness resistant to historical change and indifferent to the various predicative differences we commonly use to distinguish individual persons from one another.

My aim in this chapter is to argue that we can resolve this difficulty by invoking the fundamental psychoanalytic distinction between a *psychical* and a *biological* sex. But, this requires that we make a further distinction between psychical *sex*, as psychoanalysis formulates it, and the idea of *gender* endemic to Anglo-American, and increasingly other varieties of, feminist and sexuality theories. In terms of its relation to this book's wider context, this chapter explores one dimension of the limitations of the politicisation of sexuality. It does this by demonstrating how the politicisation of sexual difference as psychoanalysis conceives it is not only clinically and theoretically disastrous, but politically distracting as well.

Considered from the broadest multilingual and cross-disciplinary perspective, there's tremendous confusion in gender and sexuality theories concerning what precisely its fundamental categories are meant to designate. It's far from clear, for instance, that the various figures engaged in the debate understand the same thing by the terms 'sex' and 'sexuality'. As far as these terms are concerned, we know where to look to discover what Freud, for example, meant by them.

The case with gender is altogether different, however. Like French and many other Romance and Germanic languages, Freud's German had no vocabulary with which to distinguish between what English designates by sex and gender. Until 'Anglo-Saxon' gender theory finally made its presence felt in a begrudging French intellectual field in the 1990s, the term *genre* held only contrasting grammatical and cultural meanings, referring to the masculine indefinite article or the Western in literature and cinema, for instance. However, it's also true that this hasn't stopped French, or potentially any other language deprived of an indigenous term for 'gender', from distinguishing, as has much French work in feminist theory since Simone de Beauvoir, between a *sexe biologique* and a *sexe social* or *culturel*. By contrast, there's no rigorous concept of gender in psychoanalysis, neither in the original Freudian texts, nor in the broad post-Freudian field in the French-language tradition.

Of course, numerous English-language analysts and therapists, many with links to the feminist movement, have more or less uncontroversially imported gender into psychoanalysis. I want to argue that this importation has had a devastating effect on our capacity to theorise correctly what psychoanalysis, with greater fidelity to Freud, refers to as sexual difference. During the past half-century, feminist theory has spent significant amounts of time distinguishing between *sex*, deemed biological or anatomical, and *gender*, variously construed as historical, cultural, social, linguistic, discursive or ideological. Most recently, post-structuralist feminists have attacked this distinction, proclaiming that biological sex is a sort of Kantian thing-in-itself, which can never be apprehended or perceived from outside the discursive frame of gender.

My own argument moves in a different direction, however. The 'gendered subject' of contemporary Anglo-American theory is fully expressed by social codes and scripts, however heterogeneous, contradictory, or incomplete we might consider these to be. Even Judith Butler's notion of gender as an unrealisable normative ideal, which condemns us to endlessly inadequate attempts at performative conformity, assumes that this ideal is nevertheless socially intelligible – that is, inscribed in what Lacan called the symbolic order. In contrast, the sexed subject of psychoanalysis is an unconscious subject, a subject defined precisely by its non-appearance within the forms of recognised social life. For psychoanalysis, gender – understood as 'masculine' or 'feminine' social identity – can only ever be a vexing question for a subject of uncertain or ambiguous sex.

In Lacanian terms, the power to bestow a firm sexual identity is always alienated in the Other. Butler's gendered subject fails to incarnate manifest and communicable ideals of gender. By contrast, the psychoanalytic subject is forced to wonder about the content of these ideals, and also whether or not he or she conforms to them. In other words, as subjects of the unconscious we engage in a futile attempt at deciphering the impossible meaning of sexual difference from the Other's enigmatic and contradictory discourse, which can range from the ideas about sexuality uttered by parental figures or the media, to a prospective partner's expectations about the qualities of an ideal mate. In short, the social meaning of masculinity and femininity, for psychoanalysis, is forever barred from knowledge. Gender identity can only take the form of a question, which the subject poses of an Other who is incapable of responding in any fully satisfying way.

This being said, there are good reasons for which gender theory has argued against the discourse of sexual difference in psychoanalysis with the claim that it perpetuates a bias against homosexuality. Indeed, much of the discourse on homosexuality in Lacan's work, and among many Lacanian theorists and clinicians, has done little to dispel the suspicion. For example, Renata Salecl's otherwise excellent edited volume *Sexuation*, which features the work of prominent Parisian Lacanian clinicians, assumes by omission that sexuation always occurs in conformity with the subject's biological sex, an assumption Lacan himself eventually and squarely denied. Clinical work by such figures as Joël Dor and Jean Clavreul subsumes all forms of homosexuality under what both authors refer to as the 'perverse structure'.[2]

By contrast, in his path-breaking book *Beyond Sexuality*, Tim Dean draws attention to Lacan's thesis that the human sexual drive is caused by a real object of enjoyment, which is sexually undifferentiated, indeed finally *asexual*. As Freud himself put it, the 'instinct' is ultimately indifferent to the object's sexual characteristics. Dean's emphasis on what he calls the libidinal object's impersonality further exonerates the psychoanalytic theory of sexuality from familiar charges of heterosexism. The link between this object and what Lacan calls sexuation (a psychical or unconscious sex), however, remains unclear in his work. If psychoanalysis posits that the drive in itself, as it were, remains indifferent to sexual difference, then how can it take account of what today we refer to as sexual preference?

Even if we assume that the final lesson of psychoanalysis on sexuality is that the notion of sexual orientation is ultimately neurotic or ideological, the onus remains on psychoanalysis to explain why many people, or most, insist that they have one. Despite its tremendous theoretical value, Dean's work sheds no new light on this perennial problem. More precisely, it fails to distinguish between the real object that causes desire – what Lacan famously called *objet petit a* – and the other, ideal object to which the subject will address itself in the inescapable dynamic of transference. This latter object, to which Lacan gave the symbol I, is the phallus in its symbolic dimension, and it acquires crucial significance in the clinical writing on male same-sex desire.

It will be helpful to examine Dean's argument in more detail by specifying the role each of Lacan's three registers plays in its development. Put in the most basic of terms, Dean advances that faecal matter functions psychically as a sort of prototype for the phallus, which is 'less a figure for the penis than, more fundamentally, a figure for the turd'.[3] This is no doubt the case on the level of the drive. However, Dean's discussion fails to take account of Lacan's insistence that the phallus is (also) a signifier. In the mother's or mother figure's speech, this signifier will come to represent for the subject's unconscious what Lacan called the name of the father (*le nom du père*). This name refers to another entity, an object, which traumatically wrenches the subject from its position at the centre of the maternal world. In short, Dean privileges the function of the real phallus at the expense of its symbolic role as the emblem of castration. 'The logic of the concept of object *a*', he writes, 'demotes or relativizes the phallus: whereas the phallus implies a univocal model of desire (insofar as all desiring positions are mapped in relation to a singular term), object *a* implies multiple, heterogeneous possibilities for desire, especially since object *a* bears no discernible relation to gender' (250).

Dean expresses reservations about Deleuze and Guattari's anti-oedipal idea that there exists a limitless number of sex-gender positions. In light of these reservations, it remains unclear how Dean's own non-dialectical model of queer sexuality beyond sexual difference differs in its fundamentals from the one he opposes. Although he ultimately reproaches Deleuze and Guattari for promulgating a voluntarist utopianism in the liberationist current, which was thoroughly quashed in Foucault's *The History of Sexuality*, Dean nonetheless supports their enterprise to the extent that they 'aim to depersonify desire'. Further, 'apart from the vocabulary of desiring-machines', continues Dean, 'their contentions seem wholly compatible with Lacan's theory of desire as unconscious and originating in the object *a*, which is itself both irreducible and prior to anything that may be made to conform to the Oedipal figure' (242).

This last comment draws attention to a weak spot in Dean's book. According to Lacan, desire is also an effect of the subject's mediation through the Other – that is, its imperfect inclusion in the field of language. For this reason, the thesis about the real's power to eclipse the (necessarily failed) representation of sexual difference remains difficult to distinguish from Deleuze and Guattari's attack against the symbolic order as such. It's more theoretically consistent to argue that the so-called beyond of Oedipus – to be perfectly precise, the beyond of language's necessary but failed mediation of sexual difference – is internal to language itself, internal to the very process of oedipalisation. In this sense, sexuality is indeed caused by *objet petit a*. However, we fail to understand Lacan's concept if we imagine the latter as some tangible object on the other side of language or representation. Rather, the partial object is a by-product of the impossibility of uttering the sexual relation; a sort of remainder of language, which wouldn't exist without language's failure to signify it.

Further, we should recall that the anatomical reference of 'the penis' in the original Freudian passages on the phallic stage was to both the penis and the clitoris. This suggests that a degree of ambivalence with respect to biological sex was embedded from the very beginning in Freud's own discussion of what he misleadingly called the penis. In this light, the conclusion supporting the tired queer-theoretical cliché according to which psychoanalysis upholds a sexist view of the relation between the phallus and biological men, can only be qualified as overhasty. Lacan eliminated any lingering ambiguity in Freud when he claimed that 'clinical facts' demonstrate that there exists 'a relation between the subject and the phallus that forms without regard to the anatomical distinction between the sexes'.[4]

In this sense, Lacan's Freudian position on the phallus is more radical than Dean's. Dean argues that the (symbolic) phallus helps legislate a social order that tends towards heterosexist normativity. In consequence, Dean must move to the level of the drive in order to find this normativity's subversion. By contrast, Lacan insists that the symbolic distribution of the phallus already remains undetermined by sex, anatomically defined. The very symbolic mechanism that attempts (and fails) to impart sexual identity can fail even to 'match' its attribution with a subject's bodily sex. As Lacan, with disarming directness, put it in *Encore*, 'everyone knows there are phallic women, and that the phallic function doesn't stop men from being homosexuals'.[5] Lacan's utterance problematises Dean's assumption that the elimination of the agency of the phallus in sexuation is a necessary condition for a genuinely anti-homophobic psychoanalytic account of sexuality.

In my own view, the properly psychoanalytic position is that despite the asexual quality of *objet petit a*, the homosexual subject, male or female, isn't immune to the effects of the fantasmatic comedy of being and having the phallus. With reference to Lacan's later work, the logic of sexuation, which upholds that there are only two possible ways in which the symbolic order can fail to signify the (hetero)sexual relation, also plays a role for the subject who will call him or herself homosexual. To state, as one should, that all nonpsychotic forms of subjectivity must submit to what Lacan called the phallic function is not tantamount to the imposition of what Dean calls a univocal model of desire. For psychoanalysis, castration's universality obtains in two different ways: the feminine way, which is based on an immediate judgment that one does not have the phallus, coupled with an affirmation of non-phallic jouissance; and the masculine way, which bases castration's lack of exception on the authority of a paternal prohibition paradoxically exempt from castration. In short, there's no escape from the requirement that the psyche, in both its masculine and feminine guises, imbue a particular signifier with the unconscious power to signify what one necessarily lacks.

While this requirement of psychic life ensures that the phallus will play a determinative role in human sexuality, it doesn't succeed in legislating a regime of sexual orientation – hetero, homo or otherwise. Yes, the drive by its nature is indifferent to the sexually differentiated attributes of the object, as Dean and Deleuze/Guattari maintain, not to mention both Freud and Lacan. But it's also true that we never experience sexuality purely on the level of the drive. Cultural discourses – language – will forever try, and forever fail, to effect, to actualise the sexual relation. Evidence for this is far from lacking. Everything from the vulgar Jungian 'men are from Mars' discourse, to the various forms of male and female genital circumcision, attest to our species' unceasing effort to put sexual difference on firmer cultural and anatomical ground.

The causal power of Lacan's *objet petit a* with respect to desire doesn't prevent the subject from connecting its separation from jouissance to a phallic third party. The signifier our unconscious selects for this third party then serves to represent the impossibility of definitive, once-and-for-all libidinal satisfaction. In short, the phallus stands in for our irremediable sense of lack. It is crucial to underline with respect to the concerns of queer theory, or more generally in the context of today's complex social realities, that the paternal function is precisely a function for Lacan. This function can and will be linked with representations that may or may not bear any relation to the biological father, or even with the person who performs the paternal role in the infant's family unit. If, as Lacan argued, the unconscious picks out the paternal metaphor from the mother's speech, then it's hardly even necessary that the father be alive, let alone 'emotionally available', as an ambient and highly normative psychologism might suggest.

For this reason, the familiar diagnostic social commentaries that wax apocalyptic about the disastrous social implications of non-traditional families or the so-called decline of paternity should be questioned from the point of view of psychoanalysis itself, even and especially when these diagnoses emerge from psychoanalytic contexts, as they often do. Further, it's likely no great secret that the discourse of the male homosexual – and it's predominantly the male form of homosexuality that will preoccupy me in what follows – is deeply marked by the phallus and whomever, for a given subject, is deemed to bear it. This issue of the relation between male homosexual desire and the problem of the phallus is precisely what Dean's analysis glosses over and Lacanian clinical discourse most often fails adequately to address.

These are the reasons why I've chosen to examine in what follows the complex mutual implication of sameness and difference in sexuality theory through the lens of the Lacanian clinical discourse on male homosexuality. More specifically, I'll engage with the work of the late Belgian analyst Serge André, in my view the most consequential to have appeared thus far as concerns the analysis of male same-sex desire in the Lacanian field. In the process, we'll have occasion to revisit a number of classic problems that have marked the history of psychoanalytic thinking about homosexuality, including the relation of the perverse structure, sometimes deemed synonymous with fetishism, to male homosexual object choice, as well as the vexed and, in the broader context of queer theory, outright suppressed problem of the psychogenesis of homosexual desire.[6]

I pose two basic questions. First: what distinguishes the male homosexual from the male, predominantly heterosexual, fetishist? Second: if male homosexuals aren't ordinarily perverts, in the structural-clinical sense of the term, then what distinguishes the one from the other? Nearly a century of analytic discourse has prevaricated, often in a quite phobic way, on these two questions. My argument will be that both questions can be answered with a single contention. The only theoretically consistent way to distinguish the neurotic male homosexual from the fetishist is to assume that the former, unlike the latter, agrees to assume what Lacan calls feminine sexuation. As we follow the logic of this argument, we'll encounter not only something of the insistence of a *sameness* that distinguishes sexual difference from other kinds of difference (ethnic, racial, economic and so on), but also a perhaps surprising indication of a distinctly sexual *difference* at work in what we call same-sex desire.

Dany, or the Paradox of Hetero-Transsexuality

Dany is a young male patient who, for some years, has anxiously asked himself if he's a transsexual. Although the prospect of a sex-change operation horrifies him, he bears witness to having felt more like a girl than a boy for most of his life. At the time of his entry into analysis at age 20, Dany has been taking female hormonal supplements, which provide him with what André calls 'a few curves'.[7] A low-level white collar worker, Dany marries a female colleague at age 19 but, even after the wedding and up to the time of his analysis, he continues to spend on average one night a week at his father's house, a widower whose wife died when Dany was 16 years old.

Dany describes to his analyst some key details of the unusual domestic relationship he has with his father. The day after his mother's death, Dany's father invites his son to sleep with him in his bed every night, rationalising this invitation by saying that he wants to convert Dany's room into a memorial space for his wife. According to André's reproduction of his patient's discourse, the father subsequently adopts the role of 'housewife', insisting on dressing his 16-year-old son every morning before leaving for work.

Dany takes advantage of his mother's death to increase the frequency of the cross-dressing practice he had been engaging in since age 6. Before her demise, Dany's mother silently tolerated her son's transvestism. Dany explains that his mother had passionately wished for a daughter while pregnant with him. After the delivery, she refused to touch her new baby for two days. Although she eventually, on the surface at least, accepts her newborn's male sex, Dany's mother insists on dressing him in girls' clothing and buying him toys associated with girls. Not without consequence, according to André, the mother gives her son the diminutive form of the name she had picked out for a daughter. As André informs his reader, the name 'Dany' (not the patient's real name) is used for both boys and girls, men and women, in the patient's cultural context. Later, at age 12, Dany reluctantly agrees to undergo surgery to lower his testicles which, as he says, had 'remained inside' his body (34).

Those are the basic facts of the case history as André presents them. Central to my concerns in this chapter, however, will be to examine not only how André interprets these facts, but also how his interpretation is informed by particular theoretical premises surrounding the relation between the notion of the perverse psychic structure in Lacanian theory and what we call male homosexuality. With these aims in mind, certain key details of the case gain special significance. For instance, we learn that his mother would allow the young Dany to put on a pair of her tights after school before his father's return from work. This detail leads André to observe that 'a complicity, never explicitly formulated, was established between Dany and his mother', and that the father, although 'not invisible [*pas inexistant*]', was 'systematically deceived, cuckolded by the couple formed by the mother and her son'. In rather too flippant a tone, André concludes that not only did the mother 'wear the pants' in the household, but she would also, when the father's attention was turned elsewhere, 'share them with her son' (35).

Those familiar with the main tropes of the history of psychoanalytic clinical writing on male homosexuality will immediately recognise this classic aetiological scenario: a retiring, absent or feminised father symbolically castrated by the mother; the latter a permissive, almost obscene figure who lends herself with gusto to clandestine incestuous enjoyments with her son. These enjoyments are held to undermine the father's presumed duty to signify or effect castration. André's analysis assumes that the mother's desire for a female child virtually guarantees that Dany's future symbolic identifications will be feminine, in other words that he'll position himself as a member of the maternal line.

Although it hits all the familiar notes in the melody of dominant analytic thinking about male homosexuality, Dany's case, according to André himself, has little in the end to do with homosexuality properly speaking. First, Dany never claims to be homosexual, never speaks of desiring another man, and marries, when all is said and done, a woman. Second, Dany's primary concern appears to lie not with the sex attributes of his object, but rather with his own sexual identity, with what André calls 'the enigma of his sex' (34). The question Dany formulates in response to the Other's enigmatic desire is not 'am I homo or heterosexual?' but rather 'am I a man or a woman?'

In addition to worrying about his sexual identity, Dany gives evidence of sadomasochistic fantasies in his unconscious life. For instance, he tells his analyst that he customarily hires female prostitutes with whom he stages a particular fantasy scenario. Its mise-en-scène sees Dany dress in tight-fitting women's clothing, pretending to do housework while his paid female partner aggressively insults him. The scene reaches its climax when the prostitute ties Dany up and flogs him to orgasm. Gradually, Dany introduces his wife to his masochistic fantasy world. Although compliant with some of his requests, she refuses to engage in any activity that threatens to cause her husband direct physical harm. Central to Dany's fantasy is the requirement that his partner enjoy her involvement in its enactment. Only in this way, André suggests, can Dany offer up his ecstasy to the Other as the fulfilment of *its* desire.

Here we encounter an example of what Lacan describes as the perverse structure: the subject offers up his services as the catalyst, the vehicle, of the Other's jouissance. This requires not only that the subject actively manipulate his partner in order 'passively' to experience masochistic enjoyment. Further, he must also receive a sort of proof from the Other that it isn't simply pretending to be a sadist, but actually derives obscene satisfaction from causing pain.

In his commentary, André leaves unexamined the fact, crucial for my own purposes, that Dany's perverse self-instrumentalisation vis-à-vis the Other's enjoyment occurs in tandem with the physical manipulation of his own body. This manipulation through hormonal supplements is designed to attenuate the evidence of his male biological sexual identity. Not only does Dany's fantasy phallicise his female partner by having her give voice to a superegoic command that must be obeyed. The fantasy also functions to calm his anxiety about his own sexual identity, by in effect 'performing' the non-coincidence between bodily sexual difference and its representation in conventional gendered domestic roles. The sadomasochistic sequence attenuates the traumatic question of Dany's uncertain sexual identity by making it difficult or impossible to answer one way or the other.

Or, perhaps, the fantasy works pre-emptively to answer the question of sexual difference before it can even be asked: if Dany, a man, can adopt a 'passive' feminine role, and if his female partner can give voice to a severe paternal superego, then sexual difference ceases to be a function of subjectivity proper – of the always failed attempt to find a symbolic home in the Other – and becomes instead a matter of self-instrumentalisation, of solving the enigma of sexual difference by impeding its castrating emergence as a question. The neurotic tends to worry about the sex of his object, anxiously subjecting himself to the multiple-choice question of sexual orientation. By contrast, the pervert offers himself up in fantasy as the object that tries to resolve the difference between the sexes by blocking, quite literally, the emergence of the problem of its impossible symbolic representation.

André is certainly correct in his assessment that Dany isn't a 'repressed' homosexual, but rather a heterosexual pervert. Insightfully, he underscores how Dany's perverse structure functions psychically as a defence against homosexuality. In short, *Dany becomes a pervert in order to avoid becoming homosexual*. In so doing, Dany saves himself from the difficulty of acknowledging the possibility that a biologically male subject is capable of desiring 'like a woman', of adopting what Freud referred to as a passive aim for the drive. According to André, the 'complicity' between Dany and his mother allows Dany to feign submission to the symbolic law of paternal authority. But, when his mother dies and the father adopts his feminine position in the diminished family structure, Dany is directly placed for the first time in a position of passivity in relation to the father. This prospect is so traumatically seductive for Dany, André contends, that his patient must construct, in defence, a masochistic fantasy with a phallic mother dominatrix in the starring role.

Dany resists the form of symbolic castration that can engender a homosexually tending desire in at least two ways. First, the masochistic fantasy scenario supports Dany's perverse desire to fuse with his partner into a unified or self-sufficient phallic object – to embody, in other words, the phallus the mother lacks on the level of her anatomical body. Second, as if to compensate for the difficulty of finding an authentically sadistic partner willing to play the required role, Dany hormonally feminises his own body, effectively protesting to the Other that in any case his desire can't possibly be homosexual because he isn't even really a man. Indeed, the psychodynamic significance of Dany's fantasy constructions finds clear expression in his response of absolute conformity with his mother's desire for a female child.

Despite the mother's apparent acceptance of her son's biological sex, André contends that the young Dany was traumatised by an unconscious wish, communicated by the mother between the lines, for a child of the opposite sex. Dany's unconscious life is structured at the most fundamental level around a libidinal dynamic of self-instru-mentalisation, which functions simultaneously as a defence against, and perverse enactment of, this desire for a girl he hears articulated in his mother's speech. Compliance with this desire requires an acknowledgment of sexual difference by way of acceptance of (phallic) lack and what goes along with it – the intolerably traumatic prospect of sexual passivity. By effectively positioning himself in fantasy as the asexual object that fills the lack in the Other, Dany's unconscious tries to stop all evidence of sexual difference from even emerging as a problem. In this way, Dany secures for himself a precarious, ersatz form of perverse castration, which is exempt from sexuation's forced choice between the libido's active and passive expressions.

Dany's analysis lasts for only a year and a half, culminating in what André calls an affirmation of the patient's masochism. According to André, the abbreviated analysis causes Dany to fail to withstand the subjective destitution that would have allowed him to traverse his perverse fantasy and attenuate its symptomatic agency. Nonetheless, Dany manages to undertake a sublimating writing practice, which grants him a modicum of satisfaction outside the challenges and dangers posed by his sexual practices. For André, writing allows Dany to engage in a form of labour that provides the psychical reassurance that comes with enabling the Other's enjoyment without having to act out his masochistic fantasy, and thereby experiencing the suffering it engenders.

The significance of the Dany case history for my concerns in this chapter lies in how it presents a concrete instance of the implication of the fetish structure in the psyche's defence against homosexuality. Without spelling it out in detail, Freud intuited this implication in his own work on perversion. 'The fetish', Freud asserts, 'saves the fetishist from becoming homosexual, by endowing women with the characteristic which makes them tolerable as sexual objects'.[8] But if the 'successful' male, more or less heterosexual, pervert is in some sense, according to Freud, a 'failed' passive homosexual (at least on the level of the passive fantasy vis-à-vis the father), then what does the clinical picture of what we might call, however improperly, the 'successful' male homosexual look like?

Indeed, a certain kind of male homosexual desire may in fact be unrelated to the perverse phallicisation of the mother we find in Dany's case. Such a male homosexuality would also be unrelated to a 'denial of sexual difference', which is the hallmark of the widest swathe of psychoanalytic writing on perversion. Rather, this male homosexuality would be situated in a 'feminine' position of passivity with respect to the phallus or father. What does this imply with respect to this presumably neurotic, as opposed to perverse, subject's castration? In short, what is the structure of (neurotic) male homosexual desire?

Although it's not certain that André's nonetheless invaluable book provides a convincing and unambiguous answer to this question, it will still be worth our while to examine another example from his casework in order to further the inquiry. This second case history will lay the groundwork for the presentation of my own views concerning both the relation of perversion to male homosexuality, and the implication of sexual difference in what we call male same-sex desire.

Philippe, or the 'Imaginarisation' of Castration

In André's historicised psychoanalytic account, male homosexuality is organised around what he calls an initiation to virility, by which access to a sexualised masculinity is non-normatively aligned with the maternal genealogical line. In André's view, such a psychic structure bears witness to a 'difficulty with respect to castration', and this difficulty plays a role in the formation of the male erotic subcultures he describes as 'more or less codified and cloistered' (159).

I'll leave it up to the reader to decide whether this description accurately identifies a key feature of male homosexual life, or rather bespeaks a fantasy, hardly unheard of among male heterosexual analysts, of male homosexual enjoyment as exotic and impenetrable, not to mention threatening to a masculine sexual identity deemed unstable or unattainable by Lacanian theory itself. For my own part, I'd merely suggest that the alternatives are not necessarily mutually exclusive. Doubtless, however, it will prove more productive to focus on the details of André's theory of male homosexuality as well as the facts of the case that serves to exemplify it.

Despite its occasionally phobic limitations, André's clinical discussion of male homosexuality has the merit of reinscribing the vectors of male homosexual desire within a phallic orbit, emphasising in the process the agency of a symbolic phallus in the male homosexual's discourse. In this way, André's approach rectifies the tendency in queer-inflected Lacanian criticism such as Dean's to theorise homosexuality strictly in relation to the real object-cause of enjoyment, abstracted from its dependence on the symbolic order, which remains, however, inconsistent and incomplete. In short, male homosexuals are neither more nor less subjected to language's opacity than any other category of subject. Moreover, they're equally obliged to separate from the gravitational field of the mother's all-consuming jouissance with the help of a phallic signifier, the signifier of lack. With this allusion to the phallus as the sign of castration, we can already see how André's considerations move us away from the paradigm of perversion characteristic of the previous case. The pervert's raison-d'être is to forestall the emergence of the mother's lack, by posing as the object that fills it. Here, by contrast, the subject is forced to tarry with this lack by finding a signifier to represent it.

In this way, André's account admirably highlights how the male homosexual psychic structure, or at least a particular version of it, features a determinate link to what Lacan calls the paternal metaphor, and more specifically to its interrogation. In brief, the paternal metaphor serves to signify for the unconscious the other thing, separate from the subject, that the mother desires. This object – the phallic object – is necessarily elsewhere, outside, in the place of the Other. This is what turns the male homosexual to the interrogation of the phallus in all its forms, not only the excremental partial object of which Dean importantly speaks, but also the idealised symbolic and imaginary forms of the phallus, which hold up the lure of virile identity. As I developed in my criticism of Dean's work, we can see how the universal *queerness* of sexuality – by which I mean sexuality's excess over sexual difference; the fact that the drive's object is ultimately *asexual* – fails to do away with the need for a (necessarily failed) process of oedipalisation, to use the old-fashioned Freudian vocabulary; or, more helpfully perhaps, for a pass through what Lacan calls the phallic function.

Indeed, Lacan's famous (or notorious) formulas of sexuation can be read as the formalisation of precisely this antinomy or disjunction between the mode through which the subject is inscribed in the symbolic order, and the queer residue of the real that deuniversalises or detotalises the phallic function. This residue can take either the masculine form of the obscene exception (Freud's 'primal father'), or the feminine form of the *pas-toute* (the law of castration is not-all).

André's concern for the male homosexual's virility boils down to the problem of how to frame the question of what we might loosely call the location of the symbolic phallus in the structure of male homosexuality. How does the male homosexual orient himself with respect to the phallus – the signifier that represents the interdiction, the impossibility, of a full and uncompromised jouissance? In short, how are we to theorise the male homosexual's sexuation?

In André's view, the elaboration of oedipal identifications, and the installation in the unconscious of the phallic signifier, are susceptible to two modes of failure he associates with male homosexuality. While one mode causes the formation of the perverse clinical structure, the other creates a more 'normal' form of neurotic subjectivity. As became apparent in the Dany case history, perverse 'homosexuality' for André bespeaks 'a failure to realise castration [*un ratage par défaut de réalisation de la castration*]'. By contrast, neurotic homosexuality is based on a second kind of failure marked by what André calls an 'excessive imaginarisation of castration'. Tellingly, however, Marc, whose case history André uses to illustrate the neurotic variation, bears consistent witness during his analysis to a 'nostalgia, which grows in intensity over the years, for a real relationship with a woman' (171). With the pseudo-homosexual case of Dany still in mind, we couldn't be blamed for wondering if André is looking for male homosexuality in all the wrong places.

Here it will be helpful, parenthetically, to bring to the fore some key details of Marc's case history. This case serves to illustrate in André's discussion the neurotic homosexual psychic structure from which Philippe's perverse structure, discussed in detail below, is distinguished. The importance of Marc's case increases by virtue of the fact that I'll want to suggest that André's diagnoses of the two analysands makes more sense put the other way round.

Describing his erotic orientation as bisexual, Marc desires nonetheless to marry a woman and have children. Despite a number of homosexual liaisons during his university years, liaisons characterised most consequentially by oral–penile contact, mutual masturbation and an atmosphere of affective warmth, Marc 'has no desire to become a homosexual', André writes (174). Instead, Marc seeks out psychoanalysis in order to overcome his impotence with women, a condition André associates with his patient's sense of horror at female genitals. Although he shows tenderness towards his son during his childhood, Marc's father adopts a more severe attitude towards him in his adolescent years. According to André, this change in the father's attitude causes Marc to seek shelter in the orbit of his mother, with whom he develops the signature 'complicit intimacy' (174).

André describes Marc's oedipal conflict as classic. Although the father's early, caring relation with his son prevents Marc from identifying symbolically with his mother, Marc's virility, according to André, is marred by his fear of the father's later, more intimidating persona. Although I agree with André that the form of Marc's castration is of the phallic or masculine variety in the sense that it's overseen by the father, in my view André goes wrong where he characterises this castration as 'overly successful' (177). With his difficulty assuming the consequences of masculine sexuation, the resulting phobia of the female sex organs and the associated fear of becoming homosexual, Marc's psychic structure appears to fit more comfortably under the rubric of perversion.

Indeed, the only case material presented in André's book featuring a patient who speaks of being penetrated by another man is Philippe, who not only serves to represent within André's typology the perverse version of the two possible homosexually inclined psychic structures, but also dies after only five sessions with his analyst in a car accident featuring a likely suicidal intent, conscious or unconscious. This is the gist of the background behind my suggestion that André gets his diagnoses mixed up. With his sexual ambivalence but overarching heterosexual orientation, Marc is the one who shows signs of the perverse structure. It's Philippe, rather, who best exemplifies the neurotic profile.

As mentioned, Philippe's analysis is cut short by his tragic death: he crashes his car into a median at the fork of a motorway, one route leading to one of his male sexual partners, and the other to his girlfriend. *Pace* André, it's entirely possible that Philippe's suicide has more to do with his failure to extricate himself from his capture by a phobic ideology that caustically abjects male sexual receptivity, than it does with the effects of a perverse or fetishistic psychic structure. In any case, according to the mainstream of analytic literature, the pervert, unlike the neurotic, rarely has problems achieving libidinal satisfaction, isn't ordinarily depressive, and for these reasons seldom comes knocking on the psychoanalyst's door.

No doubt my hypothesis requires a closer look at André's presentation of Philippe's case. My aim will be to show that cases like Philippe's can be mistaken for instances of perversion because of an ambient phobia of male anal eroticism, from which analytic literature often fails to extricate itself. Another factor is a hardly uncommon resistance within the Lacanian clinical field itself to the entirely orthodox Freudian thesis according to which many subjects of both biological sexes are *cross-sexuated*. This is to say that these subjects confront the impasse of jouissance in language in a manner associated with the other sex.

Philippe is a young, university-educated man who interrupts his post-secondary studies to become a fashion model for industry magazines and couture houses in Milan and elsewhere. Although he enjoys tremendous professional success, a condition of paralysing anxiety brings him to analysis and causes him to ask himself the question: 'am I or am I not homosexual, and must I live in this manner?' (180). Although left without comment by André, Philippe's formulation of the question concerning the nature of his desire betrays the considerable extent of his internalisation of phobic value judgments about what we call sexual orientation. Nevertheless, during his analysis Philippe speaks of frequenting what André calls hard homosexual establishments, and engaging in oral sex with a number of his male acquaintances in the fashion world. Although he considers acts of fellatio and mutual masturbation with male friends a normal feature of life in his professional environment, Philippe suffers painful intuitions of guilt in response to his desires with respect to other men.

Further, Philippe's discourse suggests that his sexual life is characterised by a significant degree of compulsiveness. As André relates, throughout this period of homosexual activity, Philippe maintains a 'more or less stable' (180) relationship with a woman. Successful sexual relations with his female partner often require, however, the conjuring of a fantasy of a man in briefs. A crisis of anxiety and confusion strikes Philippe when a male acquaintance invites him for an evening of sexual activity featuring fist-fucking. Fascinated and repulsed in equal measure, Philippe responds non-committally. He proceeds to wander through the streets of Milan in a state of acute disorientation, impulsively giving away the contents of his wallet to a woman who asks him for money. Managing to direct his ambulation to Milan's famous Duomo, Philippe experiences a full-on attack of panic while gazing upwards at a statue in the dome of the cathedral depicting the Lord God placing a crown on Jesus's head.

André's interpretation of this key sequence of events provides crucial evidence of the clinical points of reference at work in his understanding of the perverse structure in its questionable relation to male homosexuality. As I've already suggested, this interpretation also bears witness to a common theoretical regression in the Lacanian clinical field. This regression detracts from the analyst's ability to come to terms with the sexuation of some neurotic subjects who think they might be, or explicitly identify as, homosexual. Had he accepted the acquaintance's sexual invitation, André explains, Philippe in his own mind would have placed himself definitively 'among the homosexuals'. More precisely, the prospect of anal penetration for Philippe carries with it what André describes as 'an acceptance of castration, here understood on the most real level' (182). We should note that André doesn't specify at this juncture which form of castration, masculine or feminine, such an acceptance would imply. Concerning the compulsive monetary offer Philippe makes to the woman on the street, André avers that his patient here 'behaves as a man' in the sense that he 'gives a gift of what he has (the phallus) to the one who lacks it' (182).

As for the final climactic event of Philippe's narrative, namely his panicked viewing of the coronation statue, André suggests that it calls into question for a second time Philippe's masculine identification. On one level, God's crowning of his son allegorises the generational transmission of the phallic signifier, and this transmission occurs in tandem with the bodily sacrifice at the centre of the scriptural Passion. This means, for André, that the episode represents on another level both a refusal of the paternal phallic gift, and the assumption of a passive position with respect to the father. Significantly, after the cathedral episode, Philippe experiences recurring attacks of panic, engages in compulsive and anonymous sexual encounters, and bears witness to fantasies of anal penetration, which incite violently guilty self-accusations. For André, the emphasis Philippe places on sensations of anal excitation during his attacks suggests 'an identification with the hole, on the model of the female genitalia (or a *cloaque* [an animal's anal or urinary orifice])' (186).

Like Dany, during his childhood Philippe entertained a relation with his mother that André qualifies as complicitous. Going further, the analyst considers his patient's choice of profession to be an unconscious response to the lavish attention the mother accorded to her son's boyhood body. Insisting on bathing him well into his adolescence, she took care, André underlines, not to call attention to his penis with her soapy touch. In this way, according to André, Philippe's mother positions her son as an imaginary phallus – a self-enclosed, asexual unity designed to keep jouissance at bay. Further marginalising the agency of the father in the familial symbolic environment, Philippe's mother confesses to her son that her marriage was a forced and desperate attempt at self-preservation in the face of a difficult material situation stemming from her own mother's death.

At this crucial point of his case history, André begins to explore the dynamic of what he calls Philippe's fetishism, insisting that the patient's homosexuality is tied structurally to a denial of 'the anatomical difference between the sexes' as well as the 'castration that revealed to him the female sex organs' (186). Yet, Philippe tells his analyst that he experienced his first orgasm while masturbating and inhaling the odour of a pair of briefs his father had left on the bathroom floor. In a searching, if not desperate, tone, André then writes that a few moments earlier Philippe had been viewing representations of the female sex organs in a book of sexual education given to him by his parents. André qualifies Philippe's first orgasm as the instigating moment of a 'central perverse fantasy' involving an acute 'desire to see men in briefs'. The perverse nature of the fantasy is rationalised through the notion that men's briefs, 'more surely than a woman's bikini', reassure Philippe that there is 'something behind the veil' (186), even if this something remains hidden from sight.

To be sure, it's a central tenet in Lacan's teaching that the phallus functions 'only when veiled'. This implies that the penis, if it's to have any chance at all of standing in for the phallic signifier of absolute and impossible jouissance, has to remain hidden from view. On my reading of the case history, however, it's not in fact clear why André chooses to qualify Philippe's enthusiasm for images of men in briefs as perverse in the strong clinical sense – that is, as a denial of sexual difference and the form of castration based on its acknowledgment in the unconscious. As we recall, André describes Philippe's anxious and directionless wandering through the streets of Milan as a consequence of what he calls a literal castration, which the prospect of being fist-fucked presents. Clearly, Philippe's marked discomfort at the moment he receives the invitation evokes a deeply traumatic fantasy of anal receptivity which, in André's own interpretation of events, presupposes a dramatic and radical experience of castration.

Set against André's account of the father's domestic marginalisation and the clinical narrative of the briefs fantasy, Philippe's case appears to deviate from the dynamic that characterises the Freudian boy's predicament. This is to say, in Lacanian terms, Philippe's castration seems at odds with the logic of masculine sexuation. We can ask at this juncture why André doesn't choose to link Philippe's psychic structure with *feminine* sexuation – that is, with the castration of the Freudian girl. In this alternative scenario, the phallic fantasy object veiled by the briefs is recharacterised, changing from a perverse manifestation of the maternal phallus (what Lacan calls the *hommelle*) to the symbolic paternal phallus, which inspires desire for the one who has it. The briefs, after all, belong to the father, and no evidence is given to support the premise of any unconscious maternal significance.

I should stress here that my main intention isn't simply to assert that André misdiagnoses his patients. Rather, the point is to underline how the logic of the analyst's interpretation fails to acknowledge the possibility that Philippe has undergone feminine castration, in other words unconsciously registers phallic lack without the intervention of the father. Even more consequentially, André's clinical logic effectively renders unthinkable the existence of what I would call an actually existing form of neurotic (as opposed to perverse), and male (as opposed to masculine), homosexuality.

I've already pointed out that the patient whom André describes as a homosexual neurotic, namely Marc, not only never has sexual relations of any kind with another man during the period of his analysis, but also never gives evidence of a consistent desire to do so. In fact, Marc frames his erotic ambitions, as if to dispel all doubt, around an explicitly heterosexual aim. In the case of Philippe, André characterises a male subject's adoption, as his object of fantasy, of a veiled image of the male member as, by definition, a fetishistic phallicisation linked to a denial of sexual difference, here construed in anatomical, as opposed to psychical, terms. Indeed, at the crucial moment when he describes Philippe's structure as perverse, André conveniently forgets the fundamental Freudo-Lacanian thesis about sexual difference – namely that it's *not* of the order of anatomy and biology.

The classic post-Freudian qualification of perversion as a denial of sexual difference, too often left in a fog of vagueness, must be qualified in such a way as to take account of what I've called cross-sexuation. If sexual difference, psychoanalytically conceived, is indeed not the same as anatomical sexual difference – a point which André, as a self-described Lacanian, would surely be forced to concede – then we can no longer assume that any male subject's libidinal investment in images and representations of masculinity or virility is a displaced manifestation of the perverse denial of the mother's castration. Under the hypothesis of cross-sexuation, the neurotic form of male homosexuality would then indeed be marked by sexual difference insofar as, psychically, the male homosexual experiences, or can experience, a specifically feminine castration. In this precise sense, what the homosexual seeks in his partner is in fact the *other* sex.

Surprisingly, perhaps, this critical assessment of André's interpretation of the case of Philippe can actually lend support to his view of male homosexual subcultures as cults of virility. It was Lacan himself, after all, who said that the display of virility is a properly feminine phenomenon.[9] Further, it's not clear why gay cultures would be so concerned with the acquisition of the accoutrements of an idealised masculine embodiment if masculinity were not precisely an object of desire, rather than something simply achieved, however problematically, through sexuation itself.

Moreover, the intense investment in embodiment characteristic of male homosexual subcultures gains further in analytic significance when we consider that, in imaginary terms, the idealised object of desire and the ego of narcissism aren't sexually differentiated for gay men as they would be for their straight counterparts. This might mean that the pursuit of virility acquires a plastic, mobile quality, which distributes its aims between the body of the desired object and the subject's own body-image. On the level of the imaginary, in other words, the sexy body the male homosexual desires 'out there' (at the disco) and the one he wants 'for himself' (by working out at the gym) are one and the same.

From I to *a*: the Beyond of Sexual Identification

These last comments evoke what can only be described as the neurotic elements of the male homosexual economy. Before exploring what might lie beyond gay neurosis, however, it will be wise to anticipate, with the dominant assumptions of contemporary queer and feminist theories in mind, a couple of the more obvious objections to what I've put forward concerning the involvement of (one type of) male homosexuality in feminine sexuation.

First, my hypothesis in no way equates male homosexuality with transsexualism. The male homosexual, although clearly vexed in childhood and adolescence by intuitions of difference with respect to other subjects who share his bodily sexual traits, doesn't generally question his *biological* sex; doesn't bear witness to being 'trapped' inside the wrong-sexed body.

Unlike Dany, for instance, Philippe doesn't ask if he's a man or a woman; his question of the Other is framed, rather, within the terms of today's post-sexological discourse of sexual orientation. Secondly, and of equal importance, the idea of cross-sexuation I wish to propose in this chapter is *indifferent to gender*. By this I mean that being cross-sexuated in the manner I've described carries no *necessary* consequences for how this subject appears in the social world with respect to dominant ideologies of masculinity and femininity. The difference of the cross-sexuated subject is therefore to be located on the level of his or her speech, more specifically with respect to the way this speech stumbles upon the real of sex – the bedrock of sexual difference, as it were – and not in terms of the positive qualities (attributes or predicates) of this subject.

Provided we divest the notion of inversion – which Marcel Proust, for one, deemed a more appropriate moniker than homosexuality – of its personalising reference to a soulful essence, and also take the reference to woman not as evidence that every gay man is a closet drag performer, but rather as a signifier for the mode in which (some) male homosexuals desire, we can agree with Leo Bersani when he writes about that prolific and hypochondriacal French novelist that:

'homosexuality' can't describe the attraction of one male to another male if, according to the popular notion that Proust appears to accept, such men have a woman's soul. As others have noted, this rules out the same-sex desire it claims to account for. Homosexuality is just an illusion; what looks like a man desiring another man is actually a woman longing for sex with a man.[10]

To be sure, Proust's literary discourse on femininity in male homosexuality is burdened by the psychological rhetoric of inversion, which the modernist sexual ideologies inherited from mid-nineteenth- to late nineteenth-century sexology. Indeed, the idea of a female soul in a male body to which the term inversion gives expression, is linked more closely in conceptual terms with the classic feminist distinction between (biological) sex and (sociocultural or psychological) gender than it is with the properly psychoanalytic notion of sexual difference. In short, the inversion idea takes for granted socially determined meanings for masculinity and femininity, and then defines the male invert along rather crude behavioural lines as the subject who gives expression to a feminine soul.

By contrast, Lacan's Freudian concept of sexuation situates itself on another level, at the impossible intersection of speech and the real. By definition, this intersection remains inexpressible within the terms of the sociosymbolic contract. Whereas the discourse of inversion implicitly defines desire in accordance with how positive qualities of the personality accord or conflict with hegemonic gender ideologies, psychoanalysis claims instead that sex is what remains after all such expressions of the subject have been exhausted. Psychoanalytically, sex refers to the mode – 'male' or 'female' – by which such expressions always fail to express the subject's sexual essence or identity.

This being said, Bersani's commentary on Proust's interpretation of inversion makes tangible an illuminating paradox. Although, indeed, the male homosexual loves 'the other as the *same*' (128), and in this sense bears witness to a desire inscribed in what Bersani calls homo-ness, this desire is subject to the real of sexual *difference* if one considers that what's inverted is the subject's sexuation, and not his soul, personality, identity or other such metaphysical construct. If we suppose that the trajectory of the male subject who will come to experience homosexual desire is, or at any rate can be, marked by the immediate and actualised (unconscious) experience of castration that Freud discusses in relation to the girl – 'she accepts castration as an accomplished fact',[11] he writes – then in speaking of the gay man, André must qualify his castration as imaginary only because he makes the following very specific and unwarranted assumption: since the male subject bears a penis, he must necessarily become a speaking subject in a fashion that positions him as having, or rather as supposed to have, the phallus.

Under the hypothesis that some male subjects experience a symbolic castration of the feminine kind, what will be imaginarised, to use André's term, is not the maternal phallus, but rather a phallus positioned on decidedly paternal, that is to say masculine, terrain. In this precise sense, male homosexual desire features no relation to the logic of fetishism, which is centred on the fantasy of the phallic mother. On the level of his neurosis, then, this male subject would tend to locate the impossible, absolute jouissance that his castration forbids him within a male body, one which can then serve as a prototype not only for his erotic object, but for his 'own' alienated, imaginary one as well. Insofar as there can be such an imaginary convergence between the gay man's fantasised object and the body he wants to incarnate or become, he seeks himself in his partner – that is, one could say, the same in the other.

However, the hyperphallic body that captures his desire emerges from the feminine space of lack. This ensures that the gay male subject can only fail to 'find himself', as it were, in his Other. That there can be no *relation* between the gay man and his partner becomes especially clear when we consider that this non-coincidence of desire and object occurs not only on the level of the subject himself, but also 'in' his partner, such that the non-relation of homosexuality might be figured as the coexistence of two instances of the same non-complementarity. This formula distinguishes somewhat the impasse of homosexuality from the one that occurs in the heterosexual non-relation. Where heterosexuality reaches an impasse by virtue of the mutually exclusive terrains of the different masculine and feminine fantasies, homosexuality hits the rock of the real in consequence of the paradoxical incompatibility of two subjects harbouring the same fantasy structure. The basic psychoanalytic point to be made here is that any attempt to theorise a homosexual relation that would compensate for, indeed *redeem*, the failure of heterosexuality is to be avoided at all costs. Any such attempt must be dismissed as necessarily ideological, and therefore 'homonormative', to put a somewhat different spin on the term Jasbir Puar's work introduces into queer theory.[12]

Now, this premise of a homosexual non-relation has the benefit of enabling an illuminating appraisal of various aspects of what we might call the male homosexual unconscious. Neurosis, for gay men as for anyone else, has the function of disguising the uncomfortable truth that there is no sexual relation, as Lacan famously said, to which we can now add *of any kind*. We can understand in this light not only the persistence within gay fantasmatics of the inaccessible and effortlessly masculine straight partner who never, of course, returns the gay subject's desire, but also the related mystique of the authentic 'top' who would derive satisfaction from penetrating only male partners.

Is it possible that the pathological coupling of the hysteric and the pervert in the heterosexual world finds a rough equivalent in the culture of male homosexuality in the form of the (active) male fetishist and the (passive) gay man? To what extent does the fetishist's inability unconsciously to acknowledge female lack cause him to seek substitutive satisfactions with a passive male partner? Would this in turn imply that the neurotic male homosexual carries a certain vulnerability vis-à-vis other male subjects who experience difficulties with masculine castration? And finally, to the extent that they elaborate their fetish according to the classic Freudian paradigm of fetishism – as a means of resisting homosexuality – do these latter subjects tend towards a phobic form of acting out, either as a means of buttressing their own resistance to (passive) homosexuality, or else repressing their sexual attraction to other men?

It will be comparatively uncontroversial, I would imagine, to claim that the more politically radical, or at any rate avowedly socialist, wings of the various gay and lesbian movements have faded into relative obscurity during the past three decades or so, largely because of broader global political trends lacking any manifest relation to sexuality. These trends resulted from the reactionary attacks, beginning in the 1970s, against the achievements of the post-war welfare state, as well as the devastating ideological consequences of the collapse of the Eastern bloc and the end of the Cold War.

From the psychoanalytic perspective, however, it's possible to say that gay men, during the period just evoked, may have succumbed, in response to increased social recognition and acceptance, to a confusion of the two psychic agencies Lacan called I and *a*. These agencies refer, respectively, to the idealised symbolic point of identification (what Freud called the ego ideal), and the traumatic, real object-cause of desire: the object located on the level of the drive.

Lacan distinguishes between these two agencies of psychic life in the context of a gloss on Freud's schema presented in *Group Psychology and the Analysis of the Ego*. 'There is an essential difference', Lacan says, 'between the object defined as narcissistic, the *i(a)*, and the function of the *a*'. He adds that 'the fundamental mainspring [*ressort*] of the analytic operation is the maintenance of the distance' between the I – identification – and the *a*.[13] The mechanism of separation that Lacan considers integral to the analytic process implies the extrication of the real object of enjoyment from both forms of the ego, imaginary and symbolic. This implies that psychoanalysis puts into effect a reversal of the dynamic Freud describes as characteristic of hypnosis. In other words, analysis forces the patient to experience the analyst as a stupid, inert, 'hypnotised' automaton devoid of concrete knowledge of its desire. Crucially, the knowledge the patient finds lacking in the analyst includes the knowledge that could relate the patient's enigmatic desire to the classificatory framework of sexual orientation.

I've speculated that one of the particularities of male homosexuality is the relative ease with which the idealised object can be integrated into the circuit of narcissism due to the shared sexual biomorphology of subject and partner. If this is indeed the case, then it might be possible that gay men, more readily than their heterosexual counterparts, try to elevate the libidinal object of the drive through idealisation as a means of circumventing its disruptive emergence. This would only underline the crucial importance for homosexually inclined men to work towards the separation to which Lacan refers. The goal is to separate the object of jouissance from the idealised, erotically invested narcissistic object. The object of jouissance is the one that effectively interrupts the subject's self-relation, and spoils its ambition to feel 'at home' in its own subjectivity.

The separation I'm attempting to evoke requires us to acknowledge that the object causing the desire that can be qualified as homosexual is not the beautiful, seemingly self-contained, gym-trained, hypermasculine body of, say, Tom of Finland's men, but rather an altogether different object – partial, decorporealised, unsettling, formless, uncanny – more akin to Tim Dean's invaluable trope of the turd. Such an acknowledgment might have the benefit not only of knocking the postmodern queer subject off the treadmill of consumerism, integration, conformity, productivity and compulsive sexual activity that continues to fuel mainstream homosexual subcultures in what is called the West. Also, it might train his eye to see those invisible subjects in the gay world who, for reasons of 'race', socioeconomic position and – here the word fits the context – gender, will never make it into the pages of *Genre*, *The Advocate*, *Têtu* or *Out*.

These are the turds of the gay social world, turds whose staunch persistence under the collective radar of the sublime gay lifestyle's enthusiasts betrays the illusory and deeply ideological truth of the post-Stonewall construct of the brotherhood of men – white, elite-educated, upper-middle-class, freshly gentrified gay village-residing – that my imagination conjures up when I hear the phrase 'gay community'.

6

From the Antisocial to the Immortal

The investigation of male homosexuality in the previous chapter is intended in part as an intervention in the psychoanalytic clinical discourse on this topic. To some readers, it may have seemed out of place. However, I view this intervention as central to the concerns of the book as a whole, because it helps to demonstrate the irreconcilability of psychoanalytic ethics with the 'sexual politics' with which several decades of feminist and homosexual theory and activism have acquainted us. Although it has often betrayed itself on this point, Freudian psychoanalysis since its inception has featured, and this is no exaggeration, a strongly anti-homophobic message. After all, it was Freud himself who announced that he had never failed to find a significant 'current of homosexuality' in the unconscious of every patient he had ever treated.[1] And famously, Freud's tenuous belief in an ideal libidinal normalisation belied by the rest of his theory only faintly tarnished his otherwise laudable and radically before-its-time response to the letter of a young homosexual's concerned American mother.[2]

Yet, psychoanalysis also teaches us that, in an important sense, sexuality as such is *beyond politicisation*. This is so to the extent that who we are, as subjects of the unconscious, is ultimately unknowable, unfathomable – a hypothesis, as Lacan rigorously argued. This hypothesis has both logical and ethical aspects. The analysis of symptoms reveals a signifying logic. This logic indexes, however unverifiably, a traumatic cause that effectively *is* the subject. Also, the speculative reconstruction of this subject, the ethical mission that Lacan sutures to the proper name 'Freud', can only be an end in itself, one which is categorically distinct from any 'good' with which some might wish, disastrously, to wed the psychoanalytic project. It was perhaps Lacan's most lasting contribution to psychoanalysis that he defended with such unwavering ferocity this unconscious subject's absolute sovereignty. For Lacan, the attribution of any normative political meaning whatsoever to the unconscious subject is tantamount to a gross ethical betrayal of Freud's analytic desire.

However inauspicious the premise at first will seem, I want to argue nonetheless that it's precisely the *apolitical* essence of the psychoanalytic subject – that is, this subject's coincidence with the monstrously inhuman kernel of humanity that subverts the very form of the political good – that allows us to link the psychoanalytic project to the tradition of revolutionary political universalism. By revolutionary I mean to describe a politics based on two primary assumptions: first, that thoroughgoing social change is not only possible, but that its possibility is signalled by the very conservative doctrine that insists on its impossibility; and second, that the possibility of this change isn't discernible from within the logic of the social situation in which this change is speculatively, counterintuitively, imagined.

My argument rests on a distinction between what, above, I termed political meaning and politics proper. Politics proper identifies the political with a rupture in established political meaning. Simply put, politics is what emerges when something happens that can't be articulated by, is dismissed as 'impossible' within, existing political and social knowledges. What psychoanalysis most consequentially shares with such a politics is its insistence on the legitimacy of a truth of subjectivity located on *another scene*: a scene distinct from, and inassimilable to, the sociosubjective world upheld and defended by what Freud called ego libido.

As we've seen, the psychoanalytic subject can't be directly known; it can only be retroactively pieced together through the analysis of its signifying dysfunction. For its part, political subjectivity, as conceived by Alain Badiou, bears a problematic relation to an event, which necessarily fails to register in the terms of available social knowledges – 'opinion', as Badiou prefers, disparagingly, to say. From the perspective of politics proper, then, we can assert that the subject of the unconscious is caused by a rupture in the field of existing political knowledge. The consequence of this is that the elaboration of this subjectivity will necessarily reform this political knowledge in previously inconceivable ways.

In his seminar *L'acte psychanalytique* (1967–1968), Lacan began to develop the idea that the necessarily failed attempt in the clinic to signify the subject can nonetheless radically transform the dynamic of this subject's relation to its sociosymbolic world. In an imperfectly analogous way, Badiou in his writing conceives of political work as the tracing of the consequences of a disruptive event, a 'truth procedure' which has the potential literally to transform what it's possible to think in a given political situation. The psychoanalytic subject and the political subject share the key feature that they remain irreducible to, unexpressed by, the ambient discourses that work to perpetuate their indiscernibility. Given the disjunction between the subject and knowledge – in other words, the fact that no proof can establish a relation between them – a curious and deeply illiberal short-circuit is established between what is falsely understood by the distinction between the subject as person and its social beyond. This short-circuit finally puts paid to the ideology of the individual by substituting for it the truth of a strangely intimate, but properly *transpersonal*, subjectivity.

In Lacanian psychoanalytic practice, only the patient can bear final witness to the event of subjectivity encountered in the clinic. It's up to the patient, not the analyst, to decide when he has gone far enough to take account of, and responsibility for, his own subjective structure. This structure is then rendered as an impersonal formula that connects what we consider most particular about subjectivity to generic and transindividual psychical paradigms (neurosis, subdivided into hysteria and obsessional neurosis; psychosis; perversion). This is what Lacan meant when he said that the analyst *ne s'autorise que de lui-même*.[3] She can only legitimate her practice, and the knowledge on which it rests, herself through what effectively amounts to a traversal of personhood.

Further, in revolutionary politics the subject encounters the event in a way that significantly shifts the terms of his world. But this 'personal' witnessing, this attitude of fidelity towards that which transforms us, violently takes us out of ourselves, all the while connecting in a properly uncanny way our most apparently intimate experience to a register of impersonality characterised by an *indifference to difference*. Subjectivated by the political event, we subtract ourselves from the field of substantive markers of identity – heterosexual or homosexual; Jew, Muslim, Hindu, Christian; black, white, yellow, brown – to 'refind' ourselves 'outside', as it were, in a movement of generic subjectivity. Transported by this modality of indifference, what distinguishes me from others, including in particular my sexuality, ceases to bear significant consequences for thought.

'It is certainly not by renouncing the concrete universality of truths in order to affirm the rights of 'minorities', be they racial, religious, national, or sexual', writes Badiou, 'that the devastation [of financial globalisation] will be slowed down'. Indeed, there most certainly exists what Badiou calls a 'despicable complicity between the globalized logic of capital and French identitarian fanaticism'.[4] For my purposes, Badiou's reference to the xenophobic and crypto-fascist policies of Jean-Marie (and now Marine) Le Pen's *Front national* can be taken to refer more generally to *identitarian passion as such* – in other words, our passionate attachment to those signifiers of belonging that serve to differentiate my individual, and our collective, interests from the interests of the shapeless people in their generic and threateningly anonymous multiplicity.

In fact, I would go even further than Badiou does. As we know, queer theory since its inception has been invested in the dismantling of categories of identity related to gender and sexuality, viewed as normative categories of social knowledge. As I've argued in a variety of contexts throughout this book, however, it's not at all clear that the 'subversion of identity' doesn't in fact reassert identity's centrality by the very means of its putative, and typically ambivalent, negation.

It's time to substitute the left-deconstructionist motif of subversion with the contrasting, properly neutral, attitude of *indifference*. Although everyone can't help but perceive 'socially constructed' differences of gender and sexuality on the level of appearances, these differences are devoid of consequences for political thought. I would only add to this thesis the proviso that for psychoanalysis, sexual difference is *not* a phenomenal difference of this kind. In this sense, the ethical indifference to difference must remain in tension with the non-heterosexist iteration of the psychoanalytic position, which I fully endorse, that there are only two (psychical) sexes.[5]

Deathly Queer

One of the most radically negative and potentially universalising formulations of queerness can be found in the work of Lee Edelman, whose provocative *No Future: Queer Theory and the Death Drive* has been adopted, alongside Leo Bersani's writing,[6] as a linchpin of the so-called antisocial turn in queer theory writ large.

Although, officially, it aims to outline a negative political logic that moves beyond a merely oppositional stance, Edelman's version of queerness defines itself nonetheless against what he calls 'reproductive futurism'.[7] This phrase refers to an all-encompassing ideological framework which, in his view, draws for its libidinal support on a fantasy centred around the image of the child. For Edelman, the seductively conservative power of this image enforces the 'absolute privilege of heteronormativity', a privilege he views as the 'organizing principle of communal relations' (2). In other words, the child is the very horizon of meaning for social life as such.

Edelman's work as a whole mounts a ferocious attack against the 'family values' fetishisation of a certain construction of childhood as a time of pre-sexual innocence that paradoxically grounds the very possibility of the future. As monotheism does for the hereafter, this ideal of childhood installs the future as society's very raison d'être. Defining queerness as a kind of immanent resistance to the terms of a social life turned to the future in this sense, Edelman enjoins his queer-identified reader to resist the calls for positive alternatives that purely negative critical enterprises such as his own routinely come up against. Significantly, Edelman develops an interpretation of Freud's idea of the death drive to oppose any and all mobilisations of the category of 'the Good'. That is, Edelman bravely denies the basic premise that a politics must advocate for any positive social value or order whatsoever.

In my view, Edelman's development of the significance of the death drive is sound to the extent that the death drive and the terms that define the social world's intelligibility make up the terms of an antinomy. In other words, the unresolvable tension between the two terms exposes an underlying disjunction between the psychic and the social that can never be rejoined. Although the text demonstrates no awareness of the link, Edelman's insistence on society's inconsistency, on the constitutive inability of any social order to effect a gesture of absolute inclusion, covers the same theoretical ground on which Slavoj Žižek treads when he writes about what he calls political ontology's 'absent centre'.[8] Žižek develops this thematic in dialogue with the work of French post-Althusserians Alain Badiou, Étienne Balibar and Jacques Rancière.

Importantly, Edelman claims that queerness signals not merely the abjected outside of social arrangements – that is, those persons or groups who cannot be represented or remain unintelligible within an existing hegemonic field. This premise assumes that with a programme of expansive reform, for instance, queers could potentially be integrated with the existing social logic. Rather, Edelman claims for queerness a more radical negativity that exposes the inconsistency of the social as such. This negativity throws the very terms of the social into incoherence or disarray.

Now, any reader with even a cursory knowledge will have already remarked that Edelman's position runs against the tenets of the most fundamental assumptions of the socialist tradition in political thought. Indeed, the admirable doctrinal discipline with which Edelman restricts his argument's articulation to a purely negative mode seems designed to provoke or invite accusations of nihilism. Edelman's enlistment of psychoanalysis, and more specifically the work of Lacan, therefore poses an urgent question concerning the problematic relationship that inheres both historically and theoretically between the Freudian tradition and revolutionary socialist politics. In short, *No Future* implies that psychoanalytic theory is incompatible with any politics based on a sense of hope for a better future. In the rest of this section I will try to develop why I think this argument is wrong.

As Edelman uncompromisingly develops the concept, the death drive discredits by implication *all political thought*, to the extent that this thought remains wedded to an idea of the future attributed with teleological, narrative, redemptive or progressive qualities. To be sure – Edelman's training is literary, not philosophical – this thematic of futurism encompasses a broad cross-section of ideas of time that haven't always been associated with one another in the philosophical tradition.

Nonetheless, the concept is designed, none too subtly, to sweep away in a single gesture all thinking about time based on any of these four basic assumptions: (a) that time has a predetermined end; in other words, that the future will come to fruition at some definitive moment; (b) that time tells a story with, as they say, a beginning, a middle and an end; (c) that the future contains a transcendental horizon, which will bestow retrospective significance on past failures, on past suffering; and (d) that things can or will get better as time goes by. In sum, Edelman's discourse aims to 'refuse the insistence of hope itself as affirmation'. In his view, this insistence 'is always affirmation of an order whose refusal will register as unthinkable, irresponsible, inhumane' (4).

The problem with Edelman's position at the most fundamental level relates to its undialectical notion of a radically pure brand of negativity. Arguably, this version of the negative sees Edelman shirk responsibility for the content of his own argument. For example, Edelman denies the 'imperative to immure [his stance or argument] in some stable and positive *form*' (4). Now, Edelman understands Lacan's concept of 'the Symbolic' to mean that 'nothing, and certainly not what we call the "good", can ever have any assurance at all' (4). The difficulty lies not in the statement itself, but rather in Edelman's assumption that it isn't a position – in other words, an argument that's as much obliged to offer support for itself as any other. Edelman's radical negativity unhelpfully ignores the enunciative paradox that makes of the denial of the legitimacy of any statement as much of a statement as any positive assertion. Further, the argument makes the unnecessary assumption that any construct of 'the good' must be amenable to symbolic accommodation; that the normativity it prescribes must conservatively uphold a positive value, which could be articulated in the terms that constitute ambient social knowledge.

Like so much of the significantly American poststructuralist political hyperscepticism with which it shares its main features, Edelman's nihilistic attack makes the associated and fatal mistake of placing *all* allusions to the future in thought under the banner of what Lacan calls the imaginary. In other words, Edelman's discussion assumes that a retrograde belief in a time to come when all social antagonism, all conflict and dissatisfaction, all psychopathology has been eradicated, inheres *analytically*, as Kant would say, in the very concept of futurity. Edelman proceeds as if there's no other way to think about the future;

all this imaginary baggage comes unalterably pre-packaged whenever we attempt to think through what comes next.

By contrast, Lacan himself had a different and subtler way of conceiving of the subject's desiring relation to time's unfolding. In his Rome Discourse, for instance, Lacan emphasised the importance to psychoanalysis of the future perfect (*futur antérieur*), the verbal tense that looks back at the past from a hypothetical moment to come.[9] Clinically, the analysand looks forward to a time when its impenetrable symptom will have acquired an explanatory meaning, which in turn has an impact of the symptom's significance in the present. The future perfect also illuminates Freud's idea that the threat of castration has a period of latency: castration anxiety will only set in after the boy's perception of female lack has retrospectively provided the threat with a concrete, redoubtable consequence. In short, the present becomes what it is only from the retrospective point of view of a future moment, at which point, of course, it has itself become part of the past.

Lacan also developed in his teaching a related idea of logical time, premised on the notion that any act or utterance must be based on what he calls anticipated certitude. Somewhat analogously, this concept implies the projection into the future of a hypothetical certainty, which provides a fictitious rationale for one's intervention in the present.[10] In other words, we can only justify a present action on the assumption that some missing piece of knowledge will become available in the future to support our decision in the here-and-now.

For Lacan, psychoanalytic temporality's dependence on an irreducible reference, however projective, to the future is a consequence of time's mediation by language, by the signifier. Thus, Edelman's speculations about a queer present made possible by the radical negation of the future abstracts undesirably from the subject's circumscription by language – the very same 'symbolic', in other words, on which the rest of his argument fundamentally depends.

We can make the same point with reference to the psychoanalytic concept of the transference. From this perspective, Edelman's argument discounts the irreducibility of our transferential investment in the Other. As Lacan argued with his axiom *les non-dupes errent* (those who are not duped err), it's never a wise move to think that our knowledge and actions don't assume an unconscious belief in the Other's future consistency – the very same consistency that our intellectual arguments and rationalisations will insistently deny.

Simply put, Edelman's argument fails to take account of desire *in time*. Therefore, the absolute present he wishes to associate with queerness simply isn't possible. *Pace* Edelman, the future can be conceived with perfect legitimacy. But this is so only if our idea of the future takes the form of the past of a projected later moment. There is no guarantee that, at this later moment, things won't be significantly different than they are now; that a horizon-changing event might by that time have taken place.

Crucially for my own argument, psychoanalytic temporality is thus a temporality of discontinuity. This temporality features moments of disorienting and unthinkable, and therefore radical, change. Not only can this change be assessed only retroactively, but future events are likely to change that retroactive assessment in such a way that the meaning or significance of the past, even the most recent past, is constantly subject to change in light of later anticipated retroactive assessments. At any point in time, in other words, something can happen which, from the perspective of a later moment, will have literally changed the past.

Edelman's framework offers an ahistorical and metaphysical binary between the present insistence of the negative and the future aspiration for meaning. Alternatively, Lacan's logic of time formulates a *dialectic* between the symbolic order's contingent closure and this closure's inevitable failure. The fact that knowledge can only fail to think through the process of radical change – a thesis, by the way, with which Badiou takes issue – doesn't mean that change never happens. On the contrary, it implies the 'impossible' possibility that what, in a given situation, could never happen can indeed take place at any time.

In this sense, Edelman's argument expresses a paradoxical *idealism of the death drive*. It mistakenly assumes that human life can be lived 'purely' on this level; that language can be perfectly reduced to the nonsense of what Lacan called *lalangue*; that social life can be lived without the effects of an Other that imposes on human interaction not only a horizon of meaning, however contingent, imperfect, incomplete or anticipated, but also an ineradicable and unconscious transferential dimension of belief. As Žižek endlessly but instructively develops Lacan's thesis, the Other's powers of determination increase in direct proportion with the denial of our own complicity in its effective functioning.

But there's a further, even more central, difficulty in Edelman's discussion. This one is not only especially germane to the concerns of this book, but also typical of queer theory's characteristically ambivalent flirtation with, and ultimate dismissal of, the category of the universal. On one level, the link Edelman posits between the death drive and the antisocial aspect of queerness makes tangible a horizon of exceptionlessness: no matter what one's professed 'orientation', sexuality *as such* grossly oversteps the species function of reproduction. This thesis was already fully elaborated by Freud in *Beyond the Pleasure Principle* (1922), for example, and further developed through what Lacan calls *plus-de-jouir* (surplus enjoyment). On another level, however, Edelman's discussion is pitched against the conceptual couplet of heteronormativity and reproductive futurism. In consequence, his celebration of the apolitical value – or anti-value – of queerness only gains significance against the backdrop of the assumption of the effectiveness of a universe of normative heterosexuality or reproductive sexuality. This assumption is then drawn upon to attribute by specious opposition a minoritarian or vanguard edge to the queer.

Although it points in the direction of a place where everyone's sexuality can be defined as queer, Edelman's notion of queerness, like so many others, is ultimately reserved for an elite constituency whose members have violated, as he conceives them, the temporal terms of reproductive futurism. More concretely, we can presume that those homosexuals who have (or have adopted) children will not be issued membership cards, despite the fact that their sexualities, just as much as the Edelmanian queer's, overstep the bounds of what is required for species survival. In the end, Edelman's argument winds up embracing the ultimate poststructuralist fetish-values of difference and particularity. Edelman's 'no future' queerness fails the test of universality because its address retains an element of differential selectivity by pitting the breeders (and the other types of parent, even the 'queer' ones) against all the rest.

Juliet Mitchell argued over 40 years ago that the classical Marxist 'dissolution of the family' thesis *à la* Friedrich Engels – very different from Edelman's, of course – was both vague and unrealistic.

According to Engels, the emancipation of women is dependent on the absolute destruction of the family form. Mitchell argued instead for a politicisation of the historical forms of the family, recognising, in anticipation of her psychoanalytic vocation, that the passionate investment of many women in maternity and early childhood would never permit the creation of a feminist consensus in favour of a radically socialised post-family utopia.[11] Indeed, there's a strange underground complicity between the radical humanist anti-familialism of classical Marxism and the radically anti- or post-humanist anti-familialist nihilism of death drive queer theory.

By assuming the possibility of a zero-degree social life devoid of any form of the family whatsoever, these discourses lie vulnerable to the charge of idealism. By contrast, there's every reason to think that the proper socialist goal in this context should be to continue to broaden contemporary understandings of the family, and to provide women (and men) with the freedom to choose to take up early childhood parental responsibilities themselves, or else share them with regulated, adequately funded and collectively organised state institutions.[12] Although it's certainly a useful tool to wield against the ideologues of family values, Edelman's polemic against 'the Child' contributes precisely nothing to the accomplishment of this socialist goal.

Last but not least, it must also be said that the elitist minoritarianism of Edelman's discussion is based on a reductive misreading of Lacan's understanding of the universal. A consideration of this misreading will help to refine my criticism of Edelman's provocative and influential argument. It will also suggest an alternative interpretation of Lacanian psychoanalysis, which calls into question Edelman's attribution to it of apolitical and nihilistic consequences. And finally, my alternative consideration will present a more orthodox Lacanian idea of the unconscious, which lends itself to productive comparison with the *genericity* that characterises Badiou's idea of political subjectivity. In other words, this political subject is indifferent to (phenomenal) differences, including those that contemporary discourse links to the problematic of sexuality. In the final analysis, psychoanalysis is incompatible with the poststructuralist differentialism that informs Edelman's interpretation of it.

As we've already seen, Edelman's argument insists on the particularity of the subject of the unconscious. To support this view, he incorporates into his discussion an extended quote from Lacan's relatively well-known seminar on ethics. As he does elsewhere in his teaching, in this seminar Lacan links his concept of the subject to an idea of truth. In the passage Edelman extracts, Lacan associates this truth with the term *Wunsch*, which Freud uses to describe the unconscious wish that dreams, for instance, serve at once to express and to disguise.

Lacan's general point in the passage is that this wish is immune to the moral judgments imposed by the socially mediated ego, which upholds the 'civilised sexual morality' that the subject will interiorise by means of its specific social identifications. This is why Lacan qualifies the wish as 'irreducible', obeying not a 'universal', but rather 'the most particular of laws'.[13] Edelman takes Lacan's pronouncement to imply that this 'stubborn particularity' in the subject – there's no question that Lacan on one level emphasises the *Wunsch*'s 'abnormal' idiosyncrasy – 'voids every notion of a general good', in fact qualifying any reference to a 'positive social value' (6) as unjustified and unjustifiable.

Unfortunately, however, Edelman leaves the rest of the quoted passage from Lacan's seminar without comment. Although the *Wunsch*, Lacan continues, follows a particular law reflecting the ego of an individual subject, he insists that it is 'universal' nonetheless. Why? For the straightforward reason that 'this particularity is to be found in every human being' (6).

The logical flaw in Edelman's discussion lies in his undialectical assumption that an assertion of particularity automatically negates the validity of all constructions of universality. In other words, the category of the universal for Edelman must convey a positive predicate that applies to all the objects to which this category aspires to refer. By contrast, the quotation from Lacan reveals that the psychoanalyst has put into operation a different, properly negative, concept of universality, one which grounds, so to speak, the concept of the subject with the premise that all particular subjects share the same estrangement from themselves – an opacity with respect to their own desires. What is universal in subjectivity is that all subjects have in common the fact that they have mistakenly taken themselves to correspond with the markers of social identity with which they have chosen to affiliate.

There's a precise correspondence here with Badiou's concept of the subject as it relates to politics. In error, we map our subjectivities in accordance with the reference points of the hegemonic social values in circulation in a given situation of discourse. At any moment, however, an event can happen that will address itself to us not as individuals – individuals with this or that 'sexuality', for example – but rather as particular incarnations of a generic humanity. This event calls us to rerecognise ourselves, as it were, or perhaps to derecognise ourselves, as participants in the elaboration of the consequences of an evanescent truth. If we allow it, if we overcome our resistance to it, this truth – the truth of Lacan's unconscious *Wunsch*, the truth of Badiou's political event – will radically transform they way we perceive our relation to the social world.

What Comes After Queer Theory? Generic Immortality

The temporal dialectic that emerges out of psychoanalysis, and which we can now relate to Badiou's doctrine of the idea, contrasts sharply with the distinction we find in Edelman's work between an investment in the future and its nihilistic negation. The psychoanalytic position, initially developed by Freud, distinguishes rather between the finitude of ontogenetic or individual life – in other words, the 'natural' cycle of life and death – and the phylogenetic or infinite immortality of what I earlier called humanity's inhuman essence.

In simpler language, I refer here to the deathly persistence of life beyond the limits of (biological) life itself. Significantly, this irreducible dimension of human life beyond the Freudian pleasure principle is also presented by psychoanalysis as a *generic* attribute, one which straddles the otherwise unbridgeable chasm of sexual difference. Subjects on both sides of the sexuation divide are *equally* in excess of a merely animal self-preservative 'instinct', which fails to stop the living being from being capable of existing not for an ideal, but rather for an *idea*.

I'd like to argue in this final section that in its most valuable and provocative moments, queer theory discourse has tried to suggest an understanding of queerness that closely resembles this psycho-analytic-Badiouian thesis about a generic and immanent human immortality. Edelman's work represents one significant attempt to link what psychoanalysis understands by the death drive to the queer problematic. The problem, however, is that far from suggesting what Edelman elaborates under the 'no future' banner, the death drive introduces a realm we can describe in precisely opposite terms. Beyond Freud's pleasure principle, in other words, there lies not the nihilistic negation of any future for humanity whatsoever, but rather the emancipatory affirmation of humanity's excess over itself, an excess that is properly *eternal* in nature. If there's no future, in other words, it's because this future is not merely already (potentially) here, but also always has been, and always will be.

Now, the relatively recent and seemingly improbable ascendancy of interest in Badiou's work in Anglophone academic circles – secondary works and especially translations have now appeared in unprecedented number and with accelerating speed – is surely not unrelated to the remarkable clarity and single mindedness with which he mercilessly denounces the traitorous compromises and shameful rationalisa-tions of so much contemporary thought. Badiou accomplishes this amazing feat by developing an ambitious and breathtakingly original alternative to the endlessly recycled poststructuralist theoretical commonplaces of the past three or four decades, which seem to become all the more familiar and predictable the more emphatically a 'post' to poststructuralism is proclaimed. Because of hegemonic queer theory's impeccable poststructuralist credentials, the possibility presents itself to read Badiou's work as a critique of queer discourse's most deep-seated assumptions.

And yet, Badiou's philosophy amounts to more than a mere reaction to poststructuralist clichés. Indeed, it polemicises against what it seems to understand as a mostly German or Frankfurt notion of critique for offering no positive alternative. Systematically, Badiou subverts all the dominant motifs of late twentieth-century cultural theory: the all-encompassing text is ruptured by the unforeseeable event; the thick historicity of genealogical temporality (not to mention the queer-nihilist negation of any and all futurity) is halted by immanent emanations of the eternal; the heterogeneous relativism of an infinity of cultural systems is thrust aside as a self-evident banality in favour of politicised sameness and universality; the post-epistemological assault on knowledge succumbs to the heroic counterattack of truth; and the omnipresent discursive or social construction of reality is supplanted by a seemingly preposterous *mathematical* ontology. No, Badiou retorts to those irrational Heideggerians and their mystical cult of the pre-Socratics: to come closer to being you must read Plato and Georg

Cantor; learn about the immanentisation of infinity, not to mention the mathematically revolutionary invention of transfinite numbers and set theory.

The polemical frame of Badiou's recent major text *Logics of Worlds* elaborates an explicitly doctrinaire distinction between his own project – redescribed as a materialist dialectic – and what he calls democratic materialism, a rubric which, for heuristic purposes, can be rendered loosely in the Anglo-American theoretical idiom as 'French poststructuralism' – the very same poststructuralism that has decisively impacted elite queer theory. Badiou announces what he understands by democratic materialism with an axiom offered on the very first page of the book: 'There are only bodies and languages'.[14] The body in democratic materialism is the animal body that enjoys and suffers; that eats, defecates, makes love, and dies. It's a body stripped of all that which 'soul' and 'spirit' have suggested in the philosophical tradition; a machinic body of production weighed down by the factual, the pragmatic, the commercial.

For Badiou, a notion of naked life construed as survival or endurance becomes the supreme value in democratic materialism. It underscores a pernicious ideology of human rights. This ideology reduces humanity to its capacity to become victimised, marginalising in the process the human powers of creation and innovation. Further, the idea of naked or animal life nurtures a vacuous relativism, which imprisons human groups within the bounds of their culturally defined difference. The properly pathetic assumption at work here is that human accomplishment is limited to what can be envisaged within the parameters of traditional life-worlds. The rhetoric of tolerance fomented by this relativism fails to disguise a hypocritical totalitarianism: those who will not tolerate tolerance are obliterated by a potent mix of military power and international law.

For its part, language is less conspicuous in Badiou's evocation of democratic materialism. Yet, the dominant role played by structuralist linguistics and its subsequent deconstruction in Anglo-American literary and cultural theory, combined with the (to some extent) analogous influence of ideas of language on twentieth-century philosophical discourses – both 'analytic' and 'continental' – makes plain the strange exoticism of Badiou's recourse to the history of mathematics to support the weight of his philosophical project.

Badiou's mathematical ontology, together with the formal logical language he elaborates in the view of founding a radically non-subjective study of the realm of appearances – a phenomenology, in that precise sense – even calls into question the relation of his project to psychoanalysis, and more specifically to Lacanian psychoanalysis. This remains the case despite two facts: first, that Badiou will routinely, and quite performatively, name Lacan as one of his 'masters'; and second, that Lacan himself invokes the language of mathematics, although not without ambivalence, as the 'ideal' for his own intervention into the fraught legacy of Freud. At any rate, the valorisation of logical and mathematic 'language' in both Badiou and Lacan puts welcome pressure on the virtually universal queer assumption concerning the embeddedness of sexuality in language or discourse – that is, in the construction and deconstruction of meaning.

Both the poststructuralist discourse on language and the language of 'discourse' in Foucault's sense of the term commit two mortal sins for Badiou – pun fully intended. First, they privilege the realms of language-signification (*il n'y a pas de hors-texte*) and discourse-power (biopolitics) over the disruptive and exceptional event. Not only does the event break radically with both language and discourse in these precise senses. Also, the event, potentially, grants us properly subjective access to a truth both eternal and universal in its address.

Second, poststructuralist language-discourse has the perhaps counterintuitive tendency to reduce the human being to 'life', a life which must remain ignorant of the immortal excess that defines humanity for Badiou, as it does for psychoanalysis. This excess is what makes the human being capable of *persevering* through an act of faith in the invigorating promise of an idea. To be sure, this perseverance can persist beyond the limit that defends the value of self-preservation. The essence, as it were, of humanity is therefore not its merely animal attributes – its various physiological and sexual needs; its physical and psychological vulnerabilities; its appurtenance to the laws of nature – but rather a properly immortal supplement, which life itself can't account for. In other words, a human life is fully capable of holding on to forms of being that don't register in life's own terms. Badiou affirms a subjectivity that can cling to their truth and trace their points of consequence more than it clings, as one says, to life itself.

This idea of an immortal essence in the human by which the human can immanently transcend itself is hardly new. Badiou traces it to Plato's eternal ideas. But it also, very conspicuously, characterises numerous religious traditions, including of course Christianity. Badiou's discourse on immortality can helpfully be read as a materialist and explicitly atheist (as opposed to secular) reinterpretation of theological discourses about eternal life. Pascal, for example, developed the idea that one can be reborn in faith for all eternity in the here-and-now; that resurrection is something that happens before you die.

Although the Christian motif of rebirth has been appropriated by conservative and fundamentalist sects, which function more or less as profit-driven corporations, the idea is surely too valuable to abandon to the reactionaries. Indeed, the transformative experience of resubjectivation developed in Badiou's philosophy teaches precisely the same lesson taught by the subtractive, de-individuating, and incorporative message articulated by Paul in the earliest days of Christianity. Lacan, too, oriented his teaching around an idea of the subjectivating effects of an inhuman, transpersonal cause (*la cause freudienne*), effectively inviting his followers to devote their lives to it.

In the psychoanalytic literature, the most consequential meditation on the uncanny complexities of life and death is surely *Beyond the Pleasure Principle* (1920). In this text, Freud makes a heroic attempt to come to terms with this immortal and inhuman essence of humanity. Two years after the end of the Great War's unspeakable carnage, the psyche's insistent revisitation of unpleasurable experiences had become all too evident to anyone involved with the care of returning military personnel.

Traumatic neurosis, but also and primarily the transference neuroses, and then finally primary masochism and its conversion to sadism, all convinced Freud that the pleasure reference will never suffice to define the human subject. Enlisted for the organism's self-preservation, what Freud called ego libido runs up against an object-oriented drive. This latter variety of libido is the one which, for Freud, compels the organism onto the terrain of what we commonly understand as sexuality. Of course, this sexuality can result in reproduction, but also, not uncommonly in the broadest historical and epidemiological terms, in death. At the heart of life, then, Freud discovers the antinomy of individual life and species life: sexual reproduction – that is to say, species immortality – comes at the cost of the individual organism's longevity. This remains the case across the broadest range of natural or biological life, to which Freud, on this level at least, considered humanity to belong.

The life and death antinomy in Freud's text is informed by the work of late nineteenth-century German evolutionary biologist August Weismann. It was Weismann who argued that living substance is divided on the cellular level between a mortal soma (body) and an immortal 'germ-plasm'. Clearly, Freud saw a connection to his own distinction between death instincts and life instincts. In the end, however, Freud breaks from Weismann's thesis. He couldn't agree with the biologist's contention that since unicellular organisms, innocent of the soma/germ-plasm split, must be immortal, death comes late onto the scene of evolutionary history, and is therefore not inherent in life as such.

Like his theories of sexuality and sexual difference, then, Freud's theory of the death instinct is explicitly offered as an alternative to the properly biological understandings available in the early twentieth century. This remains the case despite the complicating fact that Freud also expressed hope that a biological explanation for the death instinct might one day be discovered. *Beyond the Pleasure Principle* struggles towards the conclusion that the paradoxically deathly immortal kernel of humanity is disjoined from any biological or evolutionary function. Viewed as the traumatic insistence of senseless jouissance, of the body's ceaseless bombardment of the mind with (representations of) an excessive and purposeless libidinal excitation, death not only inheres in life *as such*, but also defiantly resists rendering as a horizon of meaning of any moral, evolutionary or even biological nature.

Lacan draws attention to these paradoxes of Freud's discourse on death in the same Rome Discourse I referred to above. In this text, Lacan further develops the psychoanalytic commentary on the properly biological definition of life. Specifically, Lacan elaborates on the notion that life and death entertain what he calls a 'polar relation' – a relation of interdependency, that is – in the very midst of biological phenomena that have been understood rather to *distinguish* life from death.[15]

To support this idea, Lacan refers to the origin of modern biological science in the late eighteenth-century work of Marie-François-Xavier

Bichat. Quite simply, Bichat defined life as the set of vital forces that resist death. Hardly unlike Freud with his idea of *Eros*, Harvard physiologist Walter Bradford Cannon refined this definition in the early 1930s by associating life with the principle of homeostasis, which he viewed as a general vital function in the organism that regulates its own physiological equilibrium. Lacan takes these examples from classical biology and physiology to support an explicitly dialectical understanding according to which life can't be conceived without positing an opposing force that tries to thwart it. Referencing Heidegger, Lacan qualifies this deathly force as 'a possibility' which is 'absolutely proper, unconditional, unsurpassable, certain, and as such indeterminate [*indéterminée*]' for the subject defined in its historicity. Lacan summarises his point by describing Freud's death 'instinct' as 'the limit of the historical function of the subject' (261–2).

It's clear that Lacan enlists these authorities in the biological and physiological sciences to buttress Freud's basic notion about duelling forces of life and death in the human organism. However, he adds a crucial distinction. Modern science situates death's resistance to life in the biologically conceived organism itself, defining this resistance as a disruptive counterprinciple weaved into the fibre of humanity's natural being. To develop an alternative psychoanalytic approach to the problem, Lacan returns to Freud's concept of repetition. For Lacan, death isn't a properly biological function of the organism. Death, rather, with its associated 'drive', is a consequence of the living being's subjection to language, to the signifier. When he plays that famous game with the cotton reel, working through the mother's traumatic absence with the help of a primordial and binary signifying structure (*fort-da*), the infant gains a modicum of mastery over nature by 'murdering the thing' (319). Also, he commits his destiny to the workings of a symbolic order that will forever exceed the limitations of his conscious knowledge.

Already by 1953, Lacan had recognised in the subject's subjection to the symbol something he called the 'eternalization' (319) of this subject's desire. In choosing this word, Lacan didn't wish merely to qualify desire as incessant and inexhaustible, although it certainly possesses both of those qualities. More radically, he meant to say that desire, on the level of what he calls its real, immanently lifts the subject out of the constraints of life; separates this subject from the chronological and teleological historicity of human time. For Lacan, desire accomplishes this not by negating the future, as Edelman would have it, but rather by affirming a sort of background or underground non-temporality – eternity, in other words. In this way, Lacan introduces a crucial distinction between phenomenal time – not just chronological time, but also lived time, Bergsonian *durée* – and the non-time of desire's real. As Freud said about negation, time doesn't exist in the unconscious.

But Lacan goes even further. Our apparent enslavement to the signifier, in other words the signifier's deathly traversal of human biological life, emancipates us from the Other's – the master's – desire. This is so because the master's menace of death will fall on deaf ears in the being who chooses to 'enjoy the fruits of its servitude' (320).

It's perhaps in this decidedly Hegelian mode that Lacan's discourse, unexpectedly perhaps, approaches most suggestively Badiou's concept of immortality. Desire in its most radical form, the real of desire that delivers us onto the threshold of the drive, discloses that 'life' in all it implies by way of compromise, accommodation, conformity, adaptation, equilibrium, reconciliation, isn't everything. It's *not-all*, we could say, in reference to the logic of feminine being.

In this context, the master is the subject who defines and upholds the terms of life; separates what can legitimately be lived from what is condemned to deathly nonexistence. Lacan's Hegelian message is that the master's definition of life is binding only for the subject who fails, as it were, to read between the lines. Despite what it incessantly tells you, life need neither be swallowed whole, nor taken on its own terms. As long as you aren't put off by its deathly look, there most decidedly *is* 'more to life than this'.

Despite the considerable differences that distinguish their discourses, Lacan and Badiou equally aim to subvert the understanding that limits what we view life to be to the level of the ordinary or the everyday. This is the understanding that considers life the stuff of unexceptional, workaday experience, governed by the logic of what merely appears. Such a life is necessarily complicit with the varieties of production that can only reproduce the status quo. At a variety of points in their work, both thinkers distinguish where they locate their privileged concepts – the real for Lacan, being and the event for Badiou – from the dimensions of opinion, commerce, representation, ideology, spectacle or even politics understood as a popular or consensual good.

Both thinkers have been similarly reproached for nurturing a sort of neo-aristocratic ideal of heroic exceptionalism. Terry Eagleton, for example, has sceptically quipped that Badiou's idea of love refers to something that can only happen on the romantic streets of Paris.[16] Yet Lacan and Badiou insist, in their respective idioms, that the privileged realm they seek to define is accessed neither through some humanistic or intentional exercise of will, nor through some gesture of sacrifice, abnegation or renunciation. Most crucially, access to this realm requires no specific qualities of status, personhood or subjectivity.

To be sure, the 'point by point' development of the consequences of a truth in Badiou, or else the refusal to give way on one's desire in Lacan, necessitate something like work or effort, something other than pure abandonment to a will or power in the realm of alterity. But, on another level, the event as such, or the (missed) encounter with the real, simply *happen*: their occurrence is on one level utterly indifferent to what this or that person might make of them. Indeed, Lacan and Badiou share the anti-humanist view that when it comes to what should be done – ethics, that is – remaining open to the encounter with the real, or the maintenance of fidelity to a truth, have the effect of wrenching oneself from oneself, of subverting personhood and identity by subtracting the subjective function from its circumscription by what partakes, ideologically, of meaning or sense.

The subject is therefore a privileged category for both Lacan and Badiou. This subject is neither the humanist subject of intentional consciousness, nor the liberal subject of rational self-interest. Lacan's subject is of course the subject of the unconscious; a subject disjoined from knowledge and re/presentation. That the Lacanian subject is 'what a signifier represents for another signifier' can be derived analytically from Lacan's elementary definition of the signifier.[17] For Badiou, the subject is derived from that feature of the human being that's capable of remaining faithful to a procedure of truth. Individual selfhood – including in particular the attachment to what Freud, after British anthropologist Ernest Crawley, called the 'narcissism of small differences'[18] – is precisely what blocks us from the kind of authentic subjectivation to which both psychoanalysis and Badiou's philosophy aspire. Lacan's Antigone embraces death as an escape from an intolerable world that forbids her from acknowledging her brother's fate. Badiou's subject, transported by passion for a scientific, political, artistic or amorous idea, pursues that idea in a way that grants emancipation from the constraints and compromises of worldly self-interest.

The human condition presents us – individually, as it were – with a choice in regard to which we don't have the luxury of remaining indifferent, sitting on the fence. Essentially, we must choose not between life and death, but rather between life and *immortality*. Agnosticism is mere self-deception. Life means existence on the level of the ordinary functioning of sociosymbolic relations, or the mundane and opinion-based democratic negotiation of antagonistic sets of interests. In other words, life is accommodation and conformity. By contrast, immortality requires a partisan commitment to pursue desire to the point where the law becomes suspended; to remain faithful to the real of the Idea and the transformative consequences it presents to the world in which it intervenes. But if the choice before us is between life and immortality, what becomes of death?

The death drive is deathly, destructive, pathological, only for the neurotic subject of psychoanalysis and the reactive subject of Badiou's philosophy. These are the pseudo-subjects who resist – set up defences against – the encounter with enjoyment, with the real of the event in any of its manifestations. It's only from the defensive, ego-predicated perspective of life – this term, even more than 'democracy', is perhaps the most ideologically loaded term of the day – that death appears as the end, as the limit beyond which there might be, but maybe not, another, better world.

In truth, death needn't be the end. It needn't cause us to proclaim, with confident nihilism, that there's no future. Rather, death is the name of the infinity of immanent gateways that open up onto the threshold of an always-present arena of immortality open to everyone, without exception, on the other side of the queer horizon's ambivalent and exhausted impasse.

Notes

Introduction

1. For historical accounts of Stonewall and its contexts, which take into consideration the link to the socialist tradition, see John D'Emilio, *Sexual Politics, Sexual Communities: The Making of a Homosexual Minority in the United States, 1940–1970*, 2nd ed. (Chicago: University of Chicago Press, 1998); and Martin Duberman, *Stonewall* (New York: Penguin, 1994). For an example of recent work on the homosexuality question from the American socialist left, see Sherry Wolf, *Sexuality and Socialism: History, Politics and Theory of LGTB Liberation* (Chicago: Haymarket Books, 2004).
2. For an example of the former, see Donald E. Hall, *Queer Theories* (London: Palgrave Macmillan, 2002). For an example of the latter, see Rebecca Beirne, ed., *Televising Queer Women: A Reader*, 2nd ed. (London: Palgrave Macmillan, 2012).
3. See in particular Janet Halley and Andrew Parker, eds, *After Sex? On Writing Since Queer Theory* (Durham, NC: Duke University Press, 2011); and David M. Halperin and Valerie Traub, eds, *Gay Shame* (Chicago: University of Chicago Press, 2010).
4. Much of this last tendency can be traced back to the influence of Leo Bersani's work, in particular his important book *Homos* (Cambridge, MA: Harvard University Press, 1995).
5. Freud develops these contentions in *Three Essays on the Theory of Sexuality, The Standard Edition of the Complete Psychological Works of Sigmund Freud*, vol. 7 (London: Hogarth Press, 1953–1974), pp. 125–248.
6. Iain Morland and Annabelle Willox, eds, *Queer Theory* (London: Palgrave Macmillan, 2004), p. 4.
7. A truth is 'indifferent to differences', writes Badiou; 'the same for all'. *Ethics: An Essay on the Understanding of Evil* (London: Verso, 2002), p. 27. I further relate Badiou's deployment of the category of the universal to the queer problematic in this book's last chapter.
8. I consider in detail Lee Edelman's *No Future: Queer Theory and the Death Drive* (Durham, NC: Duke University Press, 2004) in this book's conclusion.

Chapter 1

1. The former phrase was introduced in Adrienne Rich, 'Compulsory Heterosexuality and Lesbian Existence', *Blood, Bread, and Poetry* (New York: Norton, 1994); the latter in Judith Butler, *Gender Trouble: Feminism and the Subversion of Identity* (New York: Routledge, 2006 [1990]).
2. Iain Morland and Annabelle Willox, eds, *Queer Theory* (London: Palgrave Macmillan, 2004), p. 3. Further references are incorporated into the text.

3. I discuss the psychoanalytic idea of sexual difference in the context of the Lacanian clinical work broaching male homosexuality in Chapter 5.

4. This is the subtitle of one of the sessions of Lacan's *The Four Fundamental Concepts of Psycho-Analysis* (London: Norton, 1998), pp. 149–60.

5. See for example Grosz, *Volatile Bodies: Toward a Corporeal Feminism* (Bloomington, IN: Indiana University Press, 1994).

6. Sarah Ahmed, 'Orientations: Toward a Queer Phenomenology', *GLQ: A Journal of Lesbian and Gay Studies* 12.4 (2006): 543–74, p. 543. Further references to this article are incorporated into the text. This essay appears in expanded form in Ahmed, *Queer Phenomenology: Orientations, Objects, Others* (Durham, NC: Duke University Press, 2006).

7. See my '"You never look at me from where I see you": Postcolonial Guilt in *Caché*', *New Formations* 70 (Winter 2011): 77–93.

8. Lacan, 'The Line and Light', *The Four Fundamental Concepts*, pp. 91–104.

9. See, for example, *Bodies that Matter: On the Discursive Limits of 'Sex'* (London: Routledge, 1993), pp. 12–16.

10. Bawer develops his conservative but anti-minoritarian argument in *A Place at the Table: The Gay Individual in American Society* (New York: Poseidon Press, 1993).

11. Oddly, Ahmed goes on to acknowledge, without providing an explanation, that Bawer's anti-anti-assimilationist strategy might provide the basis for 'a new angle on queer politics' (569). She does this, however, without retracting her allegation that this strategy amounts to a normalising and regressive project of 'assimilationism' (568). It would seem that the onus is on Ahmed to go one way or the other.

12. Simone de Beauvoir famously develops this argument, laying blame at the feet of both the patriarchy and women's narcissistic complicity in their own victimisation. See *The Second Sex*, trans. Constance Borde and Sheila Malovany-Chevallier (New York: Vintage, 2011).

13. A member of the so-called antisocial wave of queer theory, Halberstam's argument can be found in her book *In A Queer Time and Place: Transgender Bodies, Subcultural Lives* (New York: New York University Press, 2005), pp. 152–3.

14. Deleuze and Guattari write about lines of flight in their development of the concept of the rhizome in *A Thousand Plateaus: Capitalism and Schizophrenia* (London: Continuum, 2001), pp. 9–10.

15. See the section 'The Minoritarian Temptation' in my *The World of Perversion: Psychoanalysis and the Impossible Absolute of Desire* (Albany, NY: State University of New York Press, 2006), pp. 184–90.

16. See Foucault, 'The Repressive Hypothesis', in *The History of Sexuality: An Introduction* (New York: Vintage, 1990), pp. 17–49.

17. Sedgwick, 'Melanie Klein and the Difference Affect Makes', in Janet Halley and Andrew Parker, eds, *After Sex? On Writing Since Queer Theory* (Durham, NC: Duke University Press, 2011), p. 293. Further references to this essay in that volume are incorporated into the text.

18. I follow Slavoj Žižek in choosing this term over the alternative 'symptomatic', rendered vague through misapplication and overuse. 'Symptomal' as I use it refers to the dissimulated enjoyment that supports

a sociosymbolic identification by paradoxically violating or transgressing the ideal it upholds. To take a classic example, the thematic of freedom and democracy in American foreign policy has been unofficially, although not so secretly, accompanied by direct military support of anti-democratic tyrants in Latin America, Africa, West Asia and beyond.

19. Agamben's development of the biopower concept can be found in *Homo Sacer: Sovereign Power and Bare Life* (Stanford, CA: Stanford University Press, 1998).

20. Puar, *Terrorist Assemblages: Homonationalism in Queer Times* (Durham, NC: Duke University Press, 2007), p. xviii. Further references are incorporated into the text.

21. Puar quotes from Kaplan's article 'Violent Belongings and the Question of Empire Today: Presidential Address to the American Studies Association, October 17, 2003', *American Quarterly* 56.1 (March 2004): 1–18.

22. See Agamben's *State of Exception* (Chicago: University of Chicago Press, 2005).

Chapter 2

1. '(Queer) Theory and the Universal Alternative', *diacritics* 32.2 (Summer 2002): 1–18. I should add that after seven years of Tory rule under the reprehensible Stephen Harper, it's become significantly more difficult to direct that smug, nation-defining look southward from Canada.

2. I single out Laclau and Mouffe in acknowledgment of the centrality of their *Hegemony and Socialist Strategy: Towards a Radical Democratic Politics* (New York: Verso, 1985) to the realignment of Marxist discourse in response to late twentieth-century social change. Further references are incorporated into the text.

3. 'Themselves' *and* ourselves, I should add, since I see no other way to describe my relation to the phenomenon under discussion.

4. See *Anti-Oedipus: Capitalism and Schizophrenia* (Minneapolis: University of Minnesota Press, 1983). I discuss Deleuze and Guattari's impact on Guy Hocquenghem's work in Chapter 4.

5. In his fascinating, career-assessing dialogues with Castro, Ignacio Ramonet poses the question of 'repressive behaviour against homosexuals' in the early days of the Cuban revolution. In his answer, Castro explains that there were three categories of persons who weren't called up for military service in those vulnerable days, one of which was homosexuals. As an alternative to military service, these persons were sent to work in UMAPs (*Unidades Militares de Ayuda a la Producción*). 'I can guarantee you that there was no persecution of homosexuals', Castro says, 'or internment camps for homosexuals'. He adds that 'machismo was an element that was very much present in our society, and there was still widespread rejection of the idea of homosexuals serving in military units'. The exemption of homosexuals from military service exacerbated homophobic prejudice in Cuba at the time. See Fidel Castro (with Ignacio Ramonet), *My Life* (London: Penguin, 2008), pp. 222–3.

6. For detailed analysis of key exceptions to this rule, see Chapter 3. One can further mention Rosa Luxemburg, Clara Zetkin, Alexandra Kollontai and Herbert Marcuse; and from among those still writing, Jonathan Dollimore, Teresa Ebert, Danae Clark, Toril Moi, John d'Emilio and David Horowitz.

7. See Butler, 'Arguing with the Real', *Bodies that Matter: On the Discursive Limits of 'Sex'* (New York: Routledge, 1993), pp. 187–222.

8. Judith Butler, Ernesto Laclau and Slavoj Žižek, *Contingency, Hegemony, Universality: Contemporary Dialogues on the Left* (London: Verso, 2000), p. 49. Further references are incorporated into the text.

9. Laclau and Mouffe wrote, for example, that 'the basic obstacle [to the left's capacity for action and political analysis] has been classism: that is to say, the idea that the working class represents the privileged agent in which the fundamental impulse of social change resides' (77). I'm hardly the first to suggest that, rather than simply discard the concept of the working class, we should work towards the delineation of the socioeconomic transformations under late capitalism that have changed its content, in particular the explosion of casual service labour. To be retained is the basic Marxian assumption that the most objectively *potentially* revolutionary constituency is the one most concretely disenfranchised in a given social formation. The question then becomes: what is the socioeconomic content, at the present historical juncture, of the concept 'working class'?

10. Introduced in 1999 during Socialist Lionel Jospin's presidency, PACS is an acronym for *Pacte civil de solidarité*, a legal union which, since its introduction, has been revised to approximate more closely the terms of civil marriage. Inequalities exist still in the areas of the sharing of social benefits and the rights of partners of the deceased. My point, however, relates rather to the very need for a separate legal category for homosexual marriage. The closer the content of the two forms becomes, the more their continued separate existence gains in absurdity.

11. Butler, *Antigone's Claim: Kinship between Life and Death* (New York: Columbia University Press, 2000), p. 2. Further references are incorporated into the text.

12. I offer a more detailed analysis of Lacan's reading of *Antigone* via Freud's theory of hysteria, Kant's analytic of the beautiful and Sade's conception of crime in 'The Guardian of Criminal Being', *The World of Perversion: Psychoanalysis and the Impossible Absolute of Desire* (Albany: State University of New York Press, 2006), pp. 139–72.

13. *The Seminar of Jacques Lacan, Book 7. The Ethics of Psychoanalysis*, ed. Jacques-Alain Miller (New York: Norton, 1992), p. 283, my emphasis.

14. I deliberately avoid the term 'sex-positive', which implies quite nonsensically that one can choose a position on sex, no pun intended, for or against.

15. Of course, I don't mean to say that so-called advanced societies have eliminated sexual violence. My point is rather that we too often forget that in many parts of the world, sex is lived in a general sense *as violence*, from cultural contexts that normalise the most radical forms of female circumcision to military occupations, such as the American one in Iraq or

the Israeli one in the West Bank, that institutionalise forms of sexualised torture and humiliation.

Chapter 3

1. I'm thinking in particular of such figures as Dennis Altman, Martin Duberman and John D'Emilio.
2. Ebert, *Ludic Feminism and After: Postmodernism, Desire and Labor in Late Capitalism* (Ann Arbor: University of Michigan Press, 1996).
3. Butler, 'Gender is Burning: Questions of Appropriation and Subversion', *Bodies that Matter: On the Discursive Limits of 'Sex'* (London: Routledge, 1993), pp. 121–42.
4. Foucault, *The History of Sexuality: An Introduction* (New York: Vintage Books, 1990), pp. 17–35. Further references are incorporated into the text.
5. See my *The World of Perversion: Psychoanalysis and the Impossible Absolute of Desire* (Albany: State University of New York Press, 2006), pp. 2–10.
6. See, for example, Chrysanthi Nigianni and Merl Storr, eds, *Deleuze and Queer Theory* (Edinburgh: University of Edinburgh Press, 2009).
7. Marcuse, 'The Conquest of the Unhappy Consciousness: Repressive Desublimation', *One-Dimensional Man: Studies in the Ideology of Advanced Industrial Society* (London: Routledge Classics, 2002), pp. 59–86.
8. Freud, 'Civilized Sexual Morality and Modern Nervous Illness', *The Standard Edition of the Complete Psychological Works of Sigmund Freud*, vol. 9 (London: Hogarth Press, 1953–1974). For a presentation of the Lacanian approach, see Todd McGowan, *The End of Dissatisfaction? Jacques Lacan and the Emerging Society of Enjoyment* (Albany: State University of New York Press, 2004).
9. Floyd, *The Reification of Desire: Toward a Queer Marxism* (London: University of Minnesota Press, 2009), p. 7. Further references are incorporated into the text.
10. A version of this paper appeared in *New Left Review* 227 (Jan–Feb 1998).
11. I further develop this last point in the final section of this chapter.
12. See Chapter 1 for a detailed discussion of Laclau and Mouffe and the post-Marxist current in political theory.
13. Henry Abelove, Michele Ana Barale and David M. Halperin, eds, *The Gay and Lesbian Studies Reader* (London: Routledge, 1993).
14. Morton, *The Material Queer: A Lesbigay Cultural Studies Reader* (Boulder, CO: Westview Press, 1996), p. 1. Further references are incorporated into the text.
15. Sedgwick, *Epistemology of the Closet* (Berkeley: University of California Press, 1990), p. 1.
16. See 1917 Collective, 'Capitalism and Homophobia: Marxism and the Struggle for Gay/Lesbian Rights', *The Material Queer*, pp. 369–79.
17. I take up this argument's significance for the end of queer theory in this book's conclusion.

18. Mieli, *Homosexuality and Liberation: Elements of a Gay Critique* (London: Gay Men's Press, 1980), p. 208. Further references are incorporated into the text.

19. Lane, 'Mieli's Transsexual Aesthetic'. I'm grateful to the author for providing me with the unpublished original English-language version of his paper.

20. I provide my own detailed discussion of these Freudian concepts in the context of a reading of Guy Hocquenghem's work in the next chapter.

21. Nina Power insightfully develops this notion for materialist feminism in her provocative and important *One-Dimensional Woman* (London: O Books, 2009).

22. See Zupančič, 'Addendum: On Love and Comedy', *The Shortest Shadow: Nietzsche's Philosophy of the Two* (Cambridge, MA: MIT Press, 2003), pp. 164–82.

Chapter 4

1. This is not to say that Hocquenghem's text has had a deep impact on sexuality theory in France. Indeed, it has long since been out of print in the original French.

2. As developed in this book's introduction, by poststructuralist queer theory I broadly refer to what's become the dominant stream of contemporary sexuality theory in the English-speaking world, as elaborated by such figures as Eve Kosofsky Sedgwick, Judith Butler and David Halperin, for example. Though this discourse is far from monolithic, it features a number of common assumptions, the most important of which is the idea that sexuality is a construction of discourse and/or power. I discuss in detail how Hocquenghem's view contrasts with the poststructuralist line in the following paragraphs.

3. Hocquenghem, *Homosexual Desire* (Durham, NC: Duke University Press, 1993), p. 73. Further references are incorporated into the text.

4. Sedgwick, *Epistemology of the Closet* (Berkeley: University of California Press, 1990), p. 1. Further references are incorporated into the text.

5. Marshall, *Guy Hocquenghem: Theorizing the Gay Nation* (London: Pluto Press, 1996), p. 6.

6. Deleuze and Guattari, *Anti-Oedipus: Capitalism and Schizophrenia* (Minneapolis: University of Minnesota Press, 1983), p. 27n. Further references are incorporated into the text.

7. Lacan, 'The Subversion of the Subject and the Dialectic of Desire in the Freudian Unconscious', *Écrits*, trans. Bruce Fink (New York: Norton, 2006), p. 689.

8. Gary Genosko's edited volume *The Guattari Reader* (Oxford: Blackwell, 1996) informatively develops the impact of antipsychiatry on Guattari's writing and clinical practice.

9. For a development of this argument, see Russell Jacoby's classic study *Social Amnesia: A Critique of Contemporary Psychology* (New Brunswick, NJ: Transaction, 1997 [1975]).

10. Freud, 'Repression' (1915), *The Standard Edition of the Complete Psychological Works of Sigmund Freud*, vol. 14 (London: Hogarth Press, 1953–1974), p. 152. Further references are incorporated into the text.

11. Freud, 'On Narcissism: An Introduction' (1914), *SE* vol. 14, p. 94. Further references are incorporated into the text.

12. See in particular the concluding 'Summary' of Freud's *Three Essays on the Theory of Sexuality* (1905–1925), *SE* vol. 7, pp. 231–43.

13. Lacan, 'The Four Fundamental Concepts of Psycho-Analysis' (London: Norton, 1998), pp. 165–6.

14. Lacan, *The Seminar of Jacques Lacan, Book XVII. The Other Side of Psychoanalysis* (London: Norton, 2007), p. 89.

Chapter 5

1. In particular, see Butler, 'Arguing with the Real', *Bodies that Matter: On the Discursive Limits of 'Sex'* (New York: Routledge, 1993), pp. 187–222.

2. See Salecl, ed. *Sexuation* (Durham, NC: Duke University Press, 2000); Joël Dor, *Structure et perversions* (Paris: Denoël, 1987); and Jean Clavreul, *Le désir et la loi* (Paris: Denoël, 1987). For my book review response to the Salecl edited volume, see *Psychoanalysis, Culture and Society* 6.1 (Spring 2001): 151–4.

3. Dean, *Beyond Sexuality* (Chicago: University of Chicago Press, 2000), p. 267. Further references are incorporated into the text.

4. Lacan, 'The Signification of the Phallus', *Écrits*, trans. Bruce Fink (New York: Norton, 2006), p. 576.

5. Lacan, *Encore: The Seminar of Jacques Lacan, Book XX*, trans. Bruce Fink (New York: Norton, 1999), p. 71.

6. Indeed, if we consider Eve Kosofsky Sedgwick's *Epistemology of the Closet* (Berkeley: University of California Press, 1990) to be one of its foundational texts, queer theory's very origins are marked by the censorship of this question, its relegation to a zone safely out of bounds (40–1). When the politicisation of sexuality reaches the point where it explicitly discourages intellectual interrogation for fear of phobic appropriation, it has, in my view, gone too far. Over two decades since the publication of Sedgwick's text, anti-homophobic criticism has surely reached a state of maturity at which resistance to such facile political posturing is no longer subject to accusations of 'internalised homophobia' and complicity with heterosexism.

7. Serge André, *L'Imposture perverse* (Paris: Le Seuil, 1993), p. 33. Further references are incorporated into the text. All translations are my own; the original French is provided in brackets when helpful.

8. Freud, 'Fetishism' (1927), *The Standard Edition of the Complete Psychological Works of Sigmund Freud*, vol. 21, ed. and trans. James Strachey et. al. (London: Hogarth Press, 1953–1974), p. 154.

9. As Lacan writes in 'The Signification of the Phallus', 'the fact that femininity finds its refuge in this mask [which "dominates the identifications in which refusals of demand are resolved"] by virtue of the fact of the *Verdrängung* inherent in the phallic mark of desire, has the curious

consequence of making virile display in the human being itself seem feminine' (291).

10. Bersani, *Homos* (Cambridge: Harvard University Press, 1996), p. 131. Further references are incorporated into the text.
11. Freud, 'The Dissolution of the Oedipus Complex', *SE* vol. 19, p. 178.
12. See Puar, *Terrorist Assemblages: Homonationalism in Queer Times* (Durham, NC: Duke University Press, 2007). I consider this text in detail in Chapter 1.
13. Lacan, *The Four Fundamental Concepts*, pp. 272–3. I develop an extended discussion of the significance of Lacan's distinction between the two terms in *The Structures of Love: Art and Politics beyond the Transference* (Albany: State University of New York Press, 2012).

Chapter 6

1. Freud, Fragment of an Analysis of a Case of Hysteria (1905), *The Standard Edition of the Complete Psychological Works of Sigmund Freud*, vol. 7, (London: Hogarth Press, 1953–1974), p. 60.
2. 'It is a great injustice to persecute homosexuality as a crime, and cruelty too', wrote Freud, who goes on to cite the additional approving authority of Havelock Ellis. See 'Letter to an American Mother', *American Journal of Psychiatry* 107 (1951): 787.
3. Lacan, 'Proposition de 67', *Autres écrits* (Paris: Seuil, 2001), p. 247. The assumption is that the subject concerned is in fact an analyst, which – 'analytically' as it were – assumes the experience of having been analysed.
4. Badiou, *Saint Paul: The Foundation of Universalism* (Stanford, CA: Stanford University Press, 2003), p. 9.
5. It should be noted that despite his emphasis on the banality of difference, sexual difference also figures in Badiou's thought, and should therefore be considered a *different* difference in his work as well. For example, see his article 'What is Love?', *Umbr(a): A Journal of the Unconscious* (1996): 37–53.
6. See, most significantly, Bersani's *Homos* (Cambridge, MA: Harvard University Press, 1995).
7. Edelman, *No Future: Queer Theory and the Death Drive* (Durham, NC: Duke University Press, 2004), p. 2. Further references are incorporated into the text.
8. Žižek's key book *The Ticklish Subject: The Absent Centre of Political Ontology* (London: Verso, 2000) did much to broaden the readership of these French authors in the English-speaking world.
9. Lacan, 'The Function and Field of Speech and Language in Psycho-Analysis', *Écrits*, trans. Bruce Fink (London: Norton, 2004), pp. 197–268.
10. Lacan, 'Logical Time and the Assertion of Anticipated Certainty', *Écrits*, pp. 161–75.
11. Mitchell comments critically on Engels' classic *The Origin of the Family, Private Property, and the State* in her own classic text, originally published in *New Left Review* in 1966 and available in reworked form in *Women: The Longest Revolution* (London: Virago, 2000).

12. Nina Power develops this criticism of Edelman's work further in her invaluable article 'Non-Reproductive Futurism: Rancière's Rational Equality against Edelman's Body Apolitic', *borderlands* 8.2 (2009): 1–16.

13. Edelman quotes from Lacan, *The Seminar of Jacques Lacan. Book VII: The Ethics of Psychoanalysis* (London: Norton, 1992), p. 24.

14. Badiou, *Logique des mondes* (Paris: Éditions du Seuil, 2006), p. 9, my translation. Further references are incorporated into the text.

15. Lacan, 'Function and Field', *Écrits*, p. 261. Further references are incorporated into the text.

16. Eagleton, 'Subjects and Truths', *New Left Review* 9 (May–June 2001).

17. The signifier is 'that which represents a subject for another signifier'. Lacan, *The Four Fundamental Concepts*, p. 207.

18. Freud, 'The Taboo of Virginity' (1918), *SE* vol. 11, pp. 191–208.

Index